THE MAKING OF FEDERAL INDIA

THE MAKING OF FEDERAL INDIA

N. GANGULEE

GYAN

Published by

GYAN

Gyan Publishing House
5, Ansari Road
Daryaganj, New Delhi-110002
Phone: 011-47034999, 9811692060
E-mail: books@gyanbooks.com

Distribution Network
gyanbooks.com
India, USA, Canada, UK, Australia

ISBN: 978-93-7169-121-5 (PB)

First Published, 1936

2nd Impression 2025

Printed at: Gyan Press, Delhi.

THE MAKING OF FEDERAL INDIA

Author: N. GANGULEE

THE MAKING OF FEDERAL INDIA

A brief survey of the development of Indian Constitutional Reform from 1911 *to* 1935

THE MAKING OF FEDERAL INDIA

"*For the later kindness done in season, though small in comparison, may cancel a greater previous wrong.*"
THUCYDIDES I. XLII.

N. GANGULEE

C.I.E., Ph.D., formerly Professor, University of Calcutta (1921-1931); *Ex-member of the Royal Commission on Indian Agriculture* (1926-1928); *Member, Imperial Council of Agricultural Research* (1929-1931); *Member, Governing Body of International Institute of Educational Cinematography* (1932–)

WITH A FOREWORD BY

THE MARQUESS OF LOTHIAN, C.H.

TO

THE STATESMEN, POLITICIANS, AND PUBLICISTS OF THE BRITISH COMMONWEALTH OF NATIONS WHOSE SYMPATHETIC CO-OPERATION IN THE MAKING OF FEDERAL INDIA IS DESIRED AS A SOURCE OF ITS STRENGTH AND HOPE, THIS BOOK IS DEDICATED

FOREWORD

I AM very glad to write a short introduction to Professor Gangulee's brief survey of the development of Indian Constitutional Reform from 1911 to the enactment of the Constitution Act. There are some things in his book which I should have described differently, and I hope that some day Sir Tej Bahadur Sapru or Mr. Jayakar, or one of the other stalwarts who have been continuously in the forefront of the battle for constitutional reform during the last fifteen years, will write its history from their own experience, for no one can present adequately the tension and drama of the story who was not throughout "on the inside." But Professor Gangulee has done a very useful work in attempting to bring into a single perspective the main outlines of Indian constitutional development from its inception in the Minto-Morley Reforms through the Round Table Conference down to the present day.

I do not believe that most people, in India or in Britain, realize the immense significance of the enactment of a Federal Constitution for India. Constitution-making seems a little at a discount to-day, because the international anarchy in which the nations live in this steadily shrinking world of ours has produced wars and dictatorships which have swept away one Constitution after another. But that is only to say that the central need of mankind is a world Constitution within which the nations can carry through reform, both social and economic, by pacific means, and cease to destroy one another by physical or economic war. Nor, I think, does Indian political opinion yet realize the immense significance of that principle of "special responsibility" vested in the Viceroy and the Governors of which the Constitution is the first formal embodiment. It places the initiative and the primary responsibility for government throughout the whole domestic field on the shoulders of Ministries responsible to the Legislatives and confines the safeguarding powers to situations in which the Viceroy and the Governors are prepared to state that ministerial policy constitutes a grave menace to the stability of government or a breach of statutory guarantees.

No doubt the Indian Constitution is imperfect. No doubt it will, in due time, need revision. But history may yet say that the substitution at this critical hour of a Constitution based on responsible Legislatures, both federal and provincial, elected on a fairly wide franchise, for the old direct British autocracy, saved India from the disasters which have overtaken Europe; from its breaking into warring fragments based on religion, race or language. The Indian Constitution may be as important a milestone as was the enactment of the American Constitution 150 years ago. Indeed I hope that ere long an Indian Abraham Lincoln will arise who will proclaim that the maintenance of Indian constitutional unity and the reform of its internal political, economic and social conditions, along constitutional lines, is of more importance to Indians than any other issue, save that its sons and daughters should take on their own shoulders the difficult and dangerous responsibility for the self-government of one-sixth of the human race without further delay.

To those who want to see how the Constitution came into being and the main ideas on which it is based, Professor Gangulee has provided a valuable introduction.

LOTHIAN

PREFACE

A DISTINGUISHED French writer, Monsieur André Siegfried, in his book "England's Crisis," observes that "the Englishman not only shrinks from the effort needed to solve his problems, but he will not even formulate them. His mental laziness is extraordinary. It bores him to think, and he is particularly hostile when anyone raises a discussion of principles upsetting his peace of mind." But, when Indian affairs took a serious turn and Britain's trade with India dwindled to a low figure, he realized that the task of finding a solution compatible with the aspiration of political India could not be left to a "muddle-through policy."

India was "a key-point in the structure of the Empire," and, therefore, the constitutional issues involving the future destinies of a sub-Continent as diverse as Europe required exhaustive investigation. The institution of that investigation, lasting over eight years, was perhaps one of the most urgent Imperial tasks that has ever been set before the Imperial Government. The Government of India Act, 1935, is based upon a triune policy, namely, unity through federation; responsibility with adequate safeguards; and provincial autonomy within the Federation, evolved in the course of a searching enquiry. In this book I have attempted to make a realistic survey of the constitutional problem and have described the various stages of discussion and negotiations which preceded the Act.

In 1935 the Empire celebrated the Silver Jubilee of King George V's reign. At the commencement of that eventful quarter of a century's reign, His Majesty laid the foundation of the new capital of India. The transference of the seat of the Government to an administrative unit independent of provincial administration prepared the way for the ultimate form of Indian Constitution being of a federal type. What was then a distant goal is now brought within the realm of practical politics. I have set out in some detail the political concessions granted to British India before and after the War, and have endeavoured to clarify the controversial issues by placing before the reader the various conflicting opinions in regard to each successive stage through which Indian constitutional development has passed during the period under review. A continuous account of the events that preceded the passing of the Government of India Act, 1935, may furnish a background which is helpful in understanding the salient features of the measure in a proper perspective. As regards the Act itself I have avoided burdening the book with its technical details, but have stated in full the broad principles underlying India's new Constitution.

How best to apply these principles to the conditions obtaining in India provoked a great deal of controversy. The debates and discussions at various stages of the investigation revealed a wide divergence of views among those who were concerned with an amicable settlement of the problem of the Indian Constitution, and the long contention raised the whirlwind of political passion and made the task infinitely difficult. I hope that in the following pages I have been able to state with accuracy the views of both the opponents and supporters of the new Constitution for India. My object here is to trace in this controversy those psychological factors which have to be taken into consideration for adjusting relations between the divergent interests concerned in the making of Federal India.

There is a legend in Indian Epic[1] that once upon a time the Gods and the Demons churned the ocean to recover the lost nectar of immortality. The process of churning caused a great upheaval; and although in the end the nectar was found, it so happened that the excessive churning produced poison. The imperative task was then to deal with the poison which threatened the lives of all creatures.

The legend has a lesson for the partners in the making of Federal India. If in the attempt to recover a "Lost Dominion" there emerges the poison of bitterness and ill-feeling, Indian problems will become more insoluble and intractable. It is unfortunate that the spirit of intolerance should have been so much in evidence in the present controversy when, to quote the words of Lord Meston, "if there was a time for the calm and non-partisan treatment of Indian affairs it is to-day." While the supporters of the measure of self-government granted to India assert that by pursuing the policy of conciliating Indian public opinion "within the limits of safety" the position of Great Britain in India will be strengthened, a large section of the British public insists that the supreme hold Britain has upon India should never be relaxed, and that on the strength of the Army and Navy lies the true assurance of Indo-British relations. There are responsible men in British public life whose utterances on the subject of the new constitutional proposals seem to imply that it is an iniquitous crime for the Indian political classes to demand a greater share in the government of their country.

On the other hand, there are Indian Nationalists who

[1] Mahavarata.

propose to attain their political goal by the threat of Civil Disobedience or by causing obstructions within the Legislatures till their demands are conceded. Simultaneously with their demand for Dominion Status, they raise the question of the right of secession, and relying on the precedent of the Irish Free State they demand also the right of repudiating debts. And when faced with the realities of the Indian situation, they were unable to offer a practical solution of some of the fundamental problems, and allowed the differences among themselves to develop into communal strife. Thus, in the place of mutual confidence and unity of purpose, there has been an amazing accumulation of mutual suspicion and dissension. The birth of a new Constitution in such an atmosphere cannot be a happy augury for the future. If the framework of the Constitution appears to some " a scheme of shreds and patches," it would nevertheless be a grievous error of judgment to indulge in bitter hostility and racial antagonism. In the last chapter of the book I have, therefore, appealed to all the partners in the making of Federal India to apply their minds to the essential task of restoring mutual confidence and goodwill. They should remember that, to quote the words of Mr. Stanley Baldwin, " the Empire was not built up on trade agreements, nor can it be maintained solely by tariffs and preferences. It can only be maintained permanently by a clear conviction of its ultimate goal—the spiritual unity of the whole British Empire. Failure to realize the wider heritage growing out of the Imperial connection involves the betrayal of a profound spiritual trust." If we are not deeply conscious of this trust, the constitutional devices provided in the Government of India Act, 1935, are bound to conjure up fatal conflicts within and without the Indian Empire.

N. Gangulee

London, 1936.

CONTENTS

CHAPTER I

POLITICAL INDIA AT THE TIME OF THE CORONATION OF KING GEORGE V

The Coronation Durbar : The Structure of the Government : Local Self-Government : At the beginning of the Twentieth Century : The Morley-Minto Reforms : The Indian States

ℭ THE CORONATION DURBAR

INDIA'S entry into the second decade of the twentieth century was marked by an event of singular importance. The decision of King George V and Queen Mary to visit India to enable the people of that distant Empire to celebrate the Coronation of their Sovereign was hailed as the advent of a new era in India's relations with Great Britain. Acting upon the conviction that the first visit of a reigning Sovereign might to a certain extent assuage Indian public opinion, which continued to agitate against the Partition of Bengal and against the repressive measures adopted by the Government in India to suppress the intransigent spirit, the Liberal Government, then in power, availed themselves of the occasion of King George's Accession to the Throne to introduce certain changes in the Indian Administration. They thought that if these changes were announced by His Majesty in person they would have a salutary effect on public opinion in India.

Their Majesties the King and Queen, attended by the Marquess of Crewe, Secretary of State for India, left Portsmouth on November 11, 1911, and arrived at Bombay on December 2; and ten days later the Imperial Durbar was held in Delhi. It was a memorable occasion, which brought the Indian Princes and the representatives of British India together for the common purpose of expressing their allegiance to the Crown. On December 15 Their Majesties each laid a foundation-stone of the New Imperial Capital.

In the declaration announcing the annulment of the Partition of Bengal, an administrative measure of Lord Curzon which evoked "justifiable discontent," and the transfer of the Capital from Calcutta to Delhi, educated Indians realized that a new step was being taken towards the evolution of India's political development. To the British statesmen, the Durbar was an overwhelming proof of the devotion of the Princes, nobles and people to Their Majesties, who had been deeply touched by "the spontaneous manifestations of an enthusiastic affection and loyalty" from all classes of Indian citizens. This enthusiasm was, however, not in any sense an indication of loyalty to the Bureaucracy; it was an expression of India's traditional reverence for Kingship. The years preceding Their Majesties' visit witnessed the most turbulent forms of popular agitation in British India, and yet the Imperial Durbar was rightly described as "the miracle of the King's touch on a huge scale." The spell of the Royal presence had appeased the spirit of revolt against the bureaucratic measures adopted to suppress it.

> "The very same crowds which have rent the air with curses on the British Raj," wrote Sir Valentine Chirol, "pressed with an equal frenzy to catch a glimpse of the Royal couple to acclaim them with cheers and blessings, and strew flowers before them wherever they passed. So deeply could Indians still be moved by their ancient sense of reverence for Kingship that after the Royal Reception in the Maidan thousands who had been too far off to see anything of it rushed forward to worship the empty seats which the Royalties had hallowed and to fight for the smallest mementoes of a ceremony which their enthusiasm invested with something of the character of a religious rite."

Just before leaving India, King George, in a telegram to Mr. Asquith, then the Prime Minister, gave his own impression about the Royal visit. The King-Emperor observed:

> "From all sources, public and private, I gather that my highest hopes have been realized. . . . All classes, races, and creeds have united in receiving us with unmistakable signs of enthusiasm and affection. The magnificent display at the Durbar was the outcome of wise and well-considered plans, brilliantly carried out through the untiring efforts of the Viceroy and those who worked under him. Our satisfaction will be still greater if time proves that our visit has conduced to the lasting good of India and of the Empire at large."

In 1912 a Bill was introduced in Parliament for carrying out the administrative changes announced by His Majesty. The Conservative opposition declared that the way in which the change of Capital was effected was unconstitutional and indefensible. The House of Commons had not been consulted about the annulment of the Partition of Bengal, which the Opposition regarded as a surrender to political agitation in India.

The Government of India in their Despatch pointed out that the reasons for retaining Calcutta as the Capital had long since lost their force, and argued that the time had come to make such changes as are required for evolving autonomous Provincial Administrations. The Despatch is one of the most valuable Indian constitutional documents. It was in this momentous Despatch that the Government of India envisaged a federal type of Central Government and elaborated the need of decentralisation and provincial autonomy.

> "The time was coming," wrote Lord Hardinge (then the Viceroy), "when India would be composed of a number of autonomous provinces, somewhat similar to the different States of the American Union, with a Federal Government directing and controlling them all, in all matters of inter-state or foreign policy and administration."

The passage in the Despatch which was welcomed by the entire educated community of India ran as follows:

> "It is certain that, in course of time, the just demands of Indians for a larger share in the government of the country will have to be satisfied, and the question will be how this devolution of power can be conceded without impairing the supreme authority of the Governor-General in Council. The only possible solution of the difficulty would appear to be gradually to give the Provinces a larger measure of self-government, until at last India would consist of a number of administrations, autonomous in all provincial affairs, with the Government of India above them all, and possessing power to interfere in cases of misgovernment, but ordinarily restricting its functions to matters of Imperial concern."

The spirit of the Hardinge Despatch and the transfer of the seat of the Central Government from Calcutta to New Delhi, making it a separate unit of administration, inspired hopes in Indian political circles that the policy of the Imperial Government would now be to prepare the country for a federal constitution. Some of the Indian Nationalists found in the Despatch "the solid basis of the reconciliation of Indian nationalism and British Imperialism."

Unfortunately the interpretation of the Despatch in the House of Lords by the Marquess of Crewe revealed that the idea of provincial self-government was illusory and that there was no hope of an early modification of the Morley-Minto reforms. He said:

> "There was a certain section in India which looked forward to a measure of self-government approaching to that which had been granted to the Dominions. He saw no future for India on those lines. The experiment of a measure of self-government, practically free from parliamentary control, to a race which was not our own, even though that race enjoyed the advantages of the best services of men belonging to our race, was one which could not be tried. It was his duty as Secretary of State to repudiate the idea that the despatch implied anything of the kind, as the hope or goal of the policy of the Government."

In a later debate his Lordship laid down what he believed to be the goal or policy. " The maintenance and perpetual continuance of British rule," he said, " is the best way of securing the happiness of the Indian people."

While there was no change in the official attitude of mind towards the problem of satisfying the aspirations of political India, Their Majesties' visit had succeeded in winning the confidence of the Indian Princes and Liberal politicians. That as Emperor of his Indian subjects he would celebrate his Coronation in person at Delhi—the first Coronation of a British sovereign in India—was regarded as an act acknowledging " in the most public and solemn form possible " the status of India within the Empire. King George's concern for the spread of education in India gave an impetus to the slow recognition of the claims of education by the Government of India. The announcement of special grants for the development of education was singularly appropriate to the central purpose of leading India to the goal of self-government.

Within three years from the date of Their Majesties' visit to India, the Empire plunged into the War; the post-war conditions were not peaceful and the problems of the Empire in relation to the world became extremely complicated. But it is gratifying to record the fact that the main features of the Indian constitutional changes envisaged at the time of King George's Coronation Durbar were translated into an Act of Parliament in the year of the Silver Jubilee of his accession to the Throne. In an estimate of this eventful quarter of a century, the history of constitutional development in India should be considered as a great achievement. We shall trace the various stages through which that development has taken place; but it may be helpful to the reader if this preliminary chapter is devoted to a brief survey of the structure of the Government of India as it existed at the time of King George V's Coronation Durbar in India.

ℭ THE STRUCTURE OF THE GOVERNMENT

After over a century's rule by the stockholders of the East India Company, the circumstances, as revealed in the Mutiny, forced Parliament to take direct control of the Indian Administration.

It must be placed to the credit of Clive's genius and foresight, that after the battle of Plassey (1757) he urged the British Government to assume full sovereignty over all the British possessions instead of tolerating the "Dual government" of the merchant-adventurers. The first step taken to control grave abuses by the merchant-administrators of their powers was the Regulating Act of 1773, and within the period of the two following decades it became necessary for Parliament to enact measures, at the end of each decade, in order to reconcile the trading interests of a Company with those of the administration of the country. By Pitt's Act of 1784, the Board of Control was set up in England and its powers were extended by the Charter Act of 1793. Things went on for about 40 years in a way which failed to produce the kind of Government the country needed for its reconstruction after the fall of the Moghul Empire. Finally, under the Charter Act of 1833, the Company had to close their commercial business and seriously take up their political and administrative duties; but it required the shock of the Indian Mutiny in 1857 to seal the fate of the greatest and strongest mercantile Corporation in the world. It should be noted here that the Charter Act of 1833 laid down the principle that no natives of India are to be excluded by reason of their birth from any appointments under the Company. Indeed, the spirit of that Act and the attitude of British administrators like Lord Bentinck, Sir Charles Metcalfe, and Lord Macaulay (then Thomas Babington Macaulay) seemed to have been inspired not only by the idealism of the Whigs, then in power, but also by the evangelical outlook of the Clapham school.

The Crown assumed responsibility for pacifying India

after the Mutiny, and the change was effected by the famous Proclamation of Queen Victoria in 1858, in which Her Majesty laid down the principle of justice that would be hereafter pursued by the Government of India. The Proclamation stated :

> " It is our earnest desire to stimulate the peaceful industry of India, to promote works of public utility and improvement, and to administer the government for the benefit of all our subjects resident therein. In their prosperity will be our greatest strength, in their contentment our security, and in their gratitude our best reward. . . ."

The Proclamation was followed by the work of pacification, entrusted to the care of Lord Canning, and the Government became engaged in the task of remodelling the machinery of administration. The office of the Secretary of State, with a Council to assist him, took the place of the Board of Control in London. The work of internal development of post-Mutiny India was commenced on lines congenial to the spirit of the Mid-Victorian Age. The Universities were established in order to create a new class of Indian intellectuals, inspiring them with Western ideals of social and economic order. In the Presidency towns High Courts were set up and a number of Codes were promulgated for the administration of justice. The financial position of the Government, rudely shaken by the Mutiny (which cost the Government about 40 millions sterling), became a matter of serious concern to the authorities. Although nearly three-fifths of the revenues were derived from inelastic sources, such as land revenue and excise, expenditure, both civil and military, had greatly increased, and the total unproductive debt of India in 1860 was nearly 100 millions sterling. It was about this time that income tax, the Government paper currency, and the system of the Budget were introduced. These financial reforms were proposed by Mr. James Wilson, M.P.,[1] who was a Secretary to the British Treasury and was

[1] He was the founder of the well-known London journal: *The Economist.*

sent to India in order to put her finances in order. So much for the civil side of the administration.

On the military side of the administration, the Army was remodelled and the proportion of British troops to Indian troops was increased. The function of the Indian Army is clearly described by Lord Curzon in his book on "The India Corps in France." He said:

> "The Indian Army in fact has always possessed and has been proud of possessing a triple function: the preservation of internal peace in India itself; the defence of the Indian frontiers; and preparedness to embark at a moment's notice for Imperial service in other parts of the globe. In this third aspect, India has for long been one of the most important units in the scheme of British Imperial defence, providing the British Government with a striking force always ready, of admirable efficiency and assured valour."

In order to achieve the goal of constructing Civil and Military Administrations suitable to the special circumstances of India, it was imperative that the structure of the Government should be stable and strong. The final authority for the governance of India was vested in the British Cabinet, of which the Secretary of State for India was a member. He had a Council to which ordinarily all matters of importance were referred for an expression of opinion. The Secretary of State for India was not, however, bound by their advice (except in matters of finance).

The executive authority in India was the Governor-General-in-Council.

The Government of India was, thus, essentially a centralized bureaucracy. The Viceroy and Governor-General of India wielded the power of a benevolent autocrat, supported "by little more than a mere handful of Europeans with the help of an immense staff of Indians holding for the most part very subordinate positions." [1]

[1] "Fifty Years in a Changing World," by Sir Valentine Chirol. Cape: 1927.

For administrative purposes, British India was divided into nine Provinces, excluding Burma; but the size of each of these Provinces is equal to some of the great countries of Europe. For instance, the Province of Madras is larger than Italy, and the Punjab exceeds the area of Great Britain. Assam, which is the smallest of all the Provinces, is really as large as England and Wales.

Legislative powers were at first confined to the Viceroy's Executive Council. After the Mutiny, a few Indians were nominated to sit with the officials on the Legislative Councils, but they could have no effective voice in making laws. Towards the latter part of the nineteenth century, in consonance with the growing political ambitions of educated Indians, the Salisbury Government was persuaded to enlarge the Councils, thus providing more facilities for Indians to express their views upon the whole field of administration. The Indian Councils Act, 1892, was piloted through the House of Commons by Mr. George N. Curzon (afterwards Lord Curzon), then Under-Secretary of State for India. Perhaps the most important feature of the Bill was that members were allowed to discuss, though not vote upon, the Budget and ask questions relating to the main aspects of administrative policy and action. The mode of election was not by electorates but by nomination. The British Liberals proposed the application of the elective principle, but, to the surprise of Indian politicians, it was withdrawn by Gladstone himself. The Bill passed through Parliament with the assurance from Mr. Curzon that it was not "a great or an heroic measure." The Indian National Congress realized that its demand for the Executive to be made responsible to a growing public opinion had not been conceded, but they were satisfied with a small beginning of the process of bringing it into close touch with bureaucracy.

¶ LOCAL SELF-GOVERNMENT

But the *real* basis of self-government had been designed when Lord Ripon (1880–1884) introduced Reforms for the creation of Local Bodies for the administration of local affairs. The members of these bodies were partly elected and partly nominated. It was hoped that local self-government would form " a vital link in the chain of organisms that make up the Government," and would " foster sedulously the small beginnings of the independent political life." But the hope was not realized. The scheme did not secure the co-operation of the classes whose co-operation was essential for its success. I believe that the electoral system devised under the Act was rendered rather defective by the low qualification for the exercise of franchise, and the powers devolved upon the local bodies were far too restricted. The vision of training Indians in the responsibility of local administration was obscured by the jealousy of officials, who were concerned more with the means and methods of control than with superintendence. Then there was the chronic financial stringency.

The District officers, who come in close contact with the masses, are known to regret the absence, or, if in existence, the ill-organised character of local institutions in villages. " There is no legal means for raising a public fund by means of local taxation for making a bridge, road, well or tank, or for clearing and repairing them. There is no local authority which has legal power to preserve a right-of-way, or prevent a nuisance ; not a scavenger or conservancy cart can be employed ; not a street lamp set up or lighted ; not a dispensary or school established or maintained by means of local taxation. This is not civilization," thus wrote Robert Carstairs of the Indian Civil Service in 1904.

And yet in the development of local bodies lies the secret of obtaining the motive power for building autonomous Provincial Governments on a democratic basis. British-India territory is divided into nine [1] Provinces, known as

[1] The North-West Frontier Province became a Governor's Province in 1931.

"Governors' Provinces," with certain areas directly under the Governor-General in Council. Each Province is divided into a number of districts which are grouped into divisions. There are about 267 districts, each of which averages roughly 4000 square miles with a population of about one million. The District Officer is the pivot of the administration and serves as the immediate link between the Government and the people.

Owing to the size of the districts, they are again divided into smaller units, such as Local Boards, Union Boards, and village *panchayats*, functioning as the primary and direct agency for rural administration. If these units are properly developed they may, in addition to being the basis of socio-economic life, be the effective training ground for civic duties and self-government. Unfortunately neither the Government nor the Indian politicians have made serious efforts to make such bodies vital parts in the constitutional structure; and I consider that, in the absence of vigorous local self-governing bodies, the basis of a representative and responsible form of government in India will remain fundamentally weak.

These explanations will, I hope, enable the reader to visualize the entire structure of the Government of India from the Secretary of State in Council in London down to the unit of a local board in rural India. On the whole this machinery of the Government, built upon the ruins of the Moghul Empire, functioned well for over half a century, under the guidance of a benevolent autocracy. But at the dawn of the twentieth century India entered upon a new phase.

ℭ AT THE BEGINNING OF THE TWENTIETH CENTURY

Good as the British Administration was, it came to be a source of friction and conflict with the stirring of a new spirit among the educated classes. The Indian National Congress was organized for the demand of administrative reforms and held its first session in 1885. The Congress not only became critical of the form of government but were determined to resist the growth of this all-powerful bureaucracy. "It is the spirit of the English Constitution which, infused through the mighty mass, feeds, unites, invigorates, vivifies every part of the Empire, even down to the minutest member," declared Edmund Burke. The work of this spirit became manifest in India. The new generation, brought up under the influence of Western thought, demanded new values in its relations with an alien government, and with the victory of Japan over Russia there arose an entirely new conception in regard to the much-vaunted superiority of the European over the Asiatic races.

At the time of such awakened political consciousness, Lord Curzon was sent to India as Viceroy. Imbued with Victorian Imperialism and with the conviction that a high standard of administrative efficiency was required to fulfil England's mission in India, he engaged himself in the scrutiny of every aspect of Indian Administration.

Lord Curzon's policy from 1902 till the close of the second part of his Viceroyalty widened the gulf between the Government and the politically conscious classes. It is truly said that his Viceroyalty "left India a little breathless"; and it is no less true to say that it left her also in despair. In despair, because he alienated even the Liberals from the Government. When the Indian National Congress veterans suggested the use of the word "Self-government" (Swaraj) as "the saving word" that would rally the integrating forces to the side of the Government, he scornfully rejected it as being "beyond the range of practical politics." The inevitable consequences followed—the faith of political India in constitutional procedure on the part of the National Congress was rudely shaken, and the disturbing forces within that body gained the upper hand. The Congress was unable to hold to its traditional position. The gospel of aggressive nationalism was being carried to the masses.

The bitterness against the Government began to increase and culminated in the adoption of the methods advocated by revolutionary societies; and also in a vigorous campaign for boycotting foreign—particularly British—goods. The moderate Indian leaders were thrown into the background.

In regard to the Indian States, Lord Curzon's policy was irritating to their *amour propre*. He openly stated that the States possessed no rights except on sufferance, and considered them "as administrative Agents of the Government of India, deriving their rights, powers, and dignities from the Crown." His general attitude towards the Princes created uneasiness in their minds, and from that time they became greatly concerned with the question of maintaining the sovereignty of the States.

In December 1905 the Conservative Government came to an end, and Sir Henry Campbell-Bannerman succeeded Mr. Balfour as Prime Minister. Mr. John Morley became Secretary of State for India. This change in the Home Government inspired hope among the older Congress leaders, who urged patience, trusting that the Liberal Party and Mr. Morley [1] would respond to their demand for some radical constitutional reforms. But the Government had to move slowly, leaving Lord Minto to adopt vigorous measures in order to suppress the growing seditious movement in India.

While Mr. Morley and Lord Minto were actively engaged in formulating their proposals for Reforms, the King-Emperor issued a Proclamation on November 2, 1908, which gave Political India an assurance in the following terms:

> "From the first, the principle of representative institutions began to be gradually introduced, and the time has come when, in the judgment of my Viceroy and Governor-General and others of my counsellors, that principle may be prudently extended. Important classes among you, representing ideas that had been fostered and encouraged by British rule, claim equality of citizenship, and a greater

[1] The educated Indians knew that he had dealt with political idealism in his "Life of Burke."

share in legislation and government. The politic satisfaction of such a claim will strengthen, not impair, existing authority and power."

ℭ THE MORLEY-MINTO REFORMS

The joint proposals of Mr. Morley and Lord Minto, after passing through the usual Parliamentary procedures, were passed into law in 1909 [1] as an attempt to appease Indian demands. The Provincial Councils were enlarged up to a maximum of 50 members in the larger Provinces and 30 in the smaller; the method of election was partly indirect and partly direct; small non-official majorities were provided in the Provincial Councils but an official majority was retained at the Centre. In addition to the Governor-General and the members of his Executive Council, some 60 members were added to the Central Legislature. The members were again given a measure of freedom to raise questions relating to administration and policy but "the argument of numbers remained with the Central Government." That is, the Reforms did not touch or affect the framework of Government. Mr. Morley's reason for retaining a permanent Government majority was that the Governor-General's Council "in its legislative, as well as its executive, character, should continue to be so constituted as to ensure its constant and uninterrupted power to fulfil the constitutional obligations that it owes, must always owe, to His Majesty's Government and to the Imperial Parliament."

It was thus an exceedingly cautious measure, and fell far short of what the Indian leaders expected. It did not invest the new Councils with any powers of control over the Government. The Councils worked under regulations which allowed discussion "of any matter of general public interest and the asking of questions." But questions might be disallowed without reason given; resolutions might be proposed, but even where carried were not binding, and they

[1] The Indian Councils Act, 1909 (9 Edw. VII, c. 4).

also might be disallowed. However, it furnished a starting-point in India's constitutional development by the introduction of direct election for Legislative Councils, though on a very limited basis. The principles embodied in the Morley-Minto Reforms are now considered as "the seeds of Parliamentary Government," although Mr. Morley himself stoutly denied having had any intention of introducing this form of government in India. His object was to give representative Indians "a larger consultative voice" in the administration of their country. But, as Sir Valentine Chirol pointed out, "the event had gone to show that representative institutions could only be Dead Sea fruit if they lacked the stimulus of real power and corresponding responsibility." The fact remains, to quote Professor Coupland, that

> "it created almost exactly the same situation as that in Canada at the time of the *Durham Report*. The system in the Provinces . . . was now a system of *representative* government without *responsible* government. What could the next step be but Durham's? Had not India, without anyone yet realizing it, begun to take her place beside the Dominions in the process of assimilation?"[1]

It has been asserted[2] that the development of responsible government in England and in the Dominions has been accompanied by a corresponding advance in India, and that the Morley-Minto Reforms were "the work of the Parliament that extended responsible government to the erstwhile Boer Republics of the Transvaal and Orange Free State." And in the matter of constitutional development, it is claimed that there has been a common law of political progress for all parts of the British Empire which "operated generally and impartially in each instance as circumstances dictate and justify." But the Morley-Minto Reforms did not appear to conform to the "common law of political progress" and were denounced as a "cynical and calculated sham."

[1] "The British Empire," by Professor R. Coupland, C.I.E.

[2] See "Political India," Chapter 1, an article by Lord Halifax. Oxford University Press: 1933.

One feature of the Reforms should be noted here—the principle of communal representation. Soon after the proposals for reform were mooted, a deputation of Moslem leaders, led by His Highness the Aga Khan, waited on the Viceroy and urged that the position of the community "should be commensurate not merely with their numerical strength but also with their political importance and value of the contribution which they made to the defence of the Empire." That this compromise was fatal to the entire principle of democracy Mr. Morley knew, but he yielded to pressure in conceding the principle in favour of the Mohammedans. Later, Lord Minto gave the community a promise that in any future scheme of reform the principle should be given full consideration. We shall note in our subsequent discussions what has been the Nemesis of dividing electorates on a communal basis.

However, it was not long before even moderate Indian opinion came to regard the Reforms as illusory. With an attitude of cold acquiescence towards it, the Indian leaders agreed to work the Reformed Council "in a conciliatory fashion." Apart from the lack of "the antecedent conditions of success," to which the authors of the Montagu-Chelmsford Report referred, there was the legacy of political ferment caused by the Partition of Bengal. The first act of the Reformed Council was to pass the Press Act, followed by the Seditious Meetings Act in 1911!

The attitude of British statesmen towards the Morley-Minto Reforms of 1909 is well expressed by Mr. J. L. Garvin in the *Observer*. He wrote:

> "There is a moderate element among the educated classes, though it has been on the whole very weak and timid in expressing itself. The enlargement and wider functions of the new Legislative Councils are to be welcomed as affording more encouragement and opportunity to the moderates. They are in this sense an experiment, but a welcome and necessary experiment. But let us repeat and make it perfectly plain to ourselves that neither these

concessions nor any concessions upon the basis of representative principles—which it is impossible for us to carry to any logical conclusion—can touch those psychological and economic roots of 'Indian unrest' which have been traced to their deepest fibre by the Special Correspondent[1] of *The Times*. We must depend in the future for the discharge of our task upon that which, from the beginning, has been the only justification of our rule—the beneficence of an impartial, peaceful, constructive administration. As the late Charles Pearson said, 'For one war we have waged in India, we have prevented twenty.' We and we alone still stand between India and war, plunder, anarchy, upon an unexampled scale. Our business is to make that administration still more vigorous and vigilant for progressive and repressive purposes alike—to rule India in no conventional spirit; to rule it even more than hitherto for the practical good and the mental development of its humbler majority, and less for the advantage either of Brahmins or moneylenders. We must do this not only in a real temper, but in the quite obvious temper, lately lacking, of unhesitating and unflinching determination to hold our own."

But about ten years later the inherent weakness of the position created by the Morley-Minto Reforms was exposed by Mr. Edwin Montagu and Lord Chelmsford in the following terms:

"We must make up our minds either to rule ourselves or to let the people rule: there is no half-way house, except of course on the highway of deliberate transition. At present we are doing neither. We are trying to govern by concession, and each successive concession has the air of being wrung from us. We keep public business going by bargaining and negotiation: not, however, the healthy bargaining of the market-place, but a steady yielding to assaults which always leave some bitterness behind on both sides. . . . The reforms which followed his (Curzon's) régime brought in a power of challenge and obstruction—

[1] Sir Valentine Chirol.

> influence without responsibility; and rather than fight, we have often to give way. We are shedding the rôle of benevolent despotism, and the people—especially those who are most friendly to us—cannot understand what rôle we mean to assume in its place."

Arguing on such lines the authors of the joint Report which formed the basis of the Reforms of 1919 proceeded to suggest the creation of a new structure. The character and function of that structure are discussed in the following Chapter.

ℭ THE INDIAN STATES

So far we have dealt mainly with British India. Since one of the principal factors in the controversy, raised over the proposal for All-India Federation, centres round the future relations of British India with the Indian Princes, it is necessary to refer to some of the features of the Indian States.

The Indian States cover an area over 700,000 square miles and contain about one-fifth of the population of India, excluding Burma. They range in size from Hyderabad, which is larger than England and Scotland together, down to Lawa, which has a population not exceeding 3,000. Some of the most picturesque tracts of India are included in the States.

In most States the population is mixed and represents all castes and creeds. The ruler of the State of Hyderabad (Deccan) is a Moslem, but his subjects are predominantly Hindus. We find the reverse in the State of Kashmir, where Moslem subjects are ruled by a Hindu Prince.

Upon the downfall of the Moghul Empire, internecine struggles among the hosts of Ruling Chiefs and Jagirdars, who formed an integral part of the Moghul system of government, became a source of constant irritation to the East India Company. As the Company's authority increased in power and prestige, they were able to exercise control over these divergent groups of Indian Ruling Chiefs. Some forty

States formed alliance with the Company by treaties and others secured their position by some form of engagement granted to them. By the middle of the nineteenth century all these States had to recognize the Company as the Paramount Power and sought to defend their independence in internal affairs over which the Company had no right to intervene. After the Mutiny, when the Company's government was transferred to the Crown by the Act of 1858, the position of the States was made clear by the Proclamation of the Queen :

> "We hereby announce to the Native Princes of India that all treaties or engagements made with them by or under the authority of the Honourable the East India Company are by us accepted and will be scrupulously maintained, and we look for the like observance on their part."

In matters of status, relations with the Paramount Power and administrative efficiency, there is a considerable variation among the States. They are generally governed by the absolute will of their Princes, subject to the degrees of internal sovereignty conceded to them by treaties and engagements with the Paramount Power. The policy of the British Government towards the States is of non-interference in their internal administration ; but, since the beginning of the nineteenth century "it became the universal principle of public policy," writes Sir Alfred Lyall, "that every State in India should make over the control of its foreign relations to the British Government, should submit all external disputes to British arbitration, and should defer to British advice regarding internal management so far as might be necessary to cure disorders or scandalous misrule. A British Resident was appointed to the Courts of all the greater Princes as the agency for the exercise of these high functions; while the subsidiary forces and the contingents furnished by the States placed the supreme military command everywhere under British direction." [1]

[1] "British Dominion in India," by Sir Alfred Lyall.

In every important State or in groups of minor States, there is an officer of the Government of India, called a Resident, or Political Agent, through whom the Paramount Power is kept in touch with affairs in the State. The Princes contend that in contravention of their internal sovereignty the political officers often interfere in the affairs of the States. What the position was at the end of the last century is described by Sir Henry Cotton, a distinguished Anglo-Indian official, in the following terms :

> "They are powerless to protect themselves. There is no judicial authority to which they can appeal. There is no public opinion to watch their interests. There is no publicity to contest the action of a Government which is able to decide their fate as it pleases. Their rank and honour depend on the pleasure of a British Resident at their court, and on the secret and irresponsible mandates of a foreign office at Simla." [1]

On the other hand, it cannot be denied that, in some instances, intervention has been necessary in the interests of the people of the States. The root cause of uneasiness, due to the vigilance of the Political Resident or Agent, lies in the preponderant interest the Princes show in maintaining their own powers and privileges rather than those of the people.

> "The complaints which we often hear," writes Sir Sivaswamy Aiyer, "from the subjects of the Indian States and the known defects of administration in many of them make it clear that many of the rulers have not yet begun to realize that the princes exist for the people and not the people for the princes." [2]

The following table shows the classification of the Indian States :

[1] "New India," by Sir Henry Cotton.
[2] "Indian Constitutional Problem," by Sir Sivaswamy Aiyer.

TABLE [1]

Class of State, Estate, etc.	Number.	Area in square miles.	Population in round number.	Revenue (in crores).[2]
1. States, the rulers of which are members of the Chamber of Princes [3] in their own right . .	108	515,000	60,000,000	42
2. States, the rulers of which are represented in the Chamber of Princes by twelve members of their order elected by themselves	127	77,000	8,000,000	3
3. Estates, *Jagirs*, etc. .	327	6,400	800,000	·74

As regards constitutional developments, in some States there are Legislative Councils and in some others there are Representative Assemblies. But in most of the States there are no such bodies.

> "Of the 108 Princes in class 1, 30 have established legislative councils,[4] most of which are at present of a consultative nature only; 40 have constituted High Courts more or less on British Indian models; 34 have separated executive from judicial functions; 56 have a fixed privy purse; 46 have started a regular graded civil list of officials; and 54 have pension or provident fund schemes. Some of these reforms are still no doubt inchoate or on paper, and some States are still backward, but a sense of responsibility to their people is spreading among all the States and growing year by year." [5]

[1] Compiled by the. Indian States Enquiry Committee.

[2] Crore = £750,000.

[3] See Chapter II.

[4] Report of the Indian States Committee, 1929.

[5] G. T. Garratt, I.C.S., writes in "An Indian Commentary" (1928), as follows: "Any experiment in the form of constitutional government in the States is heralded as a great advance, but the Princes have learnt only too well from the British Government how easy it is to institute Legislative Councils and Assemblies which are merely debating societies."

States such as Travancore and Baroda are far ahead of British India in respect of progress in education.

The Princes as an Order are staunchly loyal to the Crown. They stood aside from the current of political agitation that swept over India in the first decade of the last century. Nevertheless, the growth of political consciousness in British India made its influence felt in the States. Both the Princes and their subjects recognized that new forces were at work in their midst which they could not possibly ignore. While the Princes were satisfied in their external relations with the Paramount Power, they found "an unmistakable contrast between the relationship in which they themselves stood to the Government of India and the relationship of their predecessors to the Honourable East India Company." [1] Relying upon the known strength of their devotion to the Crown, the Princes persistently worked towards the attainment of their goal of developing their States into compact political entities based on their sovereign rights. While the Paramount Power looked upon such efforts with suspicion, it realized the utmost importance of the islands of Indian States as breakwaters to the wave of political agitation in the Continent of India.

In one sentence King George described Political India at the time of his Coronation. Replying to an address of the Calcutta University, the King Emperor observed: "On every side I trace the signs and stirrings of new life." As we follow the narrative of the political events of the last twenty-five years in India, we shall see how the forces of that new life have reacted upon the political relationship of India with Great Britain.

[1] "The British Crown and the Indian States," by the Directorate of the Special Organization of the Chamber of Princes. P. S. King & Son: 1929.

CHAPTER II

DYARCHY

India and the War : Steps towards Constitutional change : The Montagu Declaration : The Government of India Act of 1919 : Unforeseen circumstances : Details of Constitutional changes : Franchise : India's reaction to the Reforms : Working of Reforms—(a) *Financial impediments,* (b) *Constitutional difficulties : Political relationships with the States : the Indian States Enquiry Committee*

ℂ INDIA AND THE WAR

THE historians have yet to analyse and evaluate the impetus given to India during and since the Great War. Her response to the call of the Empire in the hour of crisis was immediate and generous. Within a month from the declaration of War the Government of India was able to inform His Majesty's Government that the Indian Princes, rich merchants, and responsible men from the various communities, had all with one accord rallied to the defence of the Empire. Thousands of Indians voluntarily offered their services to the Government either on the War-front or in India for recruiting and other purposes. Legislative Councils voted all the emergency measures and War contributions asked for, and the Indian Congress showed political judgment by subordinating all controversies to the vital question of winning the War. The Indian Expeditionary Force was despatched to France, but with a plea from Lord Hardinge, who was then the Viceroy, that the Indian soldiers should be allowed to stand shoulder-to-shoulder on the battle front and that there should be no discrimination in treatment towards them. Over 621,000 Indian combatants and about 475,000 non-combatants were sent overseas from the beginning of the War to the end of 1919, and India's special War contribution was about £131 million.[1]

But it was not so much the assistance rendered to the Government in "men, money and munitions" that came as a surprise to the people of Great Britain. The important factor was India's attitude towards the Empire. Her loyalty was put to the test and she was not found wanting.

I think it is a narrow view to hold that Great Britain's promise of "a new angle of vision" (a phrase used by Mr. Asquith) in Indian affairs was the reward of India's loyalty. Political reform cannot be treated as a gift to be received by India as the price of her services during the War. The truth is, that in the midst of the War crisis, Indian political classes gave abundant positive proof of the development of a sense of political responsibility which the Imperial Government could not very well ignore. To critical students of international politics, it became clear that the position of European Powers in Asia after the War would have to be adjusted and that the conflict was sure to stimulate the nascent patriotism of Asiatic races into insurgent nationalism. By reason of her close association with the British Empire, the forces let loose in the War would have to be reckoned with in the sub-Continent of India. It therefore does credit to British political sense that during the War period, India's relation to the rest of the Empire should become an absorbing subject of interest among a group of British students of politics, who surveyed, as accurately as possible, the existing structure and mechanism of the Government of India and stimulated discussions on various problems arising from them.

[1] Increased military and political charges on account of the War upon Indian Budget were nearly 150 crores; and it is estimated that increase in civil expenditure due mainly to the exigencies of the War was about 25 crores. Crore = £750,000.

But the exigencies of circumstances called for a decision in regard to India's future political status even in the midst of preoccupations of the War. After the winter of 1915 it appeared that the struggle on the Western Front and elsewhere would be a long one, and consequently further mobilisation of the resources of the Empire might be necessary. In 1916 the Government of India had to follow intensive methods of recruitment and also to make adequate preparation for the supply of war material. Above all, the essential need was to preserve peace within the border of India.

The cry that the War in which India was participating was being fought for freedom had some effect upon a section of Indian intelligentsia, who persuaded some to believe that England's hour of danger was India's opportunity for breaking away from the Empire. A number of revolutionary societies were formed, possibly under the instigation of Germany, and the troubles brewing in the Moslem countries had begun to react upon the North-Western Frontier Province and the Punjab. A plan for an organized rebellion was formed in 1915. The co-operation of Afghanistan, Turkey and Russia was sought by the instigators, working under the spell of England's enemies to embarrass her position in India. In August 1916 the Government came to know of the plot through some letters which fell into their hands, and the conspiracy proved abortive.

Internal disorders broke out in many places throughout India. In the Punjab the slogan that " we should commit dacoity on the Government and awaken the whole of the Punjab " was spread through the *Ghadr* party. The revolutionary doctrines began to reach the Sikhs and the Pathans, the tribes that supply the bulk of the Indian troops. But, while such recrudescences of revolt had to be suppressed, the Imperial Government foresaw the necessity of strengthening their position in India by recognizing the claims of Nationalism, which was bound to receive fresh impetus from the post-war developments in the near East. The War had greatly weakened most of the bureaucratic governments and their reconstruction would have to be based on a different footing. Then there was the general question of the influence of European power in Asia which had to be borne in mind:

> "Great Britain was, in 1919 and 1920, intensely unpopular throughout the East," says the late Sir Henry Dobbs. "India was in turmoil; Afghanistan attacked us; Persia repudiated her treaty with us and bitterly suspected our motives; the Persian Divines in the Holy Cities of Iraq shared the feelings of their Mother Country, and stirred up the Shiah tribes; the Turks of Anatolia had revived and were pushing against both the British and the French; Egypt was convulsed by hatred of the British protectorate." [1]

The policy adopted by the Imperial Government in India was, therefore, based on two principles, namely, (1) determined efforts to suppress the revolutionary movement, and (2) the grant of a measure of constitutional Reforms with a view to leading India to the status of a self-governing member of the British Commonwealth.

But the outcome of drastic measures taken to control the forces of Indian Nationalism was the growing conviction that India had gone back to the autocratic regime of Lord Curzon, and that she could not expect much from her loyal response to England's crisis. The situation is well summed up in the following observation of a well-known British journalist:

> "After the first delighted recognition of India's wonderful response to the call of the Allies, blindness and repression on the part of the Executive had chilled the educated classes and stimulated all forms of extremism." [2]

By the end of 1915 the moderating influence of the Indian National Congress yielded to the creed of the "left

[1] "Britain's Work in Iraq": article by Sir Henry Dobbs, G.B.E., in *The United Empire*, March 1933.

[2] "Sir William Wedderburn and the Indian Reform Movement," by S. K. Ratcliffe, 1923.

wing" party. Under the clarion call of Tilak and Mrs. Besant, the Home Rule League was formed, bringing within its fold the Nationalist leaders who were dissatisfied with the "mere moonshine" of the Morley-Minto Reforms. The Home Rule agitation was thus set afoot and rent the political sky with the slogan of India for the Indians, which reminded one of the Irish situation in the latter part of the last century. The significant development of the Home Rule crusade was the increasing association with it of those leaders of the Congress who had so far believed in the fulfilment of India's political aspirations through the support of British Liberalism. In the case of most of them it was an association of despair.

ℭ. STEPS TOWARDS CONSTITUTIONAL CHANGE

Lord Chelmsford, the Viceroy, became anxious to meet the situation by making it known that he was contemplating drawing up a scheme of post-war reforms and that his Government would gladly welcome practical suggestions from Indian politicians in regard to any change in the mechanism of the Government of India.

In October 1916, nineteen elected members of the Imperial Legislative Council addressed a memorandum to the Viceroy on the subject. They suggested (1) half the members of the Imperial and Provincial Executive Councils to be Indians elected by the people, (2) a substantial elected majority in all Legislative Councils, (3) fiscal autonomy and the right of voting supplies, (4) abolition of the Council of the Secretary of State for India, (5) provincial autonomy, (6) a position similar to that of self-governing Dominions in any scheme of Imperial Federation, and (7) right to carry arms, enlistment in territorial units and eligibility for commissions in the Army on conditions similar to those for Europeans.

The Indian National Congress at its session at Lucknow endorsed the proposals by passing a resolution that the Indian demands consisted of measures that would "lift her from the position of a Dependency to that of an equal partner in the Empire with the self-governing Dominions."

But the Home Rule agitation, led by Mrs. Besant, continued to gain momentum and succeeded in drawing the leaders of all the All-India Moslem League into a pact (known as the Lucknow Pact) for pressing their united demand for full and immediate self-government. The pact was a compromise. Its sponsors probably did not realize that an agreement based on separate electorates for Mohammedans would constitute not merely "a very serious hindrance to the development of the self-governing principle," but a definite menace to India's future political status. Their immediate objective was to impress on the authorities that there was an imperative necessity for granting self-government to India and that the question could not be put aside on any plausible plea.

Meanwhile Lord Chelmsford had sent a despatch to Mr. (now Sir) Austen Chamberlain, then Secretary of State for India, suggesting means for conferring some concessions in regard to political power upon the representatives of the Indian people. The Viceroy's anxiety arose from the growing solidarity among the politically-minded Indians in their demand for Home Rule for India. "To the many problems with which the Cabinet were confronted during the summer of 1917," writes Lord Ronaldshay, "was added that of the future of government of India. The situation in India itself was such that the Viceroy considered it his duty to press for a very early statement of the views and intentions of the Home Government." [1] It should be noted here that in the cataclysm of War, the normal Cabinet system was suspended in Great Britain and the War Cabinet was supreme. The Cabinet had misgivings and doubts in regard to making a definite promise of self-government for India which might set a *fixed* goal of a Parliamentary system of government on a democratic basis. But in May 1917 the Secretary of State wrote:

[1] "The Life of Lord Curzon," by Lord Ronaldshay.

"It is not too much to say that upon a right decision at this critical time depends the peace and contentment of India for years and perhaps generations to come."[1]

Mr. Chamberlain left the India Office in July as a result of the Report of the Mesopotamian Commission. The matter did not proceed further until Mr. Edwin Montagu came to the India Office. As Under-Secretary in the Asquith Government he was familiar with Indian affairs, and it was in his hands that Lord Chelmsford's views on India's constitutional advance received close attention. He was finally able to persuade the Cabinet to agree to make a definite statement in regard to Government's intention to introduce a measure of constitutional reform in India.

A great deal of controversy stirred the War Cabinet and the India Office over the use of the term "Self-Government" in a pronouncement which would definitely commit His Majesty's Government to a form of government based on the Parliamentary system.

Lord Curzon, who was in the War Cabinet, took a prominent part in the controversy and finally took a hand in the drafting of the announcement. The expression "responsible government" seemed to him "rather safer" than the word "Self-Government." What subtle distinctions between these two expressions were in Lord Curzon's mind he had not explained in the course of the controversy; but it is certain that neither the interpretation of the announcement nor its full implications were envisaged by him. In the course of a debate in the House of Lords (December 1919) on the Government of India Bill, he said:

"This is a great experiment. I would not have quarrelled with anybody who used the words 'daring experiment'! I am not certain that I should cavil even at the word 'rash.'"

But Lord Curzon was not alone in complaining that the Secretary of State for India was "proceeding at breakneck speed" and that he was launching a hazardous experiment.

[1] Quoted in "The Life of Lord Curzon," by Lord Ronaldshay.

"Some of us, like Lord Birkenhead, then Lord Chancellor, and no doubt previously consulted on the legal aspects, had misgivings and doubts," writes the Rt. Hon. Winston S. Churchill.[1]

ℂ THE MONTAGU DECLARATION

On August 20, 1917, in reply to a question in the House of Commons, Mr. Montagu, with the full authority of the Cabinet, made an announcement in the following terms:

> "The policy of His Majesty's Government, with which the Government of India are in complete accord, is that of the increasing association of Indians in every branch of the administration and the gradual development of self-governing institutions with a view to the progressive realization of responsible government in India as an integral part of the British Empire. . . . I would add that progress in this policy can only be achieved by successive stages. The British Government and the Government of India, on whom the responsibility lies for the welfare and advancement of the Indian peoples, must be judges of the time and measure of each advance, and they must be guided by the co-operation received from those upon whom new opportunities of service will thus be conferred and by the extent to which it is found that confidence can be reposed in their sense of responsibility."

A few months later the Secretary of State went to India and, after consulting with prominent Indian political leaders, he and the Viceroy drew up a joint Report (April 1918) laying down general principles on which, in their judgment, a Bill should be drafted. A quotation from their Report will show what future they had envisaged in regard to India and her relations with the Empire:

> "Our conception of the eventual future of India is a sisterhood of states, self-governing in all matters of purely local interest. . . . Over this congeries of states would preside a central Government, increasingly responsible to

[1] India: Speeches by the Rt. Hon. Winston S. Churchill (Thornton Butterworth, Ltd.), 1931.

the people of all of them; dealing with matters, both internal and external, of common interest to the whole of India; acting as arbiter in interstate relations, and representing the interests of all India on equal terms with the self-governing units of the British Empire. In this picture there is a place also for the Native States."

The reception given to the Report by Indian politicians was what its authors anticipated. It was acclaimed as a remarkable document unlike anything generally issued by the Indian official world, and its contents as a positive evidence of His Majesty's Government's intention to conciliate the growing desire of Indians for political responsibility. All political groups awaited eagerly the new era, and Gandhi, though not actively engaged in the political field at the time, "considered the scheme an honest attempt to fulfil the pledge of Government and advised that it should receive careful and sympathetic handling." [1]

The Montagu-Chelmsford Report was remitted to a Select Committee of both Houses, under the chairmanship of Lord Selborne, while the task of working out certain details of the proposals was entrusted upon three Committees. An assurance of expediting the Reforms was conveyed to the people of India by the promise of a Bill in the King's Speech, and eventually the Government of India Act, 1919,[2] passed through all its stages without a division on any fundamental issue.

¶ THE GOVERNMENT OF INDIA ACT, 1919

The policy of the Government, as stated in the announcement, was elaborated in the preamble to the Government of India Act, 1919, which runs as follows:

(i) "Whereas it is the declared policy of Parliament to provide for the increasing association of Indians in every branch of Indian Administration, and for the gradual development

[1] "Life of Gandhi," by Gray and Parekh.
[2] 9 and 10 Geo. V, c. 101.

of self-governing institutions, with a view to the progressive realization of responsible government in British India as an integral part of the Empire:

(ii) "And whereas progress in giving effect to this policy can only be achieved by successive stages, and it is expedient that substantial steps in this direction should now be taken:

(iii) "And whereas the time and manner of each advance can be determined only by Parliament, upon whom responsibility lies for the welfare and advancement of the Indian peoples:

(iv) "And whereas the action of Parliament in such matters must be guided by the co-operation received from those on whom new opportunities of service will be conferred, and by the extent to which it is found that confidence can be reposed in their sense of responsibility:

(v) "And whereas concurrently with the gradual development of self-governing institutions in the Provinces of India it is expedient to give to those Provinces in provincial matters the largest measure of independence of the Government of India which is compatible with the due discharge by the latter of its own responsibilities."

I have quoted both the announcement and the preamble at length in order to enable the reader to follow the subsequent constitutional developments; for the preamble was at once the centre of the controversies that arose and of the great constitutional charter given to the peoples of India. I have also set out in detail the causes which had forced the Indian question to the front at a time when the Government was so fully absorbed in the Great War, an unbiassed estimation of which would show that the announcement of August 20, 1917, was not merely "a graceful act of recognition" of India's service during the War; nor the Act of 1919 merely a reward for India's loyalty to the Empire in the hour of a crisis. The Indian soldiers who laid down their lives in the War were surely not inspired with the ideal that their sacrifice would secure for India a measure of political concessions. And those who willingly offered their services and contributions to the War had no thought of "buying" political power after the cessation of the struggle. The instinct of self-interest and the spirit of loyalty induced the Princes to rally their forces in aid of the Empire, and they, too, had no political objective to gain. It is not true that India's participation in the War won for her a pledge for "responsible and representative form of government"; nor is it correct to label the Act as having contained a "Jephthah-like" pledge; or commitments injudiciously made. The assertion frequently made that the Reforms were given to India at a time of War fatigue under the influence of some form of neurosis could not be logically maintained from what transpired between the Imperial Government and the Government of India over a period of three years beginning from 1916.

The true explanation is that the announcement of August 20, 1917, was made in response to the forces, both external and internal, that were evolved in India's relationship with Great Britain. And the convergence of these forces so reacted on Indian politico-economic life as to convince the Government of India and the British Government and people that a new orientation was required. The most that can be said as regards the influence of the War was that it may have hastened a little an inevitable change.

The Royal Proclamation, dated December 23, 1919, which announced the passing of the Government of India Act, 1919, to the peoples of India, declared why "a definite step on the road to responsible government" was taken.

The King-Emperor said:

> "I have watched with understanding and sympathy the growing desire of my Indian people for representative institutions. Starting from small beginnings, this ambition has steadily strengthened its hold upon the intelligence of the country. . . . In truth, the desire after political responsibility has its source at the roots of the British connection with India. It has sprung inevitably from the deeper and wider studies of human thought and history which that

connection has opened to the Indian people. Without it the work of the British in India would have been incomplete."

ℭ. UNFORESEEN CIRCUMSTANCES

But stars of ill-omen presided over the nativity of the Act and their malign influences seemed to have affected the Reforms throughout. The Defence of India Act, a War-time measure, expired in 1917, and the Government on enquiry came to the conclusion that it should be empowered to deal with the revolutionary spirit that existed in endemic form in certain Provinces, and also with the situation that might develop in consequence of anti-British propaganda in certain foreign countries. The Government decided to appoint a Committee "to investigate and report on the nature and extent of the criminal conspiracies connected with the revolutionary movement in India," and the Committee, under the chairmanship of Sir Sidney Rowlatt, a Judge of the English High Court of Justice, reached India a month after Mr. Montagu's arrival. The Committee concluded its investigation by April 1918, but the Report, known as the "Rowlatt Report," was not released till October.

In order to implement the main recommendations of the Committee, the Government introduced two draft Bills into the Legislative Council in February 1919, one (The Criminal Law Amendment Bill No. I of 1919) proposing some radical changes in the criminal law, and the other (The Criminal Emergency Powers Bill No. II of 1919) adequately empowering the Executive to cope with emergency. At once a storm of protest was raised against these Bills, and the Government had to abandon the first, but passed the second into law on March 1919, through the support of the officials in the Legislative Councils. About two weeks before the enactment of the "Rowlatt Bill," Gandhi launched an organized campaign to resist the action of the Government, but not before he had begged the Viceroy to veto the Bill.

He held that the Bill, which sanctioned extra-legal methods, might be employed against legitimate political agitation; that distrust of the police has been a marked feature of almost all popular movements in India, and through the newly-acquired powers police methods might be ruthlessly employed against the people; and lastly, that repressive measures should not precede the proposed constitutional benedictions upon India.

While the agitation against the Rowlatt Bill was gaining in intensity, affairs in the North-West Frontier and in Afghanistan had become a source of anxiety to the authorities in the Punjab. For our purpose here it is not necessary to recount the history that led to the incident within the boundary of the Jallianwala Bagh at Amritsar on April 13, 1919; nor should we recall the excessive punishments of humiliation inflicted on the citizens after the tragedy. "It was a black day in the annals of British rule," wrote the late Sir Valentine Chirol. "That is an episode," observed Mr. Winston Churchill in the House of Commons, "which appears to me to be without precedent or parallel in the modern history of the British Empire." A Committee of Enquiry, presided over by Lord Hunter, a former Solicitor-General for Scotland, came to the conclusion that "the action taken by him (General Dyer) had been in complete violation of the principles that should rule the employment of military force in support of civil authority." The Commander-in-Chief in India removed him from his employment, and the Army Council decided not to offer him further employment outside India. But the bitterness the incident produced poisoned the soul of India and it became difficult even for Britain's friends in India to retain confidence in the Government. When, about two years later, His Royal Highness the Duke of Connaught went to India to inaugurate the new Indian Legislatures, he realized this, and spoke of "the shadow of Amritsar lengthening darkly over the land."

The second star of ill that cast an evil eye upon the inauguration of Reforms was the Treaty of Sèvres, the terms of which were published in the summer of 1920. The treaty imposed humiliating terms on the Turks by proposing to drive them from Constantinople. The Mohammedans in India felt that " the lighthouse of Islam " was attacked by the British and that " their loyal support to the cause of the Allies during the War counted for nothing in the day of victory." The revolt was organized under the designation of the Khilafat movement, which joined hand in hand with the Congress agitation in order to embarrass the Government.

The net result of these two incidents—the Amritsar tragedy and the Treaty of Sèvres—was the widening of the psychological chasm between the British and the Indian intelligentsia. Thus, the goodwill which alone would have animated the inauguration of Reforms was wholly absent, and the agitation continued to aggravate the situation, in the midst of which His Royal Highness the Duke of Connaught delivered a Royal message to the people of India proclaiming the beginnings of "*Swaraj* within My Empire" and " the widest scope and ample opportunity for progress to the liberty which my other Dominions enjoy."

The new Indian Legislatures were inaugurated on February 9, 1921. On this occasion Lord Chelmsford explained the character of the change that was introduced in the structure of the Government. He said :

> " There are changes of degree so great as to be changes of kind, and this is one of them. For the first time the principle of autocracy, which had not been wholly discarded in all earlier reforms, was definitely abandoned ; the conception of the British Government as a benevolent despotism was finally renounced ; and in its place was substituted that of a guiding authority whose rôle it would be to assist the steps of India along the road that, in the fulness of time, would lead to complete self-government within the Empire. In the interval required for the accomplishment of this task, certain powers of supervision, and, if need be, intervention, would be retained, and substantial steps towards redeeming the pledges of

the Government were to be taken at the earliest moment possible."

Before we survey the working of the new Legislatures let us briefly review the constitutional changes effected by the Government of India Act, 1919.

ℂ DETAILS OF CONSTITUTIONAL CHANGES

The Act fully retained the authority of the Imperial Government but attempted to introduce certain changes in the Government of India. Nothing like a Federation was contemplated. In working out devices for reconciling diverse elements that exist in India within the framework of a unitary Constitution, the Act established a form of government in the Provinces known as "Dyarchy." The term was unfamiliar to most Indians and was derided as a "hurly-burly innovation," and became an appropriate subject for humorous treatment. Sir Harcourt Butler writes:

> "In India it has almost become a term of abuse. I have heard one man shouting to another 'you are a dyarchy.' 'I will beat you with a dyarchy,' said one Indian boy to another, and when questioned as to what a dyarchy was replied, 'a new kind of tennis racket.' I have been received in a Burma village by a dyarchy band braying against a home-rule band with all the vigour of village faction, neither having the least idea what home rule or dyarchy meant." [1]

To those who received the gift it meant "Double government." Under the scheme all the subjects of administration were divided into two categories, Central and Provincial. There were 47 Central subjects and the rest were devolved upon the Provincial Governments. These Provincial subjects of administration were again classified into two groups—"Reserved" and "Transferred." That is, subjects such as Law and Order, Finance, Land Revenue, Famine Relief,

[1] "India Insistent," by Sir Harcourt Butler (Heinemann), 1931.

numbering 36 in all, were designated as " Reserved," and were placed in the hands of the Governors with their Executive Councils; and subjects such as Education, Agriculture, Public Health, Local Self-Government, numbering 20 in all, handed over to Indian Ministers responsible to the Legislature, came to be known as " Transferred." Thus, the Provincial Executive consisted of these two halves with the Governor as the co-ordinating authority.

The structure of the Provincial Legislative Councils under the Reforms underwent many striking changes. The Act provided that at least 70 per cent. of the numbers of a Legislative Council should be elected members (in the case of Burma the percentage is 60), and that not more than 20 per cent. should be nominated by the Governor from members of the permanent Civil Service and the balance of 10 per cent. from non-officials.

The Central Legislature would consist of:

(*a*) A Second Chamber, called a Council of State, containing 60 members, of whom 33 shall be elected and 27 nominated;

(*b*) A Lower House, called the Legislative Assembly, consisting of 145 members, of whom 104 shall be elected and 41 nominated. The latter would include 26 officials.

The life of the Assembly would be three years, but the Governor-General would have power to prolong or shorten the life of the Central Legislature.

The reader will gather from these provisions that while the elements of responsibility had been introduced in the Provincial Legislature, though restricted in their scope to " Transferred " subjects, they were not provided for in the Central Legislature. The main structure of the Central Government remained unitary. The only change was the enlargement of the Central Legislature as the initial step towards the creation of representative institutions at the Centre. We should bear in mind that the Reforms were not designed to be anything more than a temporary expedient and that the purpose aimed at was to test the representative form of government, somewhat on the lines of the British Parliamentary system, under conditions obtaining in India.

Before reviewing the working of the Reforms, it will be desirable to outline the franchise adopted for the Central and Provincial Legislatures.

ℂ FRANCHISE

The foundation of democratic institutions rests on Franchise. The issues involved in the creation of an electorate under the special conditions obtaining in India are extremely difficult. The system adopted by the Morley-Minto Reforms has been noted in the previous chapter. That system was scrapped under the Reforms of 1919 in favour of a direct electorate. Its adoption was indeed a real "leap in the dark." The circumstances under which direct election came to be regarded as a better method of election to the Provincial Legislatures are stated in the Montagu-Chelmsford Report. Its authors held that the system of indirect election which existed in the Morley-Minto Reforms should be swept away because of the unreality which characterized the Councils owing to the absence of any genuine relationship between the representative and the original voter. The intention was indeed generous, but the remedy was suggested without a full analysis of the basic problem; or adequate consideration of the implications of the change. The unreality and absence of genuine relationship between the representative and the voter were no doubt there; but it was due not in the least to indirect election as such, but to the most unsatisfactory manner in which the local self-governing bodies were at that time constituted and functioning.

The real remedy against the weakness which was found to exist in the franchise would have been retention of the indirect system with a simultaneous overhauling of the entire machinery of local self-government. But then the Report on the Indian Constitutional Reforms dismissed local self-government in a little over a page! Successive Commissions and Committees have not sought to rectify this mistake. In order to remedy the defects arising from direct franchise, the Indian Statutory Commission recommended, as will be seen in the following Chapters, an extension of that system. The history of direct election to the Provincial Legislatures has been a history of which no one can be proud, and from which no one can take any lessons for the future until local self-government becomes an accomplished fact in Indian politics. The system of direct election under the present social and economic conditions obtaining in India will not mitigate the grave risk of the exploitation of the illiterate and helpless masses by a dominant enfranchised oligarchy; nor will the perpetuation of direct election result in what is implied by the phrase "effective representation." The only argument in favour of the system of direct election seems to me to be, that Indian political leaders are generally enamoured of direct election because it leaves political power concentrated in the hands of the propertied and literate classes.

In accordance with the proposal of the Montagu-Chelmsford Report, a special Committee[1] was appointed to "measure the number of persons who can in the different parts of the country be reasonably entrusted with the duties of Citizenship." The aim was the extension of franchise, bearing in mind that its limitations should be determined rather with reference to administrative difficulties than "to any *a priori* considerations as to the degree of education" or other restricting tests. The franchise under the new Constitution was therefore based on (1) residence in a constituency; (2) the possession of certain property qualifications as measured by the payment of a prescribed minimum of land revenue or rent, or local rates (in rural areas), or municipal rates (in urban areas), or income tax; (3) a certain form of military service to the State.

[1] The Southborough Franchise Committee.

The franchise of the Second Chamber (The Council of State) was different, based partly on a high property qualification and partly on records of public service. The Chamber was designed to constitute a body of "Elder Statesmen." As regards the Legislative Assembly, its electorate numbers about one million; the qualification for which was kept fairly high but variable in order to meet the conditions of the different Provinces.

The total number of electors in all the Provinces (including Burma) was over seven millions—that is, about one in every nine adult males. The following table shows the proportion of electors to population :

THE PROVINCIAL ELECTORATE[1]

Under the Reforms of 1919

Provinces.	Proportion of electors to population (per cent.).	Proportion of male electors to adult male population (per cent.).	Proportion of female electors to adult female population (per cent.).
Madras	3·2	11·6	1·0
Bombay	3·9	13·4	0·8
Bengal	2·5	9·7	0·3
United Provinces . .	3·5	12·4	0·4
Punjab	3·4	11·9	0·5
Bihar and Orissa . .	1·1	4·6	—
Assam	3·7	14·2	0·2
Central Provinces and Berar	1·3	5·2	—
Burma	17·4	60·3	4·6

The electorate was undoubtedly small; but it should be realized that the task for the new Constitution was to call into being an electorate which did not exist in order to work a Constitution which was to bear the semblance of responsible government. We should have no quarrel with

[1] The figures are based on 1926 returns except in the case of Burma, where they are for 1928.

the size of the electorate at this stage, but its defects produced "the anomalous result of conferring the franchise on several people who are illiterate, while at the same time denying the vote to considerable numbers of adult literates." [1] The electoral system, owing to the adoption of property qualifications as the general basis for franchise, excluded the general body, the poor, nearly all the women and the bulk of the Depressed classes. It resulted in a discriminatory enfranchisement of various classes in the Punjab, where the agrarian legislation known as the Alienation of Land Act of 1900 precluded members of non-agricultural tribes from dispossessing members of agricultural tribes of land. Again, junior members of the family under the Indian joint family system could not be enfranchised. These were some of the outstanding defects of the franchise under the Reforms of 1919. The planning of constituencies for the Provincial Legislatures had seriously prejudiced the representation of minority communities. Some of the rural constituencies were as large as the whole of Scotland ; and the reader may well imagine how such unwieldy constituencies, under Indian conditions, would fulfil the purpose of a democratic political system.

I am often asked what use has been made of the vote by the enfranchised population. It is true that the novelty of the election campaign, which must be a source of attraction to the voters, provided them with some excitement. The success of the campaign, is, however, dependent on party organization. From the figures quoted opposite, showing percentage of votes polled, it is clear that the electorate responds whenever there is an effective organization for rousing enthusiasm in the election. The first election was held in 1920, when the Congress took no part in it and left the electoral field to the Liberals, who were handicapped by their want of organization. But the increase in the percentage of votes polled in two successive elections was

[1] See "The Key to Freedom and Security in India," by An Indian Student of Political Science. Oxford University Press : 1933.

largely due to the determination of the Congress to sweep the polls.

Province.	Percentage of votes polled in the election of:		
	1920	1923	1926
Madras	24·9	36·3	48·6
Bombay	16·2	38·4	39·0
Bengal	33·4	39·0	39·2
United Provinces	33·0	42·2	50·2
Punjab	32·0	49·3	52·4
Bihar and Orissa	41·0	52·0	61·0
Central Provinces	22·5	57·7	61·9
Assam	16·4	37·5	35·0

From what I have seen in Bengal and the United Provinces, especially in rural constituencies, the above figures do not indicate either success of the electoral system or awakening of political interest among the voters. My own observation confirms my conviction that under the existing social and economic conditions, the rural voters cannot exercise franchise independently and that their votes are mostly determined by the influence of landlords, moneylenders, lawyers' touts, priests, and a host of other agents. But these problems must have arisen at the initial stage of all modern democracies. Since the dominance of vested and sectional interests presents a special difficulty in India, the proper solution is likely to be found in evolving such an electoral system as will have organic relation with local bodies.

In our discussion upon the subject of franchise, we cannot overlook another fatal deficiency in the Indian electoral system, namely, communal electorates. The authors of the Joint Report regretted the necessity of retaining them, the principle of which was unfortunately recognized in the Morley-Minto Reforms. The Communities in India could not arrive at an agreed settlement and therefore the Government of India Act, 1919, had to make provision for communal electorates. We shall see in our subsequent reference to the communal problem that the system not only retards the growth of democratic institutions in India, but greatly aggravates one of the fatal maladies of Indian social life.

With this brief survey of the structure of the Reforms of 1919, we now turn to the reception given to the measure by the Indian political and other interests.

ℭ INDIA'S REACTION TO THE REFORMS

The publication of the Montagu-Chelmsford Report in July 1918 resulted in a complete schism between the two sections of the Congress. The moderates threw themselves on the side of the reform proposals and decided to lend their support for the success of the measure of responsible self-government embodied in them. The leader of this group, Sir Surendranath Banerjea, in a speech in the Imperial Legislative Council, commented upon the Report in the following terms:

> "Taking this report as a whole, I think it must be conceded that it affords a striking illustration of a change in the angle of vision on the part of our rulers, and I venture to assert that it ought to be accompanied by a similar transformation in our attitude in regard to the Government of the country. . . . They have now stretched out to us the hand of fellowship and friendship, and I invite my countrymen to grasp it with alacrity and enthusiasm, and in co-operation with British statesmanship to march forward to the accomplishment of those high destinies which, under the providence of God, are reserved for our people."

Neither the Amritsar tragedy nor the Khalifat movement deflected the moderates from their determination to pursue the course of co-operation, and, therefore, they parted company with the Congress.

The Congress, on the other hand, under the influence of extreme nationalism, regarded the proposals as falling far short of Indian aspirations. In a manifesto issued by the

Nationalists it was asserted that the Report was radically wrong in principle and that they condemned it *in toto.*

Tilak declared that the proposed scheme was "entirely unacceptable," and the leader of the Home Rule agitation, Mrs. Besant, rejected it as being "unworthy to be offered by England or to be accepted by India." A special session of the Congress (August 1918) was convened to consider the Report, but the general trend of its opposition was to strike a bargain before the Bill emerged from the Joint Select Committee. A year later its opposition became violent, as we have seen, not because of inadequate reforms but of the passing of the Rowlatt Act and the incidents that followed. Subsequently the Congress, under the leadership of Gandhi, accepted his programme of non-co-operation at its session in 1919 held at Amritsar. While the great majority were in favour of refusing any gift "from blood-stained hands," a section of the Congress was in favour of standing as candidates for the Reformed Councils. For the three years following this session of the Congress, Gandhi's creed reigned supreme in the Indian national movement, till in 1923 circumstances obliged the Nationalists to change the battle-front.

The Moslem leaders were on the whole satisfied with the Reforms, especially in regard to the retention of communal electorates; but at the time of the inauguration of the new Constitution they were rather pre-occupied with the future of Turkey! They persuaded themselves to believe that the interference with the Sultanate, as designed in the Treaty of Sèvres, would mean giving offence to the religious law of Islam. And we have seen that Gandhi entered into an alliance with the Khalifat movement in order to find a common cause of grievance against the Imperial Government. Though the alliance was short-lived, and served no useful purpose, it induced the Government of India to protest against certain provisions imposed upon Turkey by the Treaty of Sèvres. The Moslem agitation in India, however, received a set-back when Turkey deposed the Khalif.

The British commercial community in India now foresaw the necessity of taking an active interest in public questions and reorganized the European Association[1] on an All-India basis. Its attitude towards the Reforms was not hostile and its representatives in the Councils and the Assembly lent support to the new Constitution when it was threatened with deadlock by the intransigent Nationalists.

The officials, with their strong conservative tendencies, accepted the new Constitution with some misgivings in regard to its smooth working; but they were prepared to give it a trial. Sir Frederick Whyte, who was appointed as the first President of the Legislative Assembly, observed that a proportion of the officials accepted the Reforms as the Duke of Wellington looked upon the Reform Bill—" ready to take the damned thing, and let it pass, because the King's Government must be carried on." It was, indeed, clear to them that the strong Central Government and the reservation of " Key " portfolios to the Executive Councils of Provincial Governments would provide sufficient safeguards against the vagaries and vicissitudes of Indian politics.

Let us now review the actual working of the Dyarchy, the avowed object of which was to introduce " responsible government " in British India.

¶ WORKING OF REFORMS

The first elections to the new Councils were held in 1920. As the Congress decided to boycott the Councils, the Liberals succeeded in gaining an easy victory at the polls; but they did not avail themselves of the opportunity of organizing the Liberal Party or of formulating a definite programme. They ignored their serious handicaps, due to a want of electoral organization, when on the other hand their rivals were consolidating their position in the country.

[1] This Association is the political organization of the British non-official community in India. Its membership is on an individual basis and not on the basis of firms as is the case of the Chambers of Commerce.

(*a*) Financial Impediments

At the very outset, the working of the new Constitution was faced with a critical financial situation. The trouble with Afghanistan (May to August 1919) and the military operations against the rebellious frontier tribes (October 1919 to May 1920) cost the Government of India about 15 millions sterling. Then came the currency disturbance. Since the closing of the Mints to the free coinage of silver in 1893, India had an exchange standard with a ratio of fifteen rupees to the sovereign (that is, one shilling and fourpence to the rupee). But it was found impossible to maintain the ratio during the War—chiefly on account of two factors, namely, (1) the heavy demand for rupee currency for the purchase of the War materials ; and (2) the rise in the price of silver. The result was that by April 1918 the rupee had risen to one shilling and sixpence and by September 1919 the ratio stood approximately at two shillings to the rupee. The Government of India sought the aid of an expert Committee,[1] which recommended the stabilization of exchange at that rate ; but, while the Government took steps to do so, gold prices started falling and finally the sterling-dollar rate collapsed. The situation played havoc with the Government finance and violently shook the fabric of trade. The attempt to stabilize the rupee had to be abandoned, but not before the Government had lost about £55,000,000.[2]

The repercussions of the currency disturbances on the general trade of the country were perhaps more devastating than any other single factor that became operative during the post-war period. The traders, large and small, lost heavily either in their business or in the frenzy of speculation the situation encouraged. The loss is estimated at hundreds of millions. The primary producers, the Indian agriculturists, were also severely hit by the dislocation of the export

[1] The Babington Smith Committee, Cmd. 527 of 1920.

[2] See " India : the New Phase," by Sir Stanley Reed and P. R. Cadell. Philip Allan : 1928.

trade, and by the rise in prices of such articles for which they were dependent on imports. In other words, almost all the circumstances which were favourable to widespread unrest were conjured up simultaneously with the inauguration of Reforms.

Further aggravation of the situation was caused by the imposition of fresh taxes in order to meet the increasing deficit which, during the five years ending 1922–23, aggregated nearly 100 crores of rupees. On the eve of the dissolution of the Assembly the finance member proposed doubling the Salt tax! The Assembly, which had already voted new taxes amounting to about £51,000,000,[1] refused to support this unpopular tax, and the Viceroy, in exercise of his special powers, certified the impost. The inevitable consequence was that the hands of the wreckers of the Constitution were greatly strengthened, and they easily displaced the sitting members of the Assembly at the following election.

But the needs of the Central Government could not be satisfied by exploiting the sources of revenues assigned for central purposes, and the question of apportionment of revenues and expenditure between the Central Government and the Provinces became a dominant issue. Rules under the Government of India Act, 1919, laid down the principle of dividing national revenue heads between the Central and Provincial Governments in relation to their respective functions. It aimed at the laudable object of making the Provinces financially independent of the Central Government in conformity with the recommendations of the Montagu-Chelmsford Report, which stated that "if provincial autonomy is to mean anything real, clearly the Provinces must not be dependent on the Indian Government for the means of provincial development." But the Government of India had deficits which were to be met by provincial contributions based on the extra amount made available to each Province by the new scheme of distribution of revenue.

[1] See "India: the New Phase," by Sir Stanley Reed and P. R. Cadell.

The settlement thus arrived at is known as the "Meston settlement."[1]

But the Meston Committee's calculations in regard to provincial finance were also upset by the world financial blizzard. In its report, the prospect of "inaugurating the new Councils without the necessity of resort to fresh taxation" was held out; but at the very beginning these anticipations proved to be chimerical. Every Province, with the single exception of the Punjab, was faced with a deficit, and almost all Provincial Governments had to balance their Budgets by extra taxation. The Government of India was then not in a position to bring some relief to this state of affairs by reducing the financial contribution from the Provinces. The situation is summed up by the Reforms Enquiry Committee as follows:

> "The difficulty arising from finance has formed one of the main obstacles to the success of the Reforms. . . . It is due to it (*i.e.* the Meston settlement) that Ministers have been unable to enter upon a policy of progressive development in the spheres of administration committed to their care. If they had been able to do so, they would have been able to provide an answer to those critics who have reiterated the allegation that the reforms were a sham, and they would also have been able to consolidate their position or else have been required to make way for other Ministers who could have enunciated a policy more acceptable to the Councils which would incidentally have assisted in the establishment of the responsibility of the Ministers to the Councils."

However, the position of the Provincial Budgets did not much improve when the financial contributions to the Central Government ceased in the succeeding years. In any case, no substantial amount was available to the departments that concerned the welfare of the masses. The Dyarchic

[1] The Financial Relations Committee was appointed, with Lord Meston as Chairman, in order to work out the details of provincial contributions to the Central Government.

Constitution enormously increased the cost of the top-heavy administration and swallowed up all available resources, leaving almost nothing for the introduction of measures calculated to assist social and economic development.

(*b*) Constitutional Difficulties

The Liberals who had welcomed the Reforms and entered the new Legislatures with the hope that they would now be marching towards the goal of responsible government, afforded their rivals an occasion for jest and gave their official supporters a surprise when they declared in the Assembly that the new Constitution was inadequate and should be revised! The obvious reply to this demand came from Viscount Peel, then Secretary of State for India, who pointed out that a period of six months could not possibly be regarded as being sufficient for the trial of the Constitutional experiment and that the question of its revision was indeed premature. In 1923, when the Nationalists replaced the Liberals in the Assembly, they reiterated the demand, and the Government agreed to institute an enquiry into the working of the Act of 1919. The terms of reference of the Reforms Enquiry Committee, known as the Muddiman Committee, were naturally restricted to such amendments as might be recommended within the limits of the Act. While the Majority Report [1] suggested certain modifications, the minority urged the abolition of Dyarchy.

The truth behind the chronic opposition to Dyarchy from its very inception was to be found in the *manner* the new Constitution started to function. It was not long before Indian leaders realized that Dyarchy was no school for freedom. In the first place, the Legislature itself had no corporate responsibility. The decision of a Minister in charge of the "transferred subjects," for example, was only a recommendation to a Governor; and in the event of his rejecting it, the Minister himself would probably resign

[1] Report of Reforms Enquiry Committee, Cmd. 2360, 1925.

without in any way affecting his colleagues. Or, the successful venture of a Minister in giving effect to his proposals would depend on a Finance Minister who belonged to the other half of the administration. This proved to be a serious handicap to the ministerial position, and in every Province this financial arrangement not only led to considerable friction but to a certain amount of irresponsibility in both the halves of the Government.

Secondly, the dividing line between the two halves of the Government became blurred in the actual working of the Constitution. It worked comparatively well in the Provinces (*e.g.* Madras, the Punjab), where the Governor ignored Dyarchy and treated the two halves of the Government as one Cabinet. In Madras, for example, Lord Willingdon held most of the meetings of the Executive Council jointly with his Executive Councillors and Ministers.

Commenting upon this development within a year of the introduction of Reforms, a visiting American Professor, Dr. C. H. Van Tyne, says: "Dyarchy is in fact become in most cases a Unitary Government in which a Governor sits in Council with all his Ministers, those responsible for the 'transferred' subjects, as well as those concerned with the 'reserved.'" But, while the policy might have been wise in avoiding friction, it resulted in offering no scope to Indian Ministers for the exercise of their responsibilities. They leaned on the Governor and his Executive Councillors, and in the eyes of the Legislature, the electorate and the public, Ministers appeared as "Government Men." In the Legislatures, they frequently needed the support of the official bloc and were seldom able to command a majority among the elected members. In short, the intention of Dyarchy was, to a great extent, frustrated by the failure to establish the principle of the responsibility of Ministers to the Legislature or the responsibility of the Legislature itself. In some quarters, the practice of treating the Dyarchic Constitution as one Government was hailed as an instance of its success; but it would have been far better if Ministers had been trained in the habit of relying on their own initiative and on the influence they might have in the Legislature. Instead of departing from the rigidity of the Statute, the Governor should have urged and encouraged his Ministers to rely upon their "*Will to Power.*"

Thirdly, the primary task of training the electorate in the exercise of their responsibility as voters was almost completely overlooked. The foundation of responsible government lay there, and yet the representatives of the various communities and interests who adorned the Legislatures did not take any decisive steps towards the creation of genuine electorates. The criticism that the present electorates were narrow and restricted was not justifiable; for the growth of an electorate must be dependent upon the nature and extent of its political education. An electorate is something more than a mere enrolment of voters.

Such is the history of the political device, Dyarchy, as applied to British India. Its principle had not made a successful appeal to British and Indian statesmen, although the politicians had accepted it as a temporary expedient. In the opinion of the Government of the United Provinces, "Dyarchy is obviously a cumbrous, complex, confused system, having no logical basis, rooted in compromise and defensible only as a transitional experiment." Perhaps Curzon knew when he startled the House of Lords by saying, "I abominate Dyarchy," that even a transitional experiment should have a logical basis. The other Provinces held the same view that the defects of Dyarchy were inherent in the system itself and that very little could be done to eliminate them without drastic alterations.

And yet, in a way, the Reforms had fulfilled their purpose. They furnished opportunities for acquainting Indian politicians with the intricacies of Government and brought them in contact with the realities of Indian problems. They made the Government, on the other hand, sensitive to Indian public opinion and gradually established a contact between the Executives and the Legislative bodies. They brought into being the various political groupings, though now formed under the impulses of communal and sectional interests, which might eventually tend to evolve into disciplined political parties.

As regards the problems concerning administration of a vast sub-Continent, it became clear to those who had the opportunities for the practical handling of affairs, that the Central Government of India would have to be strong under any circumstances, and that it must remain as the co-ordinating element whatever might be the form of the Provincial Government. However, the cry for the re-examination of the Indian Constitution was raised, and in our next chapter we shall see what steps had to be taken in order to meet this demand.

ℂ. POLITICAL RELATIONSHIPS WITH THE STATES

For a clear comprehension of the problems of the Indian Constitution, it is necessary to note here the position of the States at the time of the introduction of Dyarchy in British India. While the Princes viewed with alarm the process of gradual "democratisation," introduced by the Government of India Act of 1919, which might ultimately alter the entire character of the Government, they availed themselves of the opportunity to renew their request for the redress of some of their grievances. They complained that the existing form of administration in British India gave "the States no share in the determination of the policy affecting their relations with the Paramount Power; or in matters of mutual concern to them and British India; and provided no impartial method of arriving at decisions which affected the interests of the States or conflicted with their interpretation of treaties or differences arising between them and the British Government."

The late Mr. Montagu during his visit to India in 1917 invited the Princes to inform him about such matters where the policy of the Paramount Power affected the interests of the States. The Princes produced a list of 23 points.

> "Of this list," writes Sir Kailas Haksar,[1] "it might be remarked that although in terms the complaints put forward bore upon disregard of the Treaties, those disregards, when analysed, were found in reality to have constituted inroads upon the economic interests and life of the States."

The Princes then put forward a plan very much like that which was subsequently proposed; that is, it was suggested that they should have a voice in the determination of All-India policy; the disputes arising between British India and the States should be decided by an impartial tribunal, and there should be a deliberative Assembly in which they as an Order could meet together and investigate questions of common concern. The framers of the Joint Report, while admitting that the interests of British India and the States could be reconciled to a certain extent in a future Constitution somewhat on a federal basis, felt that the case of the Indian States at this stage might be met by bringing into existence a permanent consultative body with the Viceroy as president. Thus, under the Reforms of 1919 the institution called the Chamber of Princes [2] was created, with the object of providing an opportunity to the Princes to express their views on matters that affect the States and British India. The Chamber of Princes was formally inaugurated by His Royal Highness the Duke of Connaught in 1921.

The Chamber consists of 108 Princes who are members in their own rights and of 12 other members chosen from 127 rulers of other States by a system of group voting. But some of the important ruling Princes have not formally joined the Chamber. We may note here the reason for their abstention as stated by Sir Sivaswamy Aiyer,[3] who writes as follows:

[1] A distinguished State official.

[2] The Sanskrit name is the NARENDRA MANDAL.

[3] A prominent Indian Liberal statesman, author of "Indian Constitutional Problems," 1928.

> "In the first place, the Princes are so jealous of their status that they are afraid of being treated as equals among themselves. Some of them are not prepared to meet each other in the Chamber on terms of apparent equality; nor are they prepared to concede the principle of decision by a majority, which is at the basis not merely of democratic rule, but also of every corporate organization. They are afraid of the levelling tendency of any organization of this sort and object to the process of levelling up, as much as to the course of levelling down. . . . Even in the matters of common interest, some of them are anxious that they should be individually consulted by the Government of India. . . ."

But in all fairness to the Princes, it should be remembered that the policy of keeping one State isolated from another, so long pursued by the Paramount Power, created circumstances which could not be easily overcome. Only during the decade 1908 1918 was that policy to some extent modified and the first official Conference of the Princes summoned by Lord Hardinge in 1916. Even then no tangible result was derived from the Conference—the Government only asked for the co-operation of the States in the collection of certain statistics about epidemics.

At any rate, the institution of the Chamber of Princes was a great step forward and marked the beginning of official recognition of their right to consult each other on matters relating to the problem of paramountcy and to their economic relations with British India. If the formal sessions of the Chamber were rather ineffective, due to its stereotyped agenda and strict Rules of Business, the informal discussions among the Princes outside the Chamber greatly fostered "a habit of co-operation" among them. Occasions were also found to meet elder statesmen of British India and to exchange views on matters of common interests.

THE INDIAN STATES ENQUIRY COMMITTEE

The political development of British India following the introduction of Reforms and its repercussions on the subjects of the States stirred the Princes to demand a clear definition of their position in the future Indian Constitution. They realized that none of the fundamental problems relating to their politico-economic relationship with British India could be solved through the ineffective Chamber of Princes. The fiscal policy of the Government of India during the post-war period had put a serious strain upon the States and greatly restricted the possibility of improving their administrations. Above all, there was no change in the procedure of the Political Department which interpreted and conducted the relationship between the Government and the States in a manner unsatisfactory to the present generation of Ruling Princes. They urged on the Viceroy a Round Table Conference with a view to arriving at a settlement. But Lord Reading did not wish to embark upon a discussion on the question of paramountcy. The basic principle of the relationship of the States to the Crown was, however, enunciated in his letter to His Exalted Highness the Nizam, dated March 27, 1926, the main conclusion of which is as follows:

> "The sovereignty of the British Crown is supreme in India, and therefore no ruler of an Indian state can justifiably claim to negotiate with the British Government on an equal footing. Its supremacy is not based only upon treaties and engagements, but exists independently of them and, quite apart from its prerogative in matters relating to foreign powers and policies, it is the right and duty of the British Government, while scrupulously respecting all treaties and engagements with the Indian states, to preserve peace and good order throughout India." [1]

As regards the right of intervention in the internal affairs of the States, Lord Reading contended that it was inherent

[1] Quoted in Sir Harcourt Butler's "India Insistent."

in the paramountcy of the British Crown and that the right might be exercised at the sole discretion of the Crown.

The Princes as an Order were alarmed at the interpretation put by the Viceroy on the fundamental rights of the States implied in their Treaties and engagements with the Crown. As the time for the re-examination of the Reforms approached they put forward various claims in regard to some matters of joint interest to British India and the Indian States. They found in Lord Irwin a Viceroy who shared their deep concern about the future relations between the Indian States and British India. To him they expressed their desire that before a new Constitution for British India was submitted to Parliament "it is essential that the opinions, wishes, and aspirations of the States should be ascertained in regard to the effect upon them, both of proposals for British India and as to the constitutional machinery which will best ensure wise, harmonious and easy co-operation between the Governments of British India and the Governments of the States in the future." [1]

In July 1927, the Viceroy accordingly convened a Conference, at which it was decided to appoint a Committee of Enquiry to examine the whole question. Sir Harcourt Butler, G.C.S.I., G.C.I.E., a distinguished administrator, was invited to be the Chairman of the Committee, the other members being the Hon. Sidney Peel and Professor Sir William Holdsworth. The terms of reference were:

(1) To report upon the relationship between the Paramount Power and the States, with particular reference to the rights and obligations arising from (*a*) treaties, engagements, and sanads, and (*b*) usage, sufferance, and other causes; and

(2) To enquire into the financial and economic relations between British India and the States and to make any recommendations that they may consider desirable or necessary for their more satisfactory adjustment.

[1] See "The British Crown and the Indian States," by the Directorate of the Special Organization of the Chamber of Princes. P. S. King & Son: 1929.

The Committee reported on February 14, 1929. In order to safeguard the interests of the Princes, it was recommended that in the future they should deal with the Viceroy as the Agent for the Crown, and not with the Governor-General in Council. What troubled the Princes was the *definition* of the powers and rights of interference of the Paramount Power. The Committee held that the Paramount Power is the Crown acting through the Secretary of State for India and the Governor-General in Council who are responsible to the British Parliament. It did not clearly define the *sphere* of the Paramount Power in its relations with the States; but declared:

> "Paramountcy must remain paramount. . . . On paramountcy and paramountcy alone can the States rely for their preservation through the generations that are to come. Through paramountcy is pushed aside the danger of destruction or annexation."

The emphasis laid in the Report upon the Sovereignty of the Indian States being subject to the Paramount Power alarmed the Princes, who, at the Session of the Chamber of Princes, severely criticized the findings of the Committee. But they waited for subsequent developments in British India in the making of its Constitution. It occurred to the Princes, as already stated, that through an appropriate federal machinery they might secure their dual objective, namely, due recognition of their treaty rights and fair adjustment of conflicting interests between the States and British India and Great Britain. We should note here that the Indian States Enquiry Committee regarded the federation of British India and the States as a remote ideal. How the forces of co-operation among the three partners (*i.e.* British India, Indian States and Great Britain) were assembled, what means were adopted for reconciling divergent interests, and what were the stages through which the "main ground plan" of an All-India Federation finally emerged are the subjects to which we shall now turn.

CHAPTER III

THE INDIAN STATUTORY COMMISSION

Appointment : Terms of Reference : Indian Opposition : Lord Irwin's Conciliatory Policy : India and the Labour Government : Lord Irwin's Announcement : Report : Recommendations—(a) *Provincial Autonomy*, (b) *Transference of Law and Order in the Provinces*, (c) *Safeguarding Provincial Constitution*, (d) *Central Government*, (e) *Central Legislature*, (f) *Defence*, (g) *Indian States*, (h) *Financial Reforms : Miscellaneous Recommendations* —(a) *Separation of Burma*, (b) *Backward tracts : Alternative Proposals : Parliament and the Report of the Statutory Commission*

¶ APPOINTMENT

FROM the preamble of the Government of India Act, 1919, it is evident that the dyarchical form of government introduced by that Act was to be for a transitional period and that it was regarded more as an experiment than as a beginning of a well-defined Constitution. It was provided in the Act that a Statutory Commission should be appointed within ten years' time

> "for the purpose of enquiring into the working of the system of Government, the growth of education, and the development of representative institutions in British India, and of reporting as to whether, and to what extent it is desirable to establish the principle of responsible government, or to extend, modify, or restrict the degree of responsible government then existing therein. . . ."

But the idea of a transitional period to be followed by Parliamentary enquiries roused suspicion among a section of Indian political opinion and became a matter of dissatisfaction among others. It was held that even for an experiment, a decade was too short and that the Constitution should be regarded as a living political organization developing its powers by its own inward law of growth.

In a previous chapter I have referred to the circumstances that resulted in bringing the dyarchical mechanism to a standstill. Here I would only recall the effects of the obstruction to the government of the country which was organized within the Councils by the Indian Nationalists from the time they entered these bodies. This intolerable friction within the Indian Legislatures agitated the public mind. In some of the Provinces the essential functions of government had to be carried on under considerable difficulties; the day-to-day administration of the "transferred" subjects had even to be left, in a few instances where no Ministry could be formed, in the hands of the Governors. Meanwhile the National Congress and other political parties clamoured for the appointment of a Commission before the expiry of the statutory period.

As the dyarchical Constitution had almost collapsed, Lord Birkenhead, then Secretary of State for India, saw no reason why the date of the appointment of the Commission should not be advanced. Perhaps the trend of development in Home politics may have induced the Secretary of State to ante-date the institution of a statutory enquiry. Such a vital Imperial question could not be entrusted to a Labour Government, and those among the ranks of the Conservative Party who had some misgivings as to the working of the Reforms of 1919 were eager to pull up the seedling Constitution and examine its roots. Besides the political sky in India was then comparatively clear; after Gandhi's release in February 1924 he had returned to his Ashram, and in the following two years there were signs of weariness among his followers. That hydra-headed monster of Hindu-

Moslem antagonism was lying low after its hideous performances in 1926. The time for an enquiry into the constitutional questions therefore seemed favourable, and by acceding to the demand of the Indian politicians the Government would have the credit of making a generous gesture. Indian politicians, however, hailed the decision of the Conservative Government as another signal victory of organized agitation.

In conformity with Section 84 A of the Government of India Act, 1919, and by an Amending Act, Mr. Baldwin, then Prime Minister, announced the appointment of the Commission (November 1927). It was to consist of seven Members of Parliament (five commoners and two Peers) and Sir John Simon was appointed Chairman. The other Commissioners were:

Viscount Burnham,
Baron Strathcona and Mount Royal,
The Hon. E. C. G. Cadogan, M.P.,
The Rt. Hon. Vernon Hartshorn, M.P.,
Major C. R. Attlee, M.P.,
The Rt. Hon. G. R. Lane-Fox, M.P.

The Commission thus represented both the Houses of Parliament and all three political parties of Great Britain.

¶ TERMS OF REFERENCE

Section 84 A of the Government of India Act, 1919, formed the basis of the terms of reference as may be seen from the actual words of the Terms of Reference. It is set forth in the Royal Warrant as follows:

"Whereas we have deemed it expedient that the Commission for which provision is made in Section 84 A of the Government of India Act should forthwith be appointed for the purpose of enquiring into the working of the system of government, the growth of education, and the development of representative institutions in British India, and matters connected therewith, and should report as to whether

> and to what extent it is desirable to establish the principle of responsible government or to extend, modify, or restrict the degree of responsible government then existing therein, including the question whether the establishment of second chambers of the local legislatures is or is not desirable: . . ."

¶ INDIAN OPPOSITION

The appointment of a purely Parliamentary Commission raised a storm of protest from the Nationalists, in which several of the Indian Liberals joined. Lord Irwin anticipated this opposition, and therefore in announcing the appointment of the Commission issued a personal statement in order to appease the minds of Indian politicians:

> " Indian opinion," said the Viceroy, " has a clear title to ask that in the elaboration of a new instrument of government, their solution of the problem, or their judgment on other solutions which may be proposed, should be made an integral factor in the examination of the question and be given due weight in the ultimate decision. It is therefore essential to find means by which Indians may be made parties to the deliberations so nearly affecting the future of their country."

It was in this statement that His Excellency suggested that the procedure of co-operating with the Indian Legislatures, through Central and Provincial Committees, might be considered by the Commission.

The statement was followed by interviews with a large number of All-India leaders. The Viceroy and all the provincial Governors tried their utmost to convince Indian political parties and groups that their co-operation was needed for the success of the investigation. Only some of the waverers, representing chiefly the minority committees and special interests, changed their minds in favour of co-operation with the Commission; the predominant sections of Indian political opinion decided to organize violent opposition to the Commission.

The boycott demonstrations were organized and followed

the Commission throughout their tours. The slogan, "Go back, Simon," became a familiar cry among the "Volunteers" of the boycott movement. There were declarations of *Hartals* and a number of disturbances took place as the result of collisions with the police. At Lahore a prominent Indian politician [1] was injured and died some weeks later. Although the movement for boycotting the Commission lacked solidarity and its organizers knew perfectly well that they could not in any way obstruct the work of the Commission, the occasion was fully exploited to persuade the people to believe that their leaders were engaged in a great struggle with the "Satanic Government" which must either be mended or ended. The fact that in the face of opposition the work of the Commission went on unhampered was regarded as a challenge thrown down by the Government. Once again men with revolutionary ideas found an opportunity for reprisals. Mr. Saunders, a junior police officer, was murdered at Lahore in the Punjab. This was followed by an occurrence in the Legislative Assembly which may have "sent a thrill through the world" but which considerably prejudiced the case for India in the eyes of the critics of India's constitutional advance. From a public gallery of the Legislative Assembly two bombs were thrown on to the official benches; and these were followed by shots from an automatic pistol. Sir John Simon was present in the chamber and witnessed the whole scene. Finally, there was a plot to wreck the Commission's special train.

Undaunted by such occurrences, appeals continued to pour forth, even from responsible Indians, that for the sake of the Motherland, the country must be united in the opposition to the Statutory Commission. It is a strange fact that Indian public men have not learnt either from their own experience or from the lessons of history that there cannot be an effective opposition based merely on a negative platform. The boycott movement not only failed to unite

[1] Lala Lajpat Rai.

the divergent political groups but had sown the seed of dissensions among them to such an extent that even a miracle could not ensure them any political harvest. It was unfortunate that the Statutory Commission should have become the starting-point of a fresh agitation.

At the outset of these hostile demonstrations, the authorities adopted a tolerant attitude in the hope that their organizers would soon realize the utter futility of organized obstructions to the Commission. In a way it would have been a very wise policy to allow the boycott movement to die of its own incoherent weakness, had not the movement gone too far in its hostility. A member[1] of the Commission records his impressions of a boycott demonstration in the following terms:

> "The authorities had apparently entered into a sort of compact with the Swarajists, allowing them to make a demonstration only at certain points of our route through the town—an almost incredible proceeding."

Referring to the behaviour of the students of the Agricultural College, Cawnpore, he writes that they

> "went quite wild, surged up against our cars and threw dust at us. It is inconceivable that Government should have allowed such a discreditable performance."

The Viceroy, however, realized that the effective means of arresting these hostilities towards the Commission would be to propitiate the rebellious spirit behind them. He therefore consulted with the Chairman of the Commission in order to devise methods by which the Indian leaders might be persuaded to co-operate with the Commission.

Sir John Simon was an adept in placating opposition, and determined to ensure a sufficient measure of co-operation in India for his mission. Under the terms of the appointment of the Commission, he was empowered to elect

[1] The Hon. E. C. G. Cadogan. See his "The India We Saw." John Murray: 1933.

representative committees to co-operate with the Commission. He therefore invited the Indian Legislatures, Central and Provincial, to appoint such committees: eight out of nine Provincial Councils agreed to do so but the Legislative Assembly remained adamant. A Central Committee representing both the Chambers, however, had to be formed in order to complete the scheme of co-operation with Indian opinion. Sir John requested His Excellency, Lord Irwin, to appoint a Central Committee to sit with the Commission throughout its labours "as a joint free conference." The Council of State readily appointed three representatives of its own body and the Viceroy nominated six members of the Legislative Assembly; and with these nine members the Central Committee was constituted. The actual contributions these committees were able to make to the Commission in their search for solutions of various special problems (*e.g.* Defence, Finance, Communal electorate, relations between the Central and Provincial Governments, etc.) were exceedingly poor. We shall refer to the Report of the Indian Central Committee later in connection with our general review of the Commission's work. Since the growth of education is an essential factor in the determination of constitutional development, an Auxiliary Committee under the chairmanship of Sir Philip Hartog was appointed for a comprehensive survey of educational problems of India. Mr. W. T. (now Sir Walter) Layton, editor of the *Economist*, acted as financial assessor to the Commission. All these arrangements for a searching enquiry into every aspect of the Indian Government, Central and Provincial, were made during a preliminary visit of the Commission in February 1928.

But the main body of Indian public opinion, represented by the Congress and a number of All-India leaders representing the Liberals and the Moslems, continued to demand that the "All-British Commission" had no right to determine the future Constitution for India. To them it was a "national insult," and some of them proposed the setting up of a Round Table Conference in the place of the Statutory Commission.

The incidents of a Nationalist boycott of Lord Milner's Commission of Enquiry in Egypt were recalled, and it was proclaimed that, as a result of a determined plan of campaign, the British Government had been forced to surrender to the claim of the Egyptian Nationalists.

But Egypt is "a bit of Europe in Africa" and occupies, by virtue of the Suez Canal, a special strategic position. She forms, indeed, an integral part in European diplomatic relations and her case is not wholly analogous to that of India. Moreover, the concessions gained by Egypt were not the outcome of the boycott demonstrations against the Milner Commission. On the contrary, the liberal spirit of its Report was, to a great extent, marred by the impatience and irreconcilable attitude of the Egyptian Nationalists. Later on they came to London for negotiations—but only after making the atmosphere unfavourable to bringing about an equilibrium in the relations between Great Britain and Egypt.

Indian political leaders did not relax their opposition when the co-operating committees of the Legislatures were appointed. Some of the boycott leaders had cherished hopes that a continued agitation against the Statutory Commission might induce Mr. Ramsay MacDonald, as leader of the principal opposition in the House of Commons, to take the necessary steps to satisfy the Indian demand. But the following telegraphic message sent to Mr. Vernon Hartshorn on February 15, 1928, by Mr. MacDonald, proved this to be an illusion. He said:

> "It is reported here that if your Commission were successfully obstructed, a Labour Government would appoint a new Commission on another and non-Parliamentary basis. As you know, the procedure now being followed has the full confidence of the Labour Party and no change in the Commission would be made."

How little did the Indian political leaders realize that the dictum of Disraeli—" India must never be made the sport of party "—was strictly adhered to by the British Parliament. As far as one could predict, in matters relating to India's relationship with Great Britain, the British political parties would ultimately act in unison.

The Indian opposition, however, induced Lord Irwin to adopt a conciliatory policy which, as we shall see in the following pages, resulted in throwing the Report of the Commission into the shade. On this point, Mr. Cadogan writes :

> " Reviewing the whole matter in the light of all that has occurred since the appointment of the Commission, it is a justifiable complaint that its Report has been 're-pudiated by the Indian intelligentsia and ignored by the Imperial Government.' " [1]

LORD IRWIN'S CONCILIATORY POLICY

The organized boycott of the Statutory Commission by the Congress, the predominant political party in India, with which some of the notable All-India leaders joined, made Lord Irwin uneasy about the success of the Commission. Gandhi's re-entry into the arena of politics, the publication of the Nehru Report,[2] the adoption of proposals for Dominion Status as the basis for the Constitution of India, the growing influence of the apostles of an aggressive nationalism in the Congress, and finally, the threat of reviving the non-co-operation campaign if the Nehru Report were not accepted by the British Parliament before the end of 1929, all these indications of revolt appeared to Lord Irwin as being fatal to the welfare of India and to her relations with Great Britain.

He had realized that the psychological background of the revolt was the want of confidence in the sincerity and

[1] See " The India We Saw," by the Hon. Edward Cadogan, C.B., M.P

[2] The Report of a Committee appointed by the All-Parties Conference of 1928 to determine the principles of a Constitution for India.

honesty of British pledges to India. During these "years of destiny," as the term of his Viceroyalty is called by Professor Coatman, he pursued with unabated patience the policy of winning the confidence of Indian Nationalists and reluctantly subordinated the consideration of problems affecting the material and moral condition of India's millions to that of political rapprochement. It was not merely the question of bringing about an understanding between England and India to which Lord Irwin had to apply his mind. He found that the evils arising from the disintegration of Indian social life had affected the entire political atmosphere. Within a short time of his arrival in India, he laid his finger on this, the weakest spot in the Indian political life, but the fierce recrudescence of Hindu-Moslem feuds continued to make remedial measures extremely difficult.

With the arrival of the Statutory Commission, Lord Irwin's single aim was to satisfy the *amour-propre* of the various political groups in India. As we proceed in our narration of events we shall see how earnestly he tried not only to bridge the gulf between England and India but also to repair the fatal cleavages that exist in Indian political and social life.

INDIA AND THE LABOUR GOVERNMENT

Mr. Ramsay MacDonald, speaking at the British Commonwealth Labour Conference (July 2, 1928), said:

> "I hope that within a period of months rather than years, there will be a new Dominion added to the Commonwealth of our nations, a Dominion of another race, a Dominion that will find self-respect as an equal with this Commonwealth. I refer to India."

The echo of this sentiment materialized in the form of a demand made in the Nehru Report, published a month later, for raising India to the rank of Dominion. Subsequently the Calcutta Congress, held in December that year, passed a resolution demanding the immediate grant of Dominion Status to India.

The attitude of the Labour Party towards India's legitimate aspirations was set out before the General Election of 1929 in *Labour and the Nation*. The manifesto declared the Party's belief "in the right of the Indian people to Self-Government and Self-Determination . . . with the object of establishing India at the earliest possible moment, and by her consent, as an equal partner with the members of the British Commonwealth of Nations." The success of the Labour Party in the General Election brought Mr. Wedgwood Benn to the India Office as Secretary of State.

With the advent of the Labour Government in June 1929, though a minority Government, the hopes of a section of Indian politicians were now raised to the height of gaining "complete independence." A number of Congress leaders declared, to use Gandhi's phrase, "peaceful war" on British rule in India. Although they were not taken seriously, the general feeling even among the more sober politicians was to give the cry their tacit approval so that their modest demand for immediate Dominion Status might be conceded by the Labour Government. There were others who saw no difference whatsoever in the attitude of a Labour Government and a Conservative Government towards India, and warned the Congress leaders not to expect much from the MacDonald Government.

II. LORD IRWIN'S ANNOUNCEMENT

Lord Irwin's visit to England in 1929 coincided with the advent of the Labour Party to office. It was also the time when the members of the Statutory Commission were drafting their Report. Lord Irwin made it clear to His Majesty's Government that it was necessary to assure Indian politicians that the goal of India's political status should not be less than that of the Dominions and that the purpose of convening a conference was to consider what steps could be taken to attain that status. Lord Irwin felt that a declaration to this effect would certainly help to create a favourable atmosphere for the reception of the Report of the Statutory Commission.

The Secretary of State for India consulted the Party leaders and the Chairman of the Commission. While there was a general agreement in regard to a Round Table Conference, the Conservative and Liberal leaders were opposed to the proposed declaration regarding Dominion Status for India. The phrase "Dominion Status" had acquired a different meaning after the Imperial Conference of 1926, and it was urged by Conservative and Liberal statesmen that it could not be appropriately used to describe the next stage of Indian constitutional reforms.

But Lord Irwin was no ordinary Viceroy of India. Ever since he took the responsibility of this high office, he realized that the duty of a Viceroy could not be adequately discharged unless it included the task of political and moral leadership. He therefore decided to issue an announcement, the salient points of which are as follows:

> 1. "In view of the doubts which have been expressed both in Great Britain and in India regarding the interpretations to be placed on the intentions of the British Government in enacting the Statute of 1919, I am authorized on behalf of His Majesty's Government to state clearly that in their judgment it is implicit in the Declaration of 1917 that the natural issue of India's constitutional progress, as there contemplated, is the attainment of Dominion Status. . . . In the full realization of this policy, it is evidently important that the Indian States should be afforded an opportunity of finding their place.
>
> 2. "The adoption by the Prime Minister of Sir John Simon's recommendation of 'a conference in which His Majesty's Government should meet representatives both of British India and of the States, for the purpose of seeking the greatest possible measure of agreement for the final proposals . . . to submit to Parliament.'
>
> 3. "It is as unprofitable to deny the right of Parliament to form its free and deliberate judgment on the problem as

it would be short-sighted of Parliament to underrate the importance of trying to reach a solution which might carry with it the willing consent of political India."

His Excellency concluded his pronouncement with these words:

> "I trust that the action of His Majesty's Government may . . . enlist the concurrence of all sections of opinion in India, and . . . break through the webs of mistrust that have lately clogged the relations between India and Great Britain."

The reaction of the pronouncement upon the Indian political situation was what Lord Irwin had expected. The Viceroy's pronouncement was greeted by all political parties in India as an effective declaration in satisfaction of their demands, and inspired the non-co-operating leaders to issue the following statement:

> "We have read with careful consideration the Viceroyal pronouncement on the question of India's future status among the nations of the world. We appreciate the sincerity underlying the declaration, as also the desire of the British Government to placate Indian opinion. We hope to be able to tender our co-operation with His Majesty's Government in their effort to evolve a scheme for a Dominion Constitution suitable to India's needs, but deem it necessary that certain acts should be done, and certain points cleared up, so as to inspire trust and ensure the co-operation of the principal organizations of the country.
>
> "We consider it vital for the success of the proposed Conference that, first, a policy of general conciliation should be definitely adopted to induce a calmer atmosphere: secondly, that political prisoners should be granted a general amnesty; and, thirdly, that the representation of the progressive political organizations should be effectively secured, and that the National Congress, as the largest among them, should have predominant representation.
>
> "Some doubt has been expressed about the interpretation of the paragraph in the statement made by the Viceroy on behalf of His Majesty's Government regarding Dominion

Status. We understand, however, that the Conference is to meet, not to discuss when Dominion Status shall be established, but to frame a scheme of Dominion Constitution for India. We hope that we are not mistaken in thus interpreting the import and the implications of this weighty pronouncement of the Viceroy. Until the new Constitution comes into existence we think it necessary that a more liberal spirit should be infused in the Government of the country, that the relations of the Executive and the Legislature should be brought more in harmony with the object of the proposed Conference, and that greater regard should be paid to Constitutional methods and practices. We hold it to be absolutely essential that the public should be made to feel that a new era has come even from to-day, and that the new Constitution is to be but the register of the fact. Lastly, we deem it an essential factor for the success of the Conference that it be convened as expeditiously as possible."

But the question of asserting India's political goal to be the attainment of Dominion Status roused a first-class political controversy in Parliament. In the House of Lords, Lord Reading, the late Viceroy of India, a prominent spokesman of the Liberals, in opening the debate emphatically objected to the use of the expression Dominion Status when the Statutory Commission had not pronounced their judgment on the future Indian Constitution. Lord Birkenhead's advice to the Commission was to treat the pronouncement "as irrelevance," but Lord Parmoor, replying on behalf of the Government, stated explicitly that "the conditions and reservations contained in the declaration of 1917 and the preamble to the Government of India Act, 1919, remained of full force and effect and applicable to Dominion Status."

These observations in the House of Lords were followed by the subsequent debate in the House of Commons when the Prime Minister, Mr. Baldwin, Mr. Lloyd George, Mr. Wedgwood Benn, Sir John Simon, and others took part. The Prime Minister argued in effect that the "man on the spot" realized the expediency of such a declaration in connection with the summons to a Round Table Conference.

Sir John Simon made it clear in a dignified speech that the advice of the Statutory Commission was not sought by the Government before the Viceregal pronouncement. Sir John said:

> "It is enough for me to say that, when for the first time the Commission were informed that the Government contemplated a statement on the subject of the Montagu Declaration, the Commission came to the conclusion that we desired, preserving our wholly independent and judicial position, not to be associated with any such statement, and I so informed the Secretary of State on 24th September. From that moment, any responsibility of the Commission in the matter ceased."[1]

The position of the Commission was further cleared by reminding all the parties concerned that the duties laid upon that body by Parliament were really of a semi-judicial character, and that it was in no sense an instrument of the Government of India or of the British Government; that it entered upon a duty laid upon it by the King-Emperor as a completely independent and unfettered body.

But the matter did not end here. A powerful and influential section of the British press and of public opinion insisted on a definite assurance from the Prime Minister that the Viceroy's declaration involved no fresh departure from the preamble to the Government of India Act, 1919. At last the controversy was set at rest by the interchange of correspondence[2] between the Prime Minister and Mr. Baldwin.

[1] Sir John Simon: House of Commons, November 7, 1929.

[2] House of Commons,
November 11, 1929.

My dear Prime Minister,

It will be within your recollection that the debate on Thursday last in the House of Commons was concluded without any answer being given by the Secretary of State for India to my second question, namely—"whether this statement (*i.e.* the Viceroy's declaration) implies any change in the policy hitherto declared, or in the time when this status may be attained."

It is true that this question was answered in the House of Lords, but

As could be imagined, the storm of this controversy made Lord Irwin's task in India extremely difficult. The Congress leaders became suspicious of the intentions of His Majesty's Government and insisted, at an interview with the Viceroy, on his giving an undertaking that the Round Table Conference [1] should meet to draw up a Constitution for immediate Dominion Status for India. The Viceroy could not possibly give such a definite promise. Thus the intransigent element in the Congress found an occasion for the advocacy of all forms of extremism and succeeded in persuading Gandhi to take an aggressive attitude towards the Viceroy's invitation to co-operation. The Congress then raised the cry of "complete independence" from British control and precipitated open hostilities with the Government.

Nevertheless, Lord Irwin's policy was not altogether frustrated by the Congress. The Indian Liberals and other

I feel that the answer should equally be given by the Prime Minister in his capacity as Leader of the House of Commons.

I am,

Very sincerely yours,

STANLEY BALDWIN.

10, Downing Street,
Whitehall, November 11, 1929.

My dear Mr. Baldwin,

I am grateful to you for your letter. The answer to both parts of the question "whether the Viceroy's declaration implies any change in the policy hitherto declared or in the time when this status may be attained" is "No."

The policy, as you will remember, is set out in the Preamble of the Government of India Act, 1919, and it stands unchanged unless and until Parliament decides to amend that Act.

I am,

Very sincerely yours,

J. RAMSAY MACDONALD.

[1] It is interesting to note that during the Viceroyalty of Lord Reading, Mr. Gandhi repeatedly demanded a Round Table Conference between the Government and the Congress; but he insisted upon "a real Conference, where only equals are to sit and there is not a single beggar." Lord Reading then refused to convene a Round Table Conference.

political groups who had boycotted the Statutory Commission rallied round the Viceroy in the endeavour to make his genuine efforts fruitful.

The circumstances following his pronouncement on the goal to which British policy in regard to India was directed, induced Lord Irwin to clarify the position in an address to the Legislative Assembly in January 1930:

> "I have never sought to delude Indian opinion into the belief that definition of a purpose, however plainly stated, could of itself, by the enunciation of a phrase, provide a solution for the problems which have to be solved before that purpose is fully realized. The assertion of a goal, however precise its terms, is of necessity a different thing from the attainment of the goal. No sensible traveller would feel that a clear definition of his destination was the same thing as the completion of his journey, but it is assurance of direction, and in this case I believe it to be something of tangible value to India, that those who demand full equality with other self-governing units of the British Commonwealth on her behalf should know that Great Britain on her side also desires to lend her assistance to India in attaining that position."

The object of this "apologia" was to conciliate the attitude of intransigence that threatened to jeopardize Lord Irwin's efforts to create a favourable atmosphere for the proposed Round Table Conference. Those Indian leaders who were outside the sphere of Congress politics came together determined to explore fully the opportunity now given to them by the proposal of a Round Table Conference in the hope that a great advance might be made towards the *ultimate* goal, which was to be Dominion Status for India.

Meanwhile another development was taking place and that from an unexpected quarter. The distant ideal of an All-India Federation was being brought to a near focus. Commenting on the Viceroy's announcement on Dominion Status for India, His Highness the Maharaja of Bikaner remarked that the Princes "have openly given expression to the belief that the ultimate solution of the Indian problem and the ultimate goal—whenever circumstances are favourable and the time is ripe for it—is federation, which word has no terrors for the Princes and Government of the States."

Since the Viceroy's announcement of October 31, 1929, the expression "Dominion Status for India" appears to have disappeared from the political vocabulary of British politicians. We shall see in our discussion on the Round Table Conferences that it was replaced by "All-India Federation."

Let us now turn to the Report of the Statutory Commission.

¶. THE REPORT

The Commission issued its Report in June 1930. Two volumes of the Report,[1] one containing a general survey of the conditions obtaining in India and the other recommendations, have been aptly described as a "magnificent treasure house of fact and comment." The Report was unanimous on all the important issues. Volume I is an excellent work of reference on India, and is an indispensable guide to a proper understanding of the background against which the constitutional edifice has to be raised. It presents "those stubborn facts which no amount of rhetoric or appeal to abstract principles can alter."

But this historic Report was not dealt with in accordance with the Parliamentary procedure usually adopted in considering such documents. It was not presented to the Houses of Parliament for consideration as the basis of a new Constitution for India. The circumstances which led to this change of method in dealing with a Report of a Statutory Parliamentary Commission may be explained by quoting an extract from a letter which Sir John Simon addressed to the Prime Minister on October 16, 1929. In

[1] Vol. I (Cmd. 3568) and Vol. II (Cmd. 3569).

the month of February that year, the Indian States Enquiry Committee [1] submitted its Report, which recommended many changes in the political, financial and economic relations between the States and British India. Although the problem of the States was outside the terms of reference of the Statutory Commission, it became increasingly clear to its members that the extremely difficult and delicate question of the future relations between the Indian States and British India should receive adequate consideration in their Report.

Sir John Simon accordingly wrote to the Prime Minister as follows :

> "As our investigation has proceeded we have become more and more impressed, in considering the direction which the future constitutional development of India is likely to take, with the importance of bearing in mind the relations which may develop between British India and the Indian States." But "the methods by which the future relationship between these two constitutional parts of Greater India may be adjusted" cannot be examined by the Commission unless their terms of reference are given such interpretation as would enable the Commission to include these problems. The Commission suggested a change in the scheme of procedure after the issue of their Report.
>
> "It seems to us," observed Sir John, "that what would be required would be the setting up of some sort of conference . . . and that in this conference His Majesty's Government would meet both representatives of British India and representatives of the States (not necessarily always together) for the purpose of seeking the greatest possible measure of agreement for the final proposals which it would later be the duty of His Majesty's Government to submit to Parliament."

The Conference which was accordingly set up is known as the Round Table Conference, the purpose and achievement of which we shall discuss in the following chapter. The recommendations of the Commission in regard to the relations

[1] See Chapter II.

between British India and the Indian States are discussed in the next section. The point we should bear in mind here is that the decision to hold " some sort of conference " and the Viceregal pronouncement of Dominion Status for India necessitated a departure from the usual procedure in dealing with the India Statutory Commission's report. It was not referred to a Joint Select Committee of Parliament.

To turn to the recommendations. They commented upon every aspect of the Indian Government, central and provincial, but avoided generalizations and expressions of vague sentiments. " You cannot put a slogan into an Act of Parliament. A Constitution is more than that," observed Sir John. The Report was, however, framed in the spirit of the Montagu Declaration and the Commission declared that:

> " The progressive realization of responsible government in British India as an integral part of the British Empire is the fixed object to the attainment of which, in co-operation with the Indian peoples themselves, British policy stands pledged; the obstacles in the way cannot be treated as defeating that object or as affording a discharge from its pursuit."

While the Commission recognized the need for an advance, it did not envisage an immediate development in terms of " Dominion Status " for India. And because of this deliberate omission of the promise of Dominion Status, the Report was described as a " dead letter " by Indian Liberals. The Congress Press denounced it in scathing terms, recalling Pandit Motilal Nehru's prophesy that the failure of the Statutory Commission was a foregone conclusion. Even the minor communities expressed their unqualified disappointment. In England the recommendations were acclaimed as sound and reasonable and " as carrying constitutional advance to the limits of wisdom and expediency."

The cry of the Congress leaders that the recommendations of the Commission were " insulting and derogatory to the dignity of India" was added to their propaganda slogans, and the Civil Disobedience Campaign was given a fresh stimulus. The Liberals, holding fast to their faith in Lord Irwin and the Round Table Conference, made desperate efforts to persuade Gandhi, who was then in prison, to declare a cessation of the Civil Disobedience Campaign so that the Congress might lend the weight of its influence in securing the greatest possible common measure of agreement. They argued, and quite reasonably, that the Round Table Conference should not be sabotaged and that a united demand from all Indian political parties would be irresistible. And so on. Gandhi and his advisers remained adamant and negotiations broke down.

ℂ RECOMMENDATIONS

For adequate appreciation of the recommendations of the Commission, we must bear in mind *four* salient features of the Indian problem : the size of the country and the growth of its population ; the intensity of local problems ; the constitutional difficulties arising from the existence of the Indian States ; and the problem of defending the country against foreign aggression. These stubborn realities cannot be lightly treated in suggesting any alteration in the framework of the Government of the country.

Secondly, the Indian masses who form the majority of the population live in rural areas and are primitive in their outlook and understanding. Agriculture is their main occupation, and the amenities of life they enjoy are extremely meagre. The intermediaries between them and the State, be they the landed gentry or the moneylending class, tenaciously maintain the feudal character of their relationship and have no desire for change that may weaken the allegiance of the masses to the dominant social and economic traditions. Although the "pathetic contentment" of the masses is to a certain extent disturbed, it cannot be urged that they have become politically conscious.

Thirdly, the communal antagonism between the two large Indian communities, the Hindus and the Moslems, is a serious obstacle in the way of the growth of a parliamentary form of government. In the five years 1923–1927, approximately 450 lives have been lost and 5,000 persons injured in communal riots. Besides these two communities, there are several minorities whose interests have to be protected.

Fourthly, to secure the stability of the Government and to maintain peace within the borders of a sub-Continent inhabited by a congeries of races and religions, a strong central authority is essential.

The first principle on which the Commission based their recommendations was to treat the future Constitution of India as a *living* political organism containing within itself requisite powers for its own development. With its own inward principle of growth, the Constitution would be elastic and consequently adaptable to such contingencies as may arise in different phases of its advancement.

The second principle underlying the recommendations was to lead India to the goal of a politically-*united* India. In view of the varying degree of development in Provinces and the existence of " Indian " India, whose interests were interwoven with British India, reform would have to proceed along the path of least resistance. The Federal idea, therefore, seemed a feasible goal to pursue ; but true Federation was attainable only when the federating units had become sufficiently developed as political entities. Under the existing circumstances Federation would not, to use the words of the Report, " spring into being at a bound." What was now necessary was to provide such conditions as would help India to reach her *ultimate* goal of an All-India Federation. The Commissioners stated that the necessary conditions for reaching this goal were (*a*) to allow the provincial constitution to exist " as a living thing," *i.e.* to make it politically conscious, and to endow it with an inherent power of development, (*b*) to select a form of Constitution which would facilitate both the devolution of power to the Province from without and simultaneously the integration from within of all provincial activities into one organism, and (*c*) to maintain the Constitution at the centre as an effective co-ordinating body, the ultimate form of which would be dependent on the gradual development of its constituent parts, namely, the Provinces and the States. The peculiar, and to a great extent, unique circumstances of India required that her Central Government should be evolved at the same time as the Provinces were in the process of growth towards full autonomy.

The third principle was to make full provision for the maintenance and efficiency of the fundamentals of Government during the period of development of provincial autonomy. Only under a strong central Government could the progress envisaged by the Commission proceed in the right direction. The proper guidance necessary for autonomous bodies (*i.e.* federating units) in matters affecting India as a whole would have to come from a dynamic central authority.

The *main* recommendations of the Commission may be briefly stated as follows :

(1) Full responsibility in the Provinces and the consequent abolition of dyarchy. (This means that the rigid division into reserved and transferred departments of the Government should disappear.)

(2) No reconstruction in the Central Government.

(3) Certain preliminary measures which, if carried out in a true spirit, might lead to federation between the Provinces and the Indian States.

For a clear understanding of the character of the Indian controversy over the Report and of the trend of events that followed its publication, it is necessary for us to look into these recommendations in greater detail.

(a) Provincial Autonomy

It is not always realized that Provinces in India are as large as some of the countries of Europe. Assam is one of the minor Provinces, but it is about as large as England and Wales. In view of the size and of the racial and linguistic differences of the Provinces, the Commission suggested the need for provincial re-distribution, based on a further enquiry by a properly constituted authority. The rigid division of the Provincial Executive into reserved and transferred subjects in the Dyarchic Constitution should be abolished, thus making the provincial cabinet unitary. Apart from certain specified purposes for which the Governor should be given statutory powers, the provincial ministry must accept the entire responsibilities of the Government; and the ministry should be responsible to the Legislature for its policy. Opinion, both in the Commission and in the co-operating committees, differed on the advantages and disadvantages of second chambers, and the Commission accordingly made no recommendation in regard to this matter. The Commission suggested, however, that whatever the decision might be in regard to second chambers, an expert Revising Body might be constituted with a view to examining legislative proposals between the Report and third reading stage.

Since the size of the Provincial Legislature was to be increased from 200 to 250 members and its life prolonged from three to five years, the Commission recommended that the existing franchise, which (excluding Burma) comprised 2·8 per cent. of the total population, should be extended to 10 per cent. This would mean an electorate of about 20 per cent. of the adult population. After ten years the Provincial Councils should have power to make a further extension of the franchise.

In view of the grave communal friction between the Hindus and the Moslems, the two rival communities, the Commission considered that communal representation would have to be continued, with a special reservation of seats for Sikhs in the Punjab. Seats for the Depressed classes should be reserved on a proportional basis, so that there might be a substantial increase in their representation in the Legislatures. Then there should be special electorates for Europeans and for Anglo-Indians. An outstanding feature of the Legislatures would be the disappearance of the official *bloc* as it existed under the Dyarchic Constitution. Regarding the problem of enfranchising women, it was recommended that, in addition to women qualified in respect of their own property, the vote should be extended to wives (over twenty-one) and widows (over twenty-five) of men voters.

In order to provide elasticity in the Constitution, it was recommended that a Provincial Legislature should have power to amend its own Constitution in certain respects after ten years.

But in the case of the North-West Frontier Province, which must, of necessity, be treated as a special problem, the character of the Constitution should be considerably different from that of the other Provinces. Here the executive control should remain with the Chief Commissioner, but a Legislative Council consisting of some forty members (half of whom would be elected) should be set up with powers of legislation, interpellation and discussion of resolutions and with certain powers of taxation and supply. The tracts in this Province known as "excluded areas" should be directly under the Central Government.

The changes involved in the above proposals were great and were likely to offer real opportunities for the development of responsible government in the Provinces.

> "It will be a most significant advance," write the authors of the Report, "not unattended with risk, but none the less in our opinion justified, to break down the boundary between reserved and transferred subjects and to put an end to dyarchy."

(b) Transference of Law and Order in the Provinces

The subject of the administration of Law and Order under the conditions obtaining in India is one of the questions that have raised a great deal of controversy and misapprehension among the British both in England and India. It is feared that owing to ever-growing communal differences and to the risk of the undue political influence and intrigue of ill-disciplined political groups, the morale of the Indian police administration will suffer. The Commission carefully considered the question in all its aspects and came to the conclusion that, in conformity to their general recommendation of the institution of full autonomy in the Provinces, the administration of Law and Order should be transferred to the legislative control. They argued that the police are now regarded as "the minions of an alien bureaucracy" and it was this impression that was largely responsible for irresponsible criticism levelled against their actions. By singling out this branch of provincial administration as a *special* preserve of the Government, it would continue to be exposed to the hostility of all parties in the Legislatures. Therefore, the logical course would be to fix responsibility for Law and Order upon them. The path of true statesmanship lay in taking the risks involved in the transfer and minimizing them by adequate safeguards in order to ensure the stability of the administration of Law and Order.

The reasons which influenced the Commission in making this recommendation were elaborated by Sir John Simon in a speech in the House of Commons (March 28, 1933). He said:

> "The Legislatures in these Provincial Assemblies, according to the present Constitution, feel no responsibility for the police service at all. They very frequently attack the police . . . they sometimes refuse to vote the necessary funds to maintain the police. . . . The result of all this is undoubtedly that, unless you change their position the police force and all the apparatus of law and order tend

to be regarded as the agent of an alien bureaucracy. . . . Other departments of Government will be in the hands of Indian Ministers. . . . The more you isolate the police and put them in a special position, the more you encourage this attitude towards them, which is very ungenerous and unfair.

"There was only one way to deal with that situation, and it was to face the cause of the trouble and see how to remove the cause. And the only way to remove the cause was to make the Provincial Government, as a whole, responsible for the police, to make it their responsibility to see that the police should be provided with the necessary funds, and to make a Minister responsible to that Legislature, a Minister who would have to answer for the working of the police and thus to fix the responsibility on the shoulders of the critics. I believe there is no other way."

The transfer of Law and Order is, however, safeguarded by investing the Governor with statutory power to take independent action in the interests of the peace and tranquillity of the Province. He would also have adequate control over the security services. The superior officers would continue to be recruited on an All-India basis and those belonging to the provincial police service would always have the protection of the Provincial Public Service Commission. Therefore no great risk of deterioration of the morale of the police service is involved in the transfer ; nor is there danger of grave menace to the peace of the Province, when the transfer is provided with safeguards as a sort of ballast to keep the day-to-day administration on an even keel. Then there are adequate "safety devices" attached to the provincial autonomous bodies, to which we now turn.

(c) Safeguarding the Provincial Constitution

The liberal grant of provincial autonomy also necessitated insertion into the constitution of provisions to ensure its working despite the obstructions that might be created by the impulses and vagaries of Indian politics. It was accordingly recommended that the Governor should be given statutory powers to carry on the King's Government in case of a breakdown. The Governor's emergency powers include the responsibility of preserving peace in the Province and of restoring rejected demands for grants, and of certifying legislation if, in his judgment, it is necessary for any special interest in the Province. He is to be empowered also to take steps to meet any liability of Government in respect of items of expenditure not subject to the legislative sanction; and for carrying out such duties as he might be called upon to discharge in the interests of the country. These provisions do not, however, involve undue interference with the functions of autonomy. The Governor is given powers for specified and restricted purposes and for meeting a state of emergency.

In view of the need of protecting the interests of the various minorities against discriminatory legislation, it is recommended that the Governor-General and the Governors of the Provinces should be given a special mandate in their Instruments of Instructions to use the power residing in them to prevent legislation prejudicial to the interests of one or more sections of the community as compared with other sections.

(*d*) Central Government

We now come to the pith of the Indian controversies, namely, the form of the Central Government under the new constitutional regime in the Provinces. The Commission dismissed without hesitation the suggestion of divided responsibility in the Central Executive, whose unity and solidarity must be fully preserved at all costs. Dyarchy, which is to be abandoned in the Provinces, cannot be tolerated at the centre. It is argued that

> "the ultimate creation of responsible government at the centre cannot be reached by constructing a Central Executive, one part of which is not responsible for the other. Such a plan is not only unworkable in itself, but

is no real advance in the direction of developing central responsibility at all."

The future Government of India will have to bear the vast responsibilities which are cast upon it by the task of guiding the Provinces during the period of the reconstruction leading to their development as autonomous bodies, and also its responsibilities towards the Indian States while developing as federating units must be considerably enhanced. Any system or change that may weaken the Central Government was, therefore, undesirable.

But the Commission realized the desirability of reducing the rigidity of the constitutional structure of the Central Government and recommended a number of changes designed to bring the Central Legislature in close touch with the Executive, although the latter, at this stage of India's constitutional development, could not be responsible to the former in the same sense as a British Cabinet was responsible to the British Parliament. Whatever may be the constitutional position now, the influence of the Indian Legislature upon the Executive is not inconsiderable and will undoubtedly grow.

The Commission recommended that the responsibility of appointing members of the Central Executive should rest with the Governor-General, and that directions in regard to number or qualifications of the members should be expressed in statutory rules and not in the statute itself. This would enable the Government of India to effect future modifications in its structure without fresh legislation by Parliament. An additional member of the Executive Council should be entrusted with the responsibility for acting as a *liaison* officer between the Government and the Legislature. Membership of the Council should be thrown open to individuals attaining an authoritative place in the Central Legislature.

The Commission repeatedly asserted that the ultimate form which the Central Government will take cannot be finally determined in the present circumstances, and that its final structure will depend on the working of the unitary Governments in the Provinces and on the formation of other federating units. As regards the difficulties of maintaining an Executive not responsible to the Legislature and invested with wide powers, it is urged that Indian politicians in the Legislature and the Central Government should concentrate on the creation of political conventions rather than on constitutional theory. Such conventions are bound to be established, making the Executive more and more *responsive* to the will of the Legislature.

(*e*) Central Legislature

The Commission proposed that the present Legislative Assembly should be reconstituted as a Federal Assembly, but its members should not be elected, as at present, by constituencies of voters. A Provincial Council would select those whom the Province sends to the Federal Assembly by voting on a system of proportional representation. In a country so vast, with a population so heterogeneous, the system of direct election would involve unwieldy constituencies or an Assembly of inordinate size. By adopting the method of "election by the elected" the difficulty is to a certain extent overcome. Besides, the adoption of indirect election has the essential advantage of establishing a closer nexus between the member of the Federal Assembly and the Provincial Councils. The Assembly would have a fixed life of five years, corresponding to the maximum length of life proposed for the Provincial Councils.

The number of members would be increased to between two hundred and fifty and two hundred and eighty, as compared with one hundred and forty-five members in the present Assembly. On the plan recommended, the composition of the Assembly would be approximately in the same proportions as at present. That is :

Non-Mohammedans	50 per cent.
Depressed classes	8 ,,
Sikhs	2 ,,
Mohammedans	28 ,,
Indian Christian / Anglo-Indians	2 ,,
Europeans	10 ,,

The Governor-General would have power to nominate not more than twelve officials for the Assembly.

The existing Council of State would be retained, but in conformity with the general scheme, seats would be allotted to Provincial Councils. The Governor-General's nominees would not exceed twenty officials. The life of the Council of State would be extended from five to seven years.

As regards the powers of the proposed Central Legislatures, both upper and lower chambers, they would inherit all the powers of the existing bodies, with the difference that in the sphere of finance the Federal Assembly would have additional functions.

(*f*) Defence

The Commission dwelt at length on the constitutional problem in relation to the defence of India, and clearly maintained that the Indian military problem cannot be regarded as a matter of purely Indian concern. The North-West frontier, for example, is not only the frontier of India ; it is really an international frontier, the defence of which is, from the military point of view, of very great importance for the safety of the whole Empire. The defence of this frontier should therefore be an Imperial function. Take the defence of India's long coast line. It is protected by the British Navy, towards which the Indian exchequer contributes only £100,000 per annum.

The Army in India exists, as in other countries, for two main objects, namely, (*a*) defence against external aggression, (*b*) the maintenance of internal order. Under the circumstances prevailing around and within the sub-Continent, the control and direction of such an army must rest in the hands of the Imperial Government. It was, therefore, recommended that the Viceroy, acting as an agent of the Imperial Government in concert with the Commander-in-Chief, should constitute the authority for the control of the Army in India. But the increased obligations of Indian defence on the part of the Imperial Government would not involve any great departure in the administration of Army in India. Only the Commander-in-Chief would cease to be a member of the Executive Council or a member of the Central Legislature. The Army Budget would not be subject to the vote of the Federal Assembly but would be authorized by certification of the Governor-General. So long as the British element forms an essential part of the Indian Army and the defence of India involves the protection of the Imperial interests, Parliament cannot relinquish these responsibilities to the Indian legislative control.

And yet the whole question of the Indian military problem has to be reconciled with the spirit of the constitutional reforms. That it is a dilemma was recognized by the Commission. The obvious solution lies in the pursuit of a deliberate policy of Indianizing the Army, subject to the adequate maintenance of military efficiency. It is, therefore, recommended that the Government of India, in co-operation with the Central Legislature, should evolve schemes for the organization, training, and equipment of certain military, and perhaps naval, forces of its own, which would contain no British element. Such schemes, if carefully drawn and steadily pressed forward, would prepare a self-governing India not only for the realization of her ultimate goal but also for the command of military forces necessary for her defence. The Commission suggested that a committee consisting of representatives of the Central Legislature and Indian States should be appointed for dealing with army affairs, and that an Army Secretary should be available in the Legislature to represent the views of the Government. As regards any troops that may be required for the maintenance of internal peace and order, the demand for their employment should come from the Governor of the Province himself.

In making their proposals for the defence of India, the Commission kept in view the probable emergence of an All-India Federation. It was emphasized that one of the best means of promoting this ideal was to place the Army in India on a proper footing so that the Indian States, as Federal constituents, may find no difficulty in serving the common interests of a federated India.[1]

(*g*) Indian States

Consistently throughout the Report of the Commission it was maintained that the constitutional evolution of India would be likely to lead to the establishment of a Federal system and that all that should now be done would be to prepare the ground for the growth of a Federation. That development could not be hurried; for there must be an organic unity between the constituent parts of a federal system. In days to come the Indian States would have to aim at participating in that system, the pattern of which could not be defined at this stage.

The Commission put forward three concrete proposals:

1. A comprehensive list of "matters of common concern" should be drawn up in consultation and by agreement.
2. There should be a definite reference in the Preamble to any new Government of India Act to the need of closer association between British India and the Indian States with the object of evolving an eventual Federal union.
3. A consultative Council containing representatives both from British India and the Indian States should be created to confer on "matters of common concern." The operative clause of the Act might make it lawful for the Crown to create such a body by proclamation.

[1] The Indian State forces have a total strength of about 50,000.

The Council would consist of thirty members, including ten representatives of the States.

(*h*) Financial Reforms

In devising a practical Constitution for India, perhaps the foremost consideration is Finance. The subject of Indian finance was dealt with by the Commission's Financial Assessor, Mr. (now Sir) Walter Layton.

The chief features of the financial situation in India are described as follows :

1. The mass of the people is extremely poor.
2. India's expenditure on the primary functions of government, such as defence and the maintenance of law and order, is as high in proportion to her wealth as that of Western nations.
3. But her expenditure on social services, such as education, health, sanitation, etc., is far behind Western standards, and indeed, in many directions, is almost non-existent. Sir Walter observed " that an unusually small proportion of the revenue raised is used in services which are of direct benefit in raising the status of the masses of the people."

It was, however, indicated that the public revenues in India could be substantially increased without imposing an intolerable burden of taxation, provided that its incidence was adjusted to the capacity of taxpayers to pay, and that taxes were not put upon primary necessities. But the only practicable means of economic and social welfare of the people would be to increase public expenditure on the " Nation-building " services. It was pointed out that " wise expenditure on social services and particularly on health and education should be remunerative in the sense of increasing the wealth-producing power and, therefore, the taxable capacity of a country."

Sir Walter, after stating several reasons why little has

been done to increase taxation, said that the constitutional position should be so adjusted (*a*) that the responsibility of imposing additional taxation is definitely laid upon those who will have to incur additional expenditure; (*b*) that sources of revenue appropriate to their requirements are available to those authorities who have urgent and expanding services to administer; and (*c*) that all parts of India should make an equitable contribution to common purposes.

But the conditions under which the dyarchical Constitutions had to function had none of the features mentioned by Sir Walter. In our survey of the working of the Reforms, we have seen how the existing financial scheme put a serious strain on the "transferred" subjects under the control and direction of the Ministers.

Sir Walter's analysis of the Indian Budget, and of the various items which compose it, shows that the chief contributing factor in the growth of revenue is customs. It is the mainstay of the Central Budget. There had been a rise of imports to the extent of about 58 per cent. in the six years 1924-29, and Sir Walter thought it likely that the increase would continue "at an even faster pace than heretofore." But the financial slump of the autumn of 1931, from which India is only just now recovering, introduced a disturbing factor. It is, however, interesting to note that customs as a source of revenue during these difficult years have remained buoyant, the yield for 1934-35 being approximately the same as in 1929-30 (about 51 crores[1]) in spite of the decline in trade. The size of the surplus emerging from the customs revenue depends largely on the extent of the reduction that can be made in expenditure on defence, and here there has been a gratifying decline from about 55 crores to just over 44 crores in 1934-35.

But, since the financial prospects in the Provinces are none too cheerful and their expanding needs have to be met by contributions from the Central Budget; and since any

[1] Crore = £750,000.

prospective surplus here is not dependable, Sir Walter considered it essential to find *new* sources of revenue, and indicates these as follows :

(*a*) Increased yield of the income tax by lowering the exemption limits, by steepening the graduation in the case of intermediate incomes, and by an amendment of the law relating to the taxation of income invested abroad. The rate is also low and a moderate increase should be possible.

(*b*) Abolition of the exemption of agricultural incomes from income tax.

(*c*) National excises on such commodities as cigarettes and matches.

(*d*) Terminal taxes.

The last item falls within the provincial sphere but the others are taxes which, Sir Walter recommended, should be collected by the Central Government. A scheme for the raising and allocation of these resources to each Province is set out, the details of which need not be given here. It will suffice for our purpose to understand the following principles on which the scheme of allocation was based :

1. That centrally collected revenues should be distributed in part according to origin and in part on a population basis.
2. That the customs duty on imported liquor should be brought into relation with the excise policy of each Province.
3. That revenues from commercial stamps should be transferred to the centre.
4. That the claims of the industrial provinces should be met by allotting one-half of the proceeds of the income tax to the province of origin. Super-tax should continue to be entirely central.

5. That Provincial Governments should be empowered to adjust taxation between their rural and urban classes by levying a surcharge on the income tax.
6. That the exemption from income tax of agricultural incomes should be abolished and the proceeds assigned to the Province of the origin.

These were, in brief, the main recommendations of Sir Walter Layton in regard to financial reforms under the proposed Indian Constitution. That the vision of a Federated India did also rise in his mind could be traced in the suggestions which are stated here. He proposed to constitute a provincial fund for which specially designated taxes, such as excise on cigarettes and matches, and the duty on salt, would be projected. The resources of this fund would be automatically distributed to the Provinces under the authority of the Federal Assembly on a *per capita* basis. This Assembly, as already stated, was to be composed of members elected by the Provincial Legislatures, and it was proposed that Finance Ministers of the Provinces should form an Inter-Provincial Council to consider proposals in regard to the fund.

Then there is an increasing necessity for consulting the Indian States on certain aspects of the financial problems that concern them. The levying of maritime customs involves the taxation of the Indian States by the Government of India, and the States have claimed a share in this revenue. In view of the fact that the States do not share the increasing cost of Imperial burdens, the Indian States Enquiry Committee suggested an expert enquiry into the matter. Sir Walter thought that in the functioning of financial reforms it was important to find a means of harmonizing the financial policy of the Indian States and of British India and therefore approved of the machinery of consultation between the two Indias to which the Statutory Commission had attached so much importance.

ℂ. MISCELLANEOUS RECOMMENDATIONS

(*a*) Separation of Burma; (*b*) Backward Tracts

Of the other recommendations, the proposal for the separation of Burma from India was important. It was argued that the existence of fundamental differences between Burma and other Indian Provinces cannot be denied and that her association with India under a single Government had been a matter of administrative convenience. Two main reasons for the separation of Burma from India are: (1) the politically-conscious Burmans are in favour of such a measure; (2) the constitutional difficulty of finding Burma a satisfactory place in any centralized system designed to advance the realization of responsible government in British India.

As regards the future Constitution of Burma, its goal would be self-government, but in such stages as the special circumstances would permit. Since the reformed Government of India would not be in a position to assume full responsibility towards Burma, it was proposed that the Province should have direct relations with London instead of New Delhi. It is through London that Burma would secure necessary co-ordination with India.

The Commission were so impressed with the urgency of effecting the separation that it was urged that a declaration announcing the change should be made as early as possible.

But, in accordance with the change in the procedure of dealing with the Report of the Commission, a Round Table Conference consisting of representatives from Burma alone was held in London. We shall have occasion to refer to its proceedings in the next chapter.

Another important recommendation of the Commission was in regard to the future administration and welfare of what are known as "backward tracts." The total extent of these tracts in British India (excluding Burma) is about

120,000 square miles, containing a population of 11¼ millions. The majority of the population, to quote the words of the Report,

> "do not ask for self-determination, but for security of land tenure, freedom in the pursuit of their traditional methods of livelihood, and the reasonable exercise of their ancestral customs. Their contentment does not depend so much on rapid political advance as on experienced and sympathetic handling, and on protection from economic subjugation by their neighbours."

The Commission recommended that the responsibility for the people living in the backward tracts should be in the hands of the Central Government. Since the administration and development of these tracts are linked with the Provinces, the Central Government should use the agency of the Governors for their administration.

We have now concluded this rapid survey of the main recommendations of the Commission. It will be interesting at this point to consider some of the alternative proposals that emanated from responsible Indian quarters during the Commission's period of investigation.

ALTERNATIVE PROPOSALS

In spite of the vigorously organized movement for withholding co-operation with the Statutory Commission, there were, as stated above, seven provincial committees and a central committee through which the Commission were able to come in contact with a large section of Indian opinion. In response to their invitation for the submission of memoranda, some eight hundred documents representing various interests were submitted to the Commission.

It is interesting to record here how it came about that the intransigent parties, while goading their volunteers to declare *hartals* and to cry the slogan, "Simon, go back," with that "peculiar raucous intonation not unlike the cry of rooks in the nesting season," were anxious to put forward their proposals drafted by what is known as the "All-Parties Conference." The proposals for securing the co-operation of the Indian Legislatures through committees and "Joint Free Conference" alarmed the boycott leaders, and they decided to form a body under the designation of the All-Parties Conference in order to draw up proposals. At a meeting of this conference, held in Bombay in May 1928, a committee was appointed under the chairmanship of Pandit Motilal Nehru "to consider and determine the principles of the Constitution for India." It was this Committee, composed of a number of distinguished "All-India" leaders, that produced the scheme embodied in the document known as the Nehru Report, published in August 1928. Consistent with their determination of boycotting the Statutory Commission, the Report was not directly submitted to that body but was proclaimed from the house-tops as having contained proposals that would satisfy "All-Parties" in India. The Committee declared that there was no half-way house between the present hybrid system (that is, Dyarchy) and genuine responsible government. The All-Parties Conference, convened for the purpose of considering the Nehru Report, unanimously passed a resolution accepting the goal of Dominion Status, "without restricting the liberty of action of those political parties whose goal is complete independence." But the sponsors of the Nehru Report failed to grasp the realities of the problems and passed lightly over the complexity of the issues at stake by vague generalizations. Take one instance. It is known that the circumstances of the North-Western Frontier Province and Baluchistan warrant special arrangements for their administration; but the Report declares that "the status of these areas must be made the same as that of the other Provinces; we cannot in justice or in logic deny the right of any part of India to participate in responsible government." Again, the demand that the administration of the Army should be placed under the control and direction of the Indian Legislature is made without fully apprehending the gravity of the entire problem of India's defence and internal security. Besides, the authors of the Report "do not accept the constitutional position that without an Indian or Dominion Army, India cannot obtain Dominion Status," and argue that "none of the colonies was in a position to assume its defence at the time when a self-governing status was granted to it."

Regarding the Indian States, the Committee came to the conclusion that the ultimate goal for India should be a federation of some description, and left this extremely intricate problem with the observation that "we hope and trust that in the light of experience gained, the Indian States may make up their mind to join formally an Indian Federation."

In formulating proposals for British India, the authors of the Nehru Report were obsessed with the idea that the British House of Commons could be taken as a suitable model for an Indian Parliament. If Japan, Turkey and Persia could adopt that model, they argued, why should not India be able to constitute her legislature upon that basis? Accordingly, they conceived the future Legislative Assembly as a body of 500 members elected by direct election. The representative character of such an Assembly would be clear to us if we realize that by "hypothecating adult suffrage, this gives a representation of one member to every 240,000 of the electors." Adult suffrage recommended by the Nehru Report would mean placing over 100 millions of electors on the roll in place of the 6½ millions now enfranchised. As an ultimate goal, adult suffrage is to be welcomed; but the immediate acceptance of the proposal would only result in chaos. The practical difficulties at the moment are great, and for their solution the authors of the Nehru Report offer no helpful suggestions.

While the Anglo-Indian press characterized the demand as "a preposterous scheme for the next stage in the country's political progress," the Calcutta correspondent of the London *Times* commented on the Nehru Report as follows:

> "It has behind it the united weight of the old liberal or moderate party and a formidable array of Knights, Companions and ex-servants of the Crown, whom the exclusion of Indians from the Statutory Commission induced to co-operate with the Swarajists. The tone of the document is admirable. The possibility of a political existence outside the Empire is not considered, but it postulates the disappearance of the Indian Empire in a single British Empire or what is calls "a well-knit Commonwealth of Nations."[1]

The comments of the *Manchester Guardian*, the well-known journal of the British Liberals, were expressed in an editorial under the title "New Constitution for India,"[2] in which the principles underlying the Report were opposed; and the paper suggested that the most that India can expect at the present time is "responsible government for Provinces" and that there cannot be any responsible government by Indians for the Central Government of India.

While the Report failed to indicate any practical solution of the difficulties in the way of constitutional advance, it succeeded in bringing Gandhi back into the arena of politics. Not because of the belief that he possessed the political wisdom so necessary in a crisis, but because his followers were anxious to exploit his capacity for the leadership of a popular movement. It was hoped that through his influence a satisfactory solution of the communal problem might be achieved. But, notwithstanding most ingenious and persuasive arguments for reconciling communal antagonism, the Nehru Report became the source for accentuating bitter controversies between the Hindus and the Moslems. The Report broke down under the stress of communal strife, the solution of which has ever since become the very crux of the Indian Constitutional problem.

[1] *The Times*, August 15, 1928.
[2] *The Manchester Guardian*, August 17, 1928.

So much for the Nehru Report. As regards the reports of the co-operating committees—the outcome of Lord Irwin's desire to secure some sort of Indian collaboration with the Commission—they were equally inadequate and did not help the Commission to any great extent in arriving at their final proposals.

> " For nearly three years the Commissioners have subjected to a winnowing process," writes the Hon. E. C. G. Cadogan, C.B., M.P., " whatever alternative suggestions have been submitted or have been made available to them, and they are quite prepared, when and if occasion arises, to demonstrate how little these are designed to solve India's difficulties." [1]

After considering the separate Reports of the co-operating Provincial Committees, the Indian Central Committee published their Report [2] in December 1929. The Report is nothing more than a series of dissenting notes in which the members of the Committee gave expression to their individual and conflicting opinions. It should be noted that upon many important issues unanimity was secured by the casting vote of the Chairman. Its main recommendations were (1) full Provincial Autonomy; (2) an explicit declaration in regard to full Dominion Status for India; (3) the introduction of the System of Dyarchy in the Central Government.

All subjects except Defence, Relations with Indian States and Foreign Affairs were to be placed in charge of Ministers responsible to the Legislature. The Council of the Secretary of State for India was to be abolished; but if it was retained, half of its members were to be appointed from the Central Legislature. It suggested the representation of Indians in the British Parliament till such time as India attained Dominion Status.

As regards franchise, the Committee proposed to double the electorate immediately with a view to enfranchising the

[1] See *Quarterly Review*, October 1930.

[2] Cmd. 3451.

entire adult population by 1951 at the latest. They proposed separate electorates for the European and Anglo-Indian communities and for the Depressed classes, and provided reservation of seats for other minorities. Three members of the Committee demanded total abolition of communal electorates.

Apart from the contents of this Report (a report of 72 pages, followed by minutes of dissent covering some 448 pages), the number and length of conflicting opinions on many fundamental issues were a bad omen for any degree of unanimity among Indian political leaders.

Two days (November 14, 1930) after the opening of the first Round Table Conference in London, the Despatch of the Government of India on the Statutory Commission was made available to the public. It commented upon the Report of the Commission and substantially agreed with the main principles underlying their recommendations. That is, the Government of India were in accord with such proposals as the abolition of Dyarchy in the Provinces, the grant of provincial autonomy, the continuation of communal electorates, and the separation of Burma from India. But it is to be noted here, that they dissented from the Report in matters relating to the control of defence and to the formation of the Central Executive Council and Constitution of the Central Legislature.

They stated in clear terms that conditions at the Centre " involve an inevitable duality or sharing of power between the Parliament and Indian Legislature." After a brief discussion of the political forces at work in India, the Despatch observed :

> " The conditions of the problem suggest to us the importance of defining as clearly as possible the purposes which Britain must continue to safeguard in India and making it plain that where those purposes are not concerned, India should be free to manage her own affairs. The British Government must satisfy itself on certain essential points, for instance, that the defence of India from external attack

which rests, and for many years must continue to rest, largely on British troops, is fully assured; that relations with foreign states, with the ultimate possibilities of war which they involve, are conducted under its authority; that the conditions of internal security are maintained; that financial obligations are provided for and the requisite financial stability and credit of the country adequately secured; that reasonable treatment is accorded to minorities; and that unfair discrimination is not practised against any section of the community. In our opinion the ultimate control of these matters must in present conditions reside in the British Parliament."

On the question of the Central Government, the Despatch commented upon the proposals of the Indian Statutory Commission as not likely to produce what the Commission desired to see, namely, a strong Central Government, and remarked as follows:

> "Indeed, they (the Commission) carry a stage further a process which we consider has already reached the limits of safety. The policy pursued in the past in developing the constitution has been to make successive advances in the Legislature while maintaining a more conservative treatment in the Executive. A stage has now been reached when the appropriate course appears to be to endeavour to bring the development in the Legislature and the Executive into closer co-ordination. . . . Responsiveness to the Legislature is difficult to combine with a strict adherence to the principle of responsibility to Parliament over the whole field."

The whole trend of the Despatch was that it would be desirable to look to some solution on the lines of a unitary Government and that All-Indian Federation could not be artificially hastened.

It was a carefully drawn document representing the views of the Government of India; but the innovation of the Round Table Conference conspired against its serious reception by any political party, whether in India or Great

Britain. The Indian critics denounced it as being wholly inadequate, in the hope of fortifying their demands at the Round Table Conference, and the British Government treated this authoritative State document merely as "part of the material upon which the Conference would work," because the Despatch did not provide "a rallying point" for opinions that were to be conciliated. The Despatch itself, strangely enough, bore no distinct marks of Lord Irwin's Liberal policy.

¶ PARLIAMENT AND THE REPORT OF THE STATUTORY COMMISSION

From the recital of all that happened since the appointment of the Statutory Commission, the reader will perceive why there should be, among certain important sections of British opinion, so much hostility to the procedure that overthrew the Commission's Report. In the first place, "that exasperating game of manœuvre and counter-manœuvre" which at last succeeded in appointing co-operating committees and their collaboration with the Commission has not been very helpful in framing practical proposals for Indian Constitutional reforms. On the contrary,

> "there can be no doubt," writes the Hon. Edward Cadogan, M.P., a Member of the Commission, "that we could have accomplished our task in a fraction of the time, probably with infinitely more satisfactory results, had the original procedure been carried out in accordance with the intention of the Imperial Parliament."

Secondly, the declaration of the Indian Princes that they would enter an All-India Federation presented an opportunity of "burking" the Report of the Commission. The opportunity was eagerly seized by the Indian politicians who missed in the Report any indication of granting "Dominion Status" to India, and they thought of the possibility of striking a better bargain through Federal plan than that offered by the Commission.

The Imperial Government, on the other hand, realized that the denial of central responsibility would leave room for dissatisfaction among those whose co-operation was necessary for the success of the New Indian Constitution, and sought to exploit the Federal idea with the object of reconciling the unitary system in the Centre with that of the parliamentary system in the Provinces. Should the latter be introduced in the Centre, the recommendations of the Commission in regard to the constitution of the future Government of India would have to be altered out of all recognition. Further, it is held that the proposals of the Commission would not provide a strong Centre. The reason is set out in a speech by Lord Irwin in the House of Lords (April 6, 1933). He said :

> "You have 145 members at the present time in the Assembly of the Central Legislature. Of those 145 some 105, if I remember rightly, are elected. The other 40 are partly officials and are partly nominated by the Governor-General. The Simon Commission recommended, if I recollect rightly, that the Assembly should consist of something like 250 members, in which there should be 6 members of Viceroy's Council and another 12 nominated members. That is 18 out of 250. As against that he has to-day 40 of what I may call reasonably probable Governor-General votes. Noble Lords will observe at once that the position of difficulty in which, as the noble Marquess Lord Reading rightly said, the Governor-General may frequently find himself to-day, would be indefinitely aggravated if he were asked to work a system of that sort with the support of only 18 out of 250 members. Therefore do not let us have any vision of a strong Centre being secured by the Report of the Statutory Commission. The Report has great merits, and reading and re-reading it I am struck with admiration of it, but it has not the merit of providing a strong Centre."

The co-operation of the Indian States in a Federal scheme is expected to provide this strength, and that is why, in an official statement of Conservative policy, Sir Samuel Hoare announced that they gave a cordial welcome to the Princes' offer to enter an All-India Federation, and that they would try their hand " at bringing about All-India Federation, in which the stabilizing forces of the Indian States will be brought into the constitutional balance." The history of their efforts is to be found in three Round Table Conferences and several committees and the results in the famous White Paper. In our subsequent chapters we shall follow these developments.

CHAPTER IV

THE ROUND TABLE CONFERENCES

First Round Table Conference : Preparation for the Second Round Table Conference : Second Round Table Conference : Congress Mandate : Third Round Table Conference : Communal Award : Indian Franchise Committee : Federal Finance Committee : Safeguards : Conference ends : General Review : Burma Round Table Conference

IN the last chapter we have related the circumstances that led to the promise of "some sort of Conference" after the Statutory Commission submitted their Report. We are now to follow the proceedings of *three* successive Conferences that were staged in London with the avowed object of arriving at the maximum amount of agreement between the various committees and the great varieties of interests.

FIRST ROUND TABLE CONFERENCE

The Conference was duly opened by King George V on November 12, 1930, and was concluded on January 19, 1931. The Prime Minister presided, and all parties in Parliament were well represented. The total number of delegates was 89, including 57 from British India, 16 representatives of the Indian States, and 16 members of the Parliamentary delegation. It should be remembered that the Indian National Congress was not represented in the Conference, and that Gandhi and many other Congress leaders were in prison at the time.

The opening of the Conference was an imposing ceremony, attended by Prime Ministers and other representatives of the Dominions. The King-Emperor, as a visible symbol of Unity of the British Commonwealth of Nations, addressed the great assembly in person.

A significant feature of the Conference was the presence of the Indian Princes, who were invited, as stated before, in accordance with the suggestion Sir John Simon made to the Prime Minister. They readily accepted the invitation.

Ever since the political movement began to gain strength throughout India, the Indian Princes have had difficulties in controlling its invasion of their dominions. They discerned in the policy of the Government a clear indication of granting a large share of responsibility to Indian Legislatures with a view to placating the intransigent spirit behind that movement. Thus, their dissatisfaction with the Indian States Enquiry Committee and growing apprehension that bold measures of constitutional reforms might be granted to British India, the repercussion of which would certainly be felt in their States, induced them to grasp the opportunity of joining in a Conference free to modify such proposals. And not only did they succeed in modifying the proposals of the Indian Statutory Commission but they completely changed the foundation on which the Statutory Commission based their Report.

At the very first session of the Conference, His Highness the Maharaja of Bikaner made a dramatic pronouncement, proposing that there should be a Federal Government embracing British India and " Indian " India in which the Princes would be prepared to take their part. The result was that, as a writer put it, the tocsin of Dominion Status ceased to sound.

Nevertheless, the first Round Table Conference, soon after its spectacular ceremonies were over, became the arena of controversy. The announcement that the distant goal as visualized by the Statutory Commission, of an All-India Federation, had been brought near by the willingness of the

Princes to join such a scheme, introduced an entirely new feature into the discussion, and was welcomed by the Imperial Government. Most of the leading Indian nominees of British India had, however, hoped that the Conference would proceed to evolve a scheme based on Lord Irwin's assurance of "Dominion Status" for India, with such temporary safeguards as would be necessary. But any attempt to insist on the expression "Dominion Status" as the basis for discussion would have created an impasse at the very outset of the Conference. Amid cheers for the ideal of an All-India Federation and protestations against a "Dominion Status Constitution" the Conference began its work.

The unanimity of the Indian delegates on the question of an All-India Federation came as a surprise to the British statesmen. But the reason for this was obvious. The Indian politicians felt that the grant of provincial autonomy without responsibility at the Centre would be a sham, and that through a Federal Constitution it might be possible for them to secure responsible self-government and central responsibility, eventually leading to the status now enjoyed by the Dominions. They persuaded themselves that the alliance of the Indian Princes would greatly strengthen India's claim to self-government and would be of substantial help in striking bargains.

The British delegates, on the other hand, saw some advantage in gaining time in making the final decision in regard to the new Constitution for India. They, too, realized that the process of adjustment would allow greater scope for bargaining. Although the Federal picture appeared so attractive, the representatives of the Conservative Party were not prepared to commit themselves to any plan unless and until its details were clearly drawn. The British delegates as a body gave a cordial welcome to the proposal and "found, so to speak, better cards in their hands than they had expected."[1]

[1] "Years of Destiny," by Professor J. Coatman: Jonathan Cape, 1932.

For weeks the details of the picture engaged the Conference and its nine sub-committees. The proper classification of federal and non-federal subjects—defence, the protection of minorities, the structure and constitution of the Federal Legislature, the franchise—all these amazingly complicated subjects made the task of arriving at a definite solution extremely difficult. And of all difficulties, the intractable problem of communal dissension once again raised its head, and the inevitable awakening of passions among the various communities laid bare the fatal malady that existed in Indian social life. Notwithstanding the sympathetic intervention of some of their British colleagues, the heroes and protectors of communal interests, at the last moment of the Conference, " filed into the drawing-room (at St. James's Palace) with downcast mien " and announced that their efforts to find a basis of agreement on the issues referred to them had been abortive.

But this tragic failure was only what one would expect from these veterans of communal interests. As I write, the remark of His Excellency Salvador de Madariaga on the failure of the Disarmament Commission comes to my mind. He said : " It was as foolish to expect a disarmament convention from such a commission as a declaration of atheism from a commission of clergymen."

The Conference, therefore, came to no definite conclusions in regard to any of these fundamental issues that confronted the Statutory Commission. The Conference only reiterated the findings of the Commission and left the entire problem in a state of uncertainty. It became clear to the Indian delegates that all political parties in Great Britain laid the greatest possible emphasis on certain safeguards and consequently, towards the end of the Conference, Sir Tej Bahadur Sapru, a prominent Indian Liberal, boldly faced the issue and declared that the progressive Indians would agree to any reasonable constitutional limitations provided they were given responsible self-government at the Centre. He demanded a definite decision in regard to this vexed question of government at the Centre being vested in a responsible legislature.

At a meeting of the Federal Structure sub-Committee, Sir Muhammed Shafi, the chief spokesman of the Moslem delegation, supported his Hindu colleague, and it now remained for the British delegation to make a pronouncement. Lord Reading, on behalf of the Liberal delegation, declared that his party was in favour of a responsible Federal Government in India, and elaborated the nature and extent of limitations to be provided in the Constitution; but the views of the Conservatives were expressed in no ambiguous terms, making it plain that they could not agree to a particular scheme at this nebulous stage of the proposal and that the foremost consideration, in their judgment, was effective safeguards for the fundamental interests of Great Britain. In a statement [1] after the Conference, Sir Samuel Hoare wrote:

> "Certainly, we Conservative members of the Round Table Conference did not conceal the doubts and fears that we honestly feel. Time after time we were compelled to refuse our assent to vague and unproved propositions. Time after time we had the unpleasant task of putting a brake upon demands for ill-considered advance. During ten weeks of almost incessant discussion, basing ourselves upon the Simon Report, we steadily maintained our position. . . . We remained on the most friendly terms with our Indian colleagues, but we firmly refused to commit ourselves to obligations that had not been defined, and we insistently declared that two preliminary conditions must be satisfied before we could consider any changes in the Central Government, namely, the condition that the Imperial safeguards must be full and effective, and the condition that any new constitution must on the face of it be workable."

However, the declaration of an All-India Federation, the ideal which was now proclaimed as being within the

[1] *Morning Post*, February 5, 1931.

scope of immediate realization, saved the face of the Conference. On the last day of the Conference (January 19, 1931) a statement was made by His Highness the Maharaja of Patiala, at that time the Chancellor of the Chamber of Princes, in which His Highness said :

> "The main principle of Federation stands acceptable, and I echo the confident hope expressed the other day by His Highness the Maharaja of Bikaner that by far the larger proportion of the States will come into the federal structure at once and that the remainder will soon follow."

But His Highness added :

> "We consider certain things to be essential. We can only federate with a British India which is self-governing and not with a British India governed as it is at present."

The views of His Majesty's Government were summed up in the Prime Minister's final speech on the same day, in which he stated that the Government was prepared to accept the principle of an All-India Federation with a Federal Executive responsible to the Legislature. The Prime Minister's words were as follows :

> "The view of His Majesty's Government is that responsibility for the Government of India should be placed upon Legislatures, Central and Provincial, with such provisions as may be necessary to guarantee, during a period of transition, the observance of certain obligations and to meet other special circumstances, and also with such guarantees as are required by minorities to protect their political liberties and rights. . . . With a Legislature constituted on a federal basis, His Majesty's Government will be prepared to recognize the principle of the responsibility of the Executive to the Legislature."

This policy was set out in a Command Paper [1] subsequently approved by both Houses. The following is a summary of the statement issued by the Prime Minister :

[1] Cmd. 3972 of 1931.

1. Responsibility for the Government of India is to be placed upon the Legislatures, Central and Provincial, with such provisions as may be necessary to guarantee during a period of transition the observance of certain obligations and to meet other special circumstances; and also with such guarantees as are required by minorities to protect their political liberties and rights.
2. The reserved powers to be so framed and exercised as not to prejudice the advance of India to full self-government.
3. The Central Government to be bi-cameral and to take the form of a Federation of All-India, embracing both the Indian States and British India.
4. The precise form of the Federal Government to be determined after discussion with the Princes and the representatives of British India.
5. The Federal Government to have only such authority over matters concerning the States as may be conceded by their Rulers.
6. With a Legislature constituted on a Federal basis, the principle to be recognized of the responsibility of the Executive to the Legislature.
7. Defence and external affairs to be reserved to the Governor-General with the necessary administrative powers.
8. The Governor-General to be given power in case of emergency to maintain the tranquillity of the State and protect the constitutional rights of minorities.
9. The transfer of financial responsibility to be subject to conditions ensuring fulfilment of the Secretary of State's obligations and maintenance of the financial stability and credit of India.
10. The Provinces to be given full autonomy with Ministries taken from the Legislature and jointly responsible to it.

11. The communal differences to be settled by agreement among the communities themselves.
12. The work of the Conference to be suspended at this point to admit of Indian opinion being consulted. In the event of non-co-operators being disposed to co-operate on the general lines of the Government's declarations, steps to be taken to enlist their services.

The decision of the Government in regard to the possible form of Constitution for India was thus made clear and succeeded in evoking a considerable enthusiasm among the Indian delegates. It was therefore surprising that the Government did not take steps to expedite the matter and frame a Bill on that basis. One of the psychological factors underlying the Indian opposition to the measure may be traced to "the miasma of delay" which had undoubtedly damped all enthusiasm. The Nationalists in India regarded dilatoriness as part of a deliberate policy of the Government—a policy of "marking time."

> "If that Conference had been followed by legislation," observes Sir Stanley Reed, an eminent British journalist in India, "all would have been well. But it was succeeded by the two barren sessions; the drawn-out sittings of the Joint Parliamentary Committee, punctuated by delays in pursuit of the red herrings drawn across the trail. In the depression of hope deferred the bright promise of the first Round Table Conference wilted, dried almost to a cinder by the arid blasts of reactionary oratory. . . ."[1]

However, the delegates returned home with the word "Federation" on their lips; but it was not long before the reaction came. All the parties concerned came to scrutinize the implications of an immediate All-India Federation, and numerous problems of a fundamental character emerged, adding to the complexities of Indian constitutional reforms. The conditions under which the Princes would agree to enter Federation seemed to make

[1] Sir Stanley Reed at the East India Association, May 21, 1935.

democracy a sham; on the other hand, the conditions demanded by the majority of British Indian politicians seemed to make the entry of the Princes into a Federal scheme hazardous. Thus something like an impasse was created.

But that was not all. The insistence with which the Princes laid emphasis on the sacred preserve of their paramountcy indicated that they felt nervous about the entry into Federation, although His Highness the Maharaja of Patiala declared in the Round Table Conference that the Princes would be willing to make sacrifices of sovereignty. In the intervening period between the first and second Round Table, some of the Princes suggested confederation as a preliminary stage towards the ultimate Federation—the view which is, as the reader may note, implicit in the recommendations of the Indian Statutory Commission. The Prime Minister of the State of Bikaner observed that: "The federation likely to be accepted by Indian Princes would tend more towards a confederation for specifically defined subjects of joint interest than towards unity or union." A similar trend of thought could be traced in other utterances of some of the Princes and their responsible officials.

The prominent Indian Liberals were, on the other hand, uneasy over two main factors, namely (1) the number and the nature of the safeguards stipulated by the Imperial Government in their statement after the Round Table Conference; (2) the absence of the Congress from the next Conference, where strenuous efforts would have to be made to modify the rigidity of limitations imposed on the proposed constitution.

¶ PREPARATION FOR THE SECOND ROUND TABLE CONFERENCE

Then came the next phase—a preparation for the second Round Table Conference. We now turn to events in India, where an exciting drama in connection with this preparation was being enacted.

Lord Irwin, determined to create an atmosphere for the acceptance of the Government policy as it emerged from the first Round Table Conference, and to offer opportunities to the Indian Liberals for bringing the Congress to the Conference, released Gandhi and thousands of his followers; and the notifications declaring the working committee (which is the Central Executive Council) of the Congress an unlawful association was withdrawn. Two days before the adjournment of the Conference in London, on January 17, His Excellency, addressing the Indian Legislature, gave definite indication of a peace-offering to the Congress. To a section of the British public, this method of treating the rebellious spirit may seem wholly unorthodox and even damaging to British prestige in India; but it was singularly successful in handling a saintly rebel. It paved the way for the capitulation of the Civil Disobedience Movement and brought its leader face to face with the realities of the constitutional problems. On the other hand, the Indian Liberal leaders' confidence in the intentions of the Government was greatly enhanced, and they hailed Lord Irwin's gesture as "a miracle of statecraft." The Indian Princes welcomed the steps taken to negotiate with Gandhi.

As a result of a prolonged series of conversations between Lord Irwin and Gandhi, a settlement was reached such as would be described in a Parliamentary document as "agreements" and in the Congress vocabulary as a "truce," a "pact," or even a "treaty." It is an undeniable fact that by entering into these negotiations, which continued for several days, requiring no less than eight interviews with the Viceroy and the Home Secretary to the Government of India, Gandhi had acquired for the Congress a considerable political prestige and for himself the position of a plenipotentiary. It was, however, inherent in the policy adopted by Lord Irwin that the prestige of the Congress should be pushed to a great height so that in the event of a fall the injury would be fatal. The reaction of the negotiations on the policy of the Congress will be traced in the course of our narration; here we will confine ourselves to such developments as led to Gandhi's co-operation in the second Round Table Conference in London.

At the outset Lord Irwin made it clear to Gandhi that any decision he might come to must involve the acceptance of the policy that India's political objective was an All-India Federation, subject to certain essential safeguards and reservations, the details of which could be discussed by the Congress representatives in the next Conference. And when Gandhi agreed to this fundamental point in the bargain Lord Irwin's purpose was fulfilled.

The second step towards the preparation of the Conference was the proposal to hold it in India. Lord Irwin's intention was to allow the generation of young Indians which had been drawn into the orbit of the political struggle to see the Conference at work with their own eyes, so that they might be convinced that the Imperial Government had fully recognized the growing political ambitions of the Indian political classes, and that the constitutional concessions now proposed were offered "in no niggling spirit." He was sufficiently conversant with the Indian mind to realize that niggardliness was fatal in dealing with so sensitive a people. The proposal to hold the Conference in India had also the advantage of bringing the British delegates in closer contact with the Indian situation than was possible in the drawing-room of St. James's Palace. The task of "fact finding" would then probably have been easy.

But the proposal met with opposition from the Conservative Party. Its India Committee passed a resolution as follows: "That this Committee welcomes the decision of Mr. Baldwin that the Conservative Party cannot be represented at any further Round Table Conferences to be held in India, as now foreshadowed by His Majesty's Government." Although the Prime Minister was in favour of accepting Lord Irwin's proposal, the attitude of the Cabinet as a whole made it impossible for him to accept it. It was then decided to hold the second Round Table Conference in

London in September 1931. Lord Irwin left India on April 18, 1931, and Lord Willingdon assumed the office of Viceroy.

After a period of fresh negotiations with Lord Willingdon over the fulfilment and non-fulfilment of his "pact" with Lord Irwin, Gandhi, at the last moment, decided to attend the Conference, to which he was appointed as "a poor humble agent acting on behalf of the Indian National Congress" at its Karachi Session in March 1931.

In the meantime, changes had taken place in the Home Government. The position of a minority Government could not long be maintained, and it became necessary to form a coalition. Under the National Government, Sir Samuel Hoare was appointed to replace Mr. Wedgwood Benn as Secretary of State for India. These changes did not, however, affect the policy of the Imperial Government in regard to the Indian Constitutional Reforms nor was there any alteration in the procedure that had already been decided upon.

¶ SECOND ROUND TABLE CONFERENCE

The total membership of the Conference was increased to 114; but most of the difficult issues were discussed at the meetings of the Federal Structure sub-Committee, whose size was also increased to 38, before they were brought to the full Conference. The problem of safeguarding the minorities was referred to a special committee. In point of fact, the Conference met only three times in plenary session for considering the Reports of the sub-Committees.

Gandhi entered the stage of the Round Table Conference with his dual personality of a saint imbued with the idea of "soul-force" as a solvent of all difficulties, and of a politician adept in the art of finesse. The atmosphere of a London Conference was not, however, suitable for playing the rôle of a saint, and when Gandhi the politician found himself faced with some intricate and stark facts which baffled his ingenuity, he took refuge in what he termed the Congress Mandate with which he was entrusted at the Karachi Session of that body. I shall presently refer to this mandate and to Gandhi's performance in the Conference. Let us pause here for a moment to review the attitude of the various sections of the delegation which reassembled after an interval of nine months.

In the first place, a group of Princes, led by His Highness the Maharaja of Patiala, having considered the implications of an All-India Federation in respect to their own States, now favoured a confederation of Indian States—a distinct change in the views expressed in the first Conference. It gradually dawned upon them that their position, especially in reference to the sovereignty of the States in the proposed Constitution, might give rise to serious complications at the present moment. Nor were they devoid of nervous feelings in regard to their future relations with the Paramount Power. They argued that a political alliance of the Indian States could be secured, consistent with the maintenance of their internal autonomy in a Confederation. It would be a preparatory stage for the growth of the federal idea, would develop the growth of the necessary materials for a federation, and would educate the country in the handling of such a complicated structure as a Federal Constitution. A loose federal structure would be ineffective and might impede the growth of a Federal Constitution. It appeared that the decision of the Congress to take part in the second Round Table Conference had put the oligarchy of the Indian States on its guard.

Some of the premier Indian States, however, adhered to the federal idea in the hope of improving their relations with the Paramount Power so that the States might really enjoy complete internal autonomy. They raised the fundamental issue of the sovereignty of the States—the subject which had caused a stir among them owing to the letter [1] which Lord Reading, when Viceroy, addressed to His

[1] See Chapter II.

Exalted Highness the Nizam of Hyderabad. At any rate the Indian Princes came to the Conference with the idea of securing an irreducible minimum of essential conditions for their entry into the Federal scheme.

The Second Group, the Indian Liberals, having earned some prestige as the mediating party between the Government and the Congress, came to the Conference encouraged by their success in bringing Gandhi to London. With him in opposition, pledged to make demands which no British Government could concede, they cherished hopes of striking a better bargain with the Government. They felt that Gandhi's presence would help them to form a satisfactory pact with the minority committee, and that once this knotty communal problem was disentangled, the conditions for modifying the proposed limitations in the Constitution would be favourable.

The Third Group, the British Conservatives, strengthened by the formation of the National Government and stiffened by the persistent "call for safeguards" from a powerful section of the Party, were determined to insist upon adequate and effective limitations being imposed upon the Constitution and expressed their views in the clearest possible language. Their position was no longer dependent, as it was at the first Round Table, upon the British Liberals. Moreover, the events in India following the Irwin-Gandhi conversations alarmed the Conservatives. The riot at Cawnpore, the Congress enthusiasm at Karachi, and the outbursts of the "red shirt movement" on the North-West Frontier were the incidents that stirred Conservative opinion.

At a meeting of the Central Council of the National Union of Conservative and Unionist Associations on June 30, 1931, the following resolution was proposed:

> "That this Council is of opinion, especially in view of the recent events in India, that before the Conservative Party is again represented on the occasion of the resumed discussions at the next Round Table Conference, they should receive a clear and definite assurance from the Government

that the proposals for an Indian Constitution are subject to the condition (as being vital and fundamental to and already forming part of the scheme) that the essential safeguards must be both real and permanent, and capable of being exercised by the Imperial Parliament in the interests of this country no less than in those of India, and also to the condition that any Resolution calculated to render possible complete independence is definitely outside the scope of discussion."

On this occasion Sir Samuel Hoare made it clear that the Round Table Conference was in no wise a "Constituent Assembly," and that if it were found possible and expedient to build up an All-India Federation now, the Conservative delegates to the Conference would do their utmost to secure adequate and effective safeguards for the maintenance of Imperial interests.

Such was the frame of mind of the different groups that reassembled in the second Round Table Conference. The obvious results ensued—the Conference achieved no unanimity on some of the fundamental issues involved in the proposed Federal Constitution. The question of safeguarding the minorities still remained undecided, and the communal antagonism unreconciled.[1] The representatives of the Indian States could not come to an agreement amongst themselves in regard to their place in the Federation and their mutual relationship within the proposed Constitution. The subject of provincial autonomy, which the Prime Minister declared to be "the surest and speediest route to Federation," had not received much consideration from the Conference as it was only a "partial advance." At last came, as usual, a declaration from the Prime Minister which was of special importance, as it now came from the head of the *National* Government. He reiterated the policy embodied in his statement made at the end of the first Round Table Conference and added that the Cabinet regarded Federation as offering the only solution of India's constitutional

[1] See Section: The Communal Award, p. 126.

problem. This emphasis on Federation was evidently designed to initiate wavering minds into the ideal which alone seemed to admit of providing the conditions in which central responsibility might be embodied in the Constitution.

The failure to arrive at any decisions upon the questions of paramount importance induced the Conference to resort to the well-known expedient of appointing committees. It was proposed to set up (1) a consultative committee; (2) a committee for examining the revision of franchise and constituencies; (3) a committee for detailed scrutiny of the financial proposals; and (4) a committee for examining specific financial problems in some of the Indian States. The last three were known as "fact finding" committees.

Perhaps the only effective decision to which the Conference agreed, was that the North-West Frontier Province should be raised to the status of a Governor's Province, with due regard to the necessary requirements of the Frontier.

The Conference came to an end on December 1. In view of the extraordinary interest and enthusiasm roused by Gandhi's presence we should enquire what assistance he was able to render in the solution of the difficulties that faced it.

¶ THE CONGRESS MANDATE

So far as the framing of the Constitution was concerned, Gandhi took his stand on the Congress demand for *Purna Swaraj*, meaning complete independence, which, he argued, was not inconsistent with "an indissoluble partnership" with the British people. In the details of the proposed Federal structure he had little interest. What he aimed at was clear from the very first pronouncement he made before the Federal Structure Committee. He wanted His Majesty's Government to realize that the Congress was not merely a powerful political organization but it was a dynamic movement that had touched and stirred the soul of the people. He recognized the difficulties in framing a workable Constitution for India, but his fervent appeal was for trust and goodwill. "For heaven's sake, give me, a frail man of 62 years gone, a little bit of chance," he cried in a speech at the plenary session. "Find a little corner for him and the organization that he represents. You distrust that organization though you may seemingly trust me." Based on mutual trust, he tried to persuade the Conference to grant India the status that would lead to "an honourable and equal partnership between Great Britain and India."

But his declaration at the outset of the Conference, that the delegates were "an ill-assorted group" and not "the chosen ones of the nation" undoubtedly created a chasm between him and his colleagues. His insistent reiteration of the Congress Mandate was not helpful in giving a shape to the constitutional proposals and only resulted in bringing into greater prominence the fundamental differences between him and the rest of the Conference.

However, we have to judge Gandhi's performance in London from the point of view of the Congress. Faithfully he delivered its mandate, argued the logic of its mission and defended its predominant position in Indian political life. In his parting words to the Prime Minister he declared that he and the Congress he represented had come to the parting of the ways and that he did not know in what direction his path would now lie. To his followers he said: "True, I have come empty-handed, but I am thankful I have not compromised the honour of the Country."

But, zealous of the power and prestige of Congress and of its methods in "ending or mending" the Government, Gandhi availed himself of the opportunity presented to him within and outside the Conference for explaining the Congress demands. He knew that he was speaking before, as it were, a world-microphone, and that the world-press was taking note of his message. Whatever might be the result of his participation in the Conference, it served well the cause of the Congress by the publicity his words received.

From the point of view of the Imperial Government, Gandhi's presence in the Conference was also fruitful of some results. It helped them to measure his influence over the various sections of Indian political opinion, and his capacity to find a practical solvent to the communal problem which the Congress so far regarded as a domestic issue, jealously guarding it so long against any outside interference; it enabled them to foresee the precise character of opposition that would come from the rank and file of the Congress; and finally, it weakened the Civil Disobedience Movement, the suspension of which, in accordance with the "Delhi pact" had already produced coma.

The Indian delegates returned home with a feeling of uncertainty in regard to the "inner policy" of the Government. The assurance that the future Indian Constitution would be an All-India Federation was not enough. They became apprehensive of the various complications that were conjured up in the course of the deliberations. All this would mean a considerable delay in coming to a decision. Besides, the Indian Princes had not fully made up their minds in regard to entering the Federation. Their indecision inspired Lord Sankey, at the close of the Conference, to make a passionate appeal in the following terms:

> "Gentlemen of the States," said the Lord Chancellor, "India is thirsting, India is calling; you have put the cup to her lips—do not delay her drinking it. You have excited the hopes of India. Hope deferred makes the heart sick, and I very much hope that as soon as possible, you or your rulers will be able to give us some definite assurance that you will enter into the Federation. It will assist everybody; it will gratify the ambitions and the aspirations of India, if we can have your positive assurance that, come what may, your entry into the Federation is a certain fact."

On their way to India, the delegates were in varying moods. The Indian Princes were now mainly concerned with the problem of paramountcy; the Indian Liberals with Central responsibility; the Minority Communities with communal representation and reservation of seats; and Gandhi with the next phase of the Congress. The promulgation of Ordinances, and the imprisonment of some of his Congress associates made his task extremely difficult. On his return to India he was faced with a tense atmosphere, and he soon found himself in Yeravda Central prison. Meanwhile, the British delegates were examining the various devices for safeguarding the Imperial interests, and the three Committees appointed by the Conference commenced their further investigation of the problems referred to them. The reports of these three Committees were placed before the third Round Table Conference.

ℂ. THE THIRD ROUND TABLE CONFERENCE

But there was a fourth committee which was a Consultative Committee in India of members of the Round Table Conference, the main purpose of which was to arrive at some definite conclusions among themselves on matters on which there existed a wide divergence of opinion among them. His Majesty's Government intended to proceed with the setting up of the Joint Select Committee after the conclusion of the Consultative Committee's work. The Consultative Committee met in India under the chairmanship of the Viceroy, but it failed to come to terms over the communal and the other outstanding problems. Once more the Indian leaders failed to compose their own differences, and once again His Majesty's Government had to stage another Conference in London "for a final review of the scheme." But the size of the third Round Table was smaller, and its agenda was more defined than that of the two which preceded it. Both the Congress Party in India and the Labour Party in England abstained from taking any part in the Conference. The British delegation included non-official Conservatives and Liberal representatives. The Indian delegation consisted of Government nominees, carefully selected from those who were likely to support Government proposals. The Indian States were represented by some of their officials. The Conference met this time at the Palace of Westminster.

¶. THE COMMUNAL AWARD

Within the intervening period between the second and third Round Table Conferences, His Majesty's Government gave their decision upon the communal question, which they reluctantly undertook to consider after the Indian politicians had given it up in despair. During the second Round Table Conference, the Prime Minister appointed an informal Conciliation Committee under the chairmanship of Gandhi; but, after a week's strenuous efforts to reach a settlement, he announced " with deep sorrow and deeper humiliation, his failure to secure an agreement with the Communities concerned,"[1] and suggested that this " sinful wrangle " would continue so long as there remained uncertainties in regard to " the fundamentals of the Constitution." He said:

> " The solution can be the crown of the Swaraj Constitution, not its foundation, if only because our differences have hardened—if they have not arisen—by reason of the foreign domination. I have not a shadow of doubt that the iceberg of communal differences will melt under the warmth of the sun of freedom."

It became increasingly clear to His Majesty's Government that the communal question was growing into a serious obstacle in the way of framing the Constitution, and that once they could clearly indicate the basic method and proportions of representation between the rival claims of different communities, the communities themselves might

[1] On this occasion Sir Tej Bahadur Sapru recorded a brief impression in his little diary as follows: " Witnessed the funeral of so-called Indian Nationalism, chief pall-bearers being . . . When will it be re-born ? "

then "find it possible to arrive at a *modus vivendi* on other communal problems."

Accordingly, the Prime Minister agreed to settle the dispute provided he was given a definite assurance by the members of the Minorities' sub-Committee that they would support his decision. Gandhi, while welcoming the Prime Minister's offer, declined to commit the Congress either to recognize the Government's power of arbitration on the communal issue or to accept their verdict if it were prejudicial to the growth of Indian national life. The matter was referred to a Consultative Committee set up after the second Round Table Conference, but they, too, having failed to come to an agreement, requested His Majesty's Government to fulfil an undertaking given by the Prime Minister to apply a provisional scheme of settlement. The terms of the settlement, known as the British Government's "Communal Award," were announced on August 17, 1932. Settlement by an outside party, not wholly disinterested, of a problem which is deeply rooted in the socio-religious systems of a country, can never be satisfactory.

The Award created 12 separate electoral compartments, namely, (1) Hindus, (2) Moslems, (3) Sikhs, (4) Anglo-Indians, (5) Britishers, (6) Depressed classes, (7) Indian Christians, (8) Commerce and Industry, (9) Landlords and Capitalists, (10) Labour, (11) University men, and (12) Women. It devised ingenious schemes for weightage and preferential representation in order to placate the various Communalist groups. At best, it could be described as a provisional patchwork of compromises between the rival claims of the Minorities.[1]

The Award was greeted with scorn and abuse from the Congress Party. Gandhi was at the time in prison, and on

[1] The Award provided that seats in the Provincial Legislatures should be distributed as follows: General (mainly Hindu), 705; Moslem, 489; Depressed classes, 61; Commerce and Industry, 54; Labour, 38; Land-holders, 35; Sikhs, 35; Europeans, 25; Indian Christians, 21; Backward Areas, 20; Anglo-Indians, 12; and Universities, 8.

the day following the publication of the Award he informed the Prime Minister that he would resist his decision

> "by declaring a perpetual fast unto death" and that "this fast will cease if, during its progress, the British Government, of its own motion or under pressure of public opinion, revise their decision and withdraw their scheme of communal electorates for the Depressed classes, whose representatives should be elected by the general electorate under a common franchise, no matter how wide it is." [1]

The situation developed by Gandhi's fast was dramatic in its effect, and undoubtedly riveted our attention on one of the gruesome evils of Hindu society. But it deflected our attention from the wider and more fundamental concepts of the Indian Constitutional development. It is not suggested here that Gandhi approved of many of the other parts of the Government decision embodied in their Communal Award. He singled out the provision of a separate electorate for the Depressed classes, with the object of awakening the Caste-Hindus to the realization of a malignant ulcer eating into their social life, which the decision did nothing to eradicate but on the contrary left untouched to work its evil on the body-politic. Here Gandhi the saint worked in consultation with Gandhi the politician.

Protest was also made by other Communities. The Sikh delegates to the Conference resigned. At a mass gathering of the Sikhs at the shrine of the Maharaja Ranjit Singh, the British Government were warned of the consequences of a "betrayal of Sikhs" in the Communal Award. They further pledged themselves to offer Civil Disobedience against the operation of this "mischievous and intriguing Award," whose main object was to set one community against another. The Nationalist-Moslem organizations recorded their disapproval of the ways and means by which the compromise was to be effected. The All-India Women's Conference expressed their opinion that the Award was

[1] Letter from Gandhi to the Prime Minister, from Yeravda Central Prison, August 18, 1932.

an attempt to inject the "poison of Communalism into the Indian body-politic." Rani Lakhshamibai Rajwade, on behalf of the All-India Women Conference, sent the following cable to the Prime Minister:

> "Our Conference read with deep sorrow the Communal Award as touching the women of India. Standing unequivocally for the principles embodied in our joint memorandum and the recent statement, we totally disapprove and strongly protest against the proposals which failed to recognize our rightful position and seek to establish in our midst communities which will remain permanently estranged from the National life."

The Hindus, who had organized themselves under a *Mahasabha* [1] for the protection of their rights, denounced the Award as being partial to the Moslems, whose position they declared would now be greatly strengthened in all Provinces. Fear, suspicion and jealousy engaged the communities in intolerable wrangles, and in the meantime, Gandhi declared his fast-unto-death. The issue here was, as stated above, the representation of the Depressed classes. Therefore, their leaders and some of the representatives of the Caste-Hindus hurried to Poona, where Gandhi was in prison, with a view to suggesting a modification of the Communal Award in reference to the Depressed classes. Following upon negotiations which lasted for about a week, their leaders were induced to renounce separate electorates for Depressed classes by an offer of a disproportionately large number of seats to be reserved for them in general electoral rolls. It was agreed that 148 seats in the Provincial Legislatures should be allotted to them (compared with 71 seats under the Premier's Communal Award); that 18 per cent. of the seats in the Central Legislature to be allotted to the general electorates should be reserved

[1] A great Assembly of the Hindus, recently organized, with a view to providing for Hinduism the same kind of opportunity for self-expression as the deliberations, for example, of the National Assembly of the Church of England have since its inception in 1920 provided for that Church.

for them; that the voting in the joint electorate should be preceded by a primary election for a panel of four representatives of the Depressed classes for each reserved seat; that the system of reserved seats and primary election should be terminated after ten years. The terms were accepted by His Majesty's Government and Gandhi broke his fast. Whether the principles involved in the agreement are sound, *i.e.* whether it will eventually provide a permanent solution of the communal problem, is a question to which few would care to hazard a reply. What is important to note here is, that in the third Round Table Conference this problem was not allowed to impede the work of the framers of the Indian Constitution.

The outstanding feature of that Conference was the anxiety of His Majesty's Government and the British delegations to bring all matters of discussion down to concrete forms. They adopted "less formal and more expeditious procedure" than that followed at its previous two sessions. They had, by this time, adequately judged the extent and depth of political acumen of the Indian spokesmen whose loquacious and intransigent tendencies were held in check by the character of the agenda and by the decision that speeches should not be published. The Conference had also the advantage of three authoritative reports on Franchise, Federal Finance, and Financial Relations with the Indian States.

¶ THE INDIAN FRANCHISE COMMITTEE

Under the chairmanship of the Marquess of Lothian, a Committee consisting of 18 members was set up with a view to submitting to His Majesty's Government "complete and detailed proposals on which to base the revision of the franchise and the arrangements of Constituencies, Central and Provincial." From the terms of reference laid down in the Prime Minister's letter to the Chairman of the Committee, it was obvious that the Committee's duty was to keep their gaze fixed on the superstructures of Indian polity rather than on the basis on which they should ideally rest, and its task was to recommend only certain changes to suit the plans for reconditioning those superstructures. In other words, the Committee's chief concern was with extending the existing franchise and suggesting the several forms of representation by which all communities and interests might find a rightful place in the Legislatures. The communal question was not included in the Committee's terms of reference.

The main recommendations of the Committee were:

(1) Complete adult franchise as demanded by the Congress was administratively impracticable and "politically unwise" at the present time. Not merely on account of the huge numbers involved in adult suffrage was it regarded as an impossible suggestion; the fact that only 8 per cent. of the adult population were literate made it unworkable. Consequently, the course of wisdom and statesmanship was not to attempt to launch the new constitution on the basis of adult franchise.

(2) Since the existing franchise was too limited, it should be extended by lowering the standard of property qualification, supplementing it by an educational qualification. The existing military service qualification should be retained, and should now be extended to those enrolled in the Auxiliary and Territorial forces.

(3) Wives of men who now possessed a property qualification for the vote, members of special constituencies created for labour, the Depressed classes, and all income tax payers should be enfranchised.

(4) Special seats at present allotted to special interests, like commerce, industry, landlords and universities, should be retained, but their number should not be increased.

(5) Since there were various disadvantages in indirect franchise, the Committee recommended that the extension proposed should be effected by the direct vote.

The reader may note that the Committee did not suggest any new basis for widening the franchise nor indicate how the best interests of the Indian masses were to be represented in the newly constituted Legislatures. According to the estimate based on the Committee's proposals, the electoral roll would increase from about 7 millions to 36 millions. That is, about 14 per cent. of the total population, and an increase of about 500 per cent. over the existing electorate. And it was this increase which was to provide the basis upon which an adequate system of representative government would be built. The Committee was, however, satisfied that the proposed electorate would be representative of the general mass of the population, and that its needs and opinions would be adequately expressed in the Legislatures through the electoral system devised by them.

In accordance with the recommendation of the Franchise Committee, the Conference accepted the principle of direct election for the Federal and Provincial Lower Houses, the extension of provincial franchise by a low property qualification, and the enfranchisement of women approximately in the proportion of two women for every nine men. It was also agreed that the existing electorates for the Provincial Councils should elect the Federal Assembly, but the Federal Upper House should be elected by indirect election from the Provincial Legislatures.

All this was smooth sailing. The conflict of Indian opinion arose on the point where the two Indias, namely, British India and Indian India, would be federated under the scheme. The Conference could not come to any decision upon the size of the two Federal Chambers, for the question is related to the allocation of seats between the two integral parts of the Federal Structure. It had been proposed at the second session of the Round Table Conference to give the Indian States 40 per cent. and 33⅓ per cent. of the seats in the Federal Assembly and Federal Senate respectively, and although this proposal still held the field, Moslem opposition to it brought in the complication of a communal proportion in the States representation. Speaking about the situation this gave rise to in the Conference, Mr. Hugh Molson, M.P., observed :

> "It looks as if this fundamental problem, which will of course determine how much power the Indian States will exercise in the Federation, would have to be referred, like the communal problems, for the arbitral decision of His Majesty's Government, but even that point has not yet been reached. British Indian delegates were willing to leave the size of the Chambers to this arbitration, but not the percentage to be given to the States ; the latter were prepared for the percentage also to be arbitrated, subject to their right not to enter the Federation if they were dissatisfied. This may be regarded as the worst deadlock which the Conference reached, and it is made more difficult because neither the British Indian nor the States' delegations were agreed amongst themselves upon their minimum terms." [1]

THE FEDERAL FINANCE COMMITTEE

The Committee [2] on Federal Finance, presided over by Lord Eustace Percy, found economic conditions in India abnormal. The index number of wholesale prices had fallen calamitously ; and there was a considerable shrinkage of trade, as the following figures of India's exports and imports show :

	Exports (crores of Rupees). 1 crore = £750,000.	Imports (crores of Rupees). 1 crore = £750,000.
1928	319	250
1929	330	253
1930	310	240
1931	220	164
1932	138	136

[1] Speech at a meeting of the East India Association, January 16, 1933.

[2] This Committee included two representatives from Indian States, but there were none from British India.

The repercussions of such an economic depression naturally affected the financial position of the Governments and local bodies, and it became necessary for the Central Government to augment its revenue by heavy import duties on sugar, spices and salt and export duties on hides and skins. The Budget was balanced, but the duties brought into operation the law of Diminishing Returns.

However, the Percy Committee strained their utmost to draw a rosy picture in the midst of the prevailing economic depression and detailed a scheme for the allocation of revenues to the Centre and to the Federal units. The sub-Committee appointed by the second Round Table Conference, under the chairmanship of Lord Peel, to consider the question of Federal finance had decided unanimously that, with the exception of the super-tax on companies, the net proceeds of the income tax should be distributed to the Provinces. But since this arrangement might lead to a Federal deficit, they recommended a system of provincial contributions to be determined by a further investigation into the entire financial problem. The Conference wrangled over the allocation of income tax but did not come to a definite agreement. It was proposed that a number of heads of income tax, as being special provincial contributions, should be permanently assigned to the Federal Government; but the representatives of the States wanted to put a minimum sum of 8¼ crores (£6,187,000) per annum for these contributions as a condition precedent to levying corporation tax in their States.

The Indian States Enquiry Committee (Financial), under the chairmanship of the Right Hon. J. C. C. Davidson, went to India with a view to "clearing the ground for Federation" by evolving a system of finance in relation to the Indian States entering into the proposed Federal Scheme. The Committee recommended that against contributions of each State to the Federal Government, there should be immunities from taxation now due to the Government of India from the States. It was urged that their price of entry should be reasonably assessed, and the adherence to the principle of "give and take" on both sides would solve the difficulties to their mutual advantage.

The Committee pointed out that a uniform distribution of benefits and burdens, either between the States or between the States and British India, could not be provided in its Report, which dealt, in the main, with the obstacles in the way of attaining such uniformity. Commenting upon the Report the *Financial News* (London) observed:

> "What emerges clearly from the whole Report is the difficulty that will be felt in many directions in reconciling the quasi-sovereign independence of the States with a really satisfactory system of federal finance."

C. SAFEGUARDS

The minorities in India, in addition to the safeguards provided for them in the form of representation in the Legislatures, were eager to have a Declaration of Fundamental Rights in the Statute. It was one of the issues on which Gandhi was insistent, as being a true solvent of the minority problem in the second Round Table Conference. To the English statesmen, such constitutional provisions, purporting to preserve the liberty of all men, were of no importance, and they were sceptical of their effectiveness. They explained to the Conference that the experience of countries where such a declaration of the abstract rights of their citizens is laid down in the Constitution confirmed their view, and suggested that a guarantee of protection of political and other rights of the various Indian Communities should be given in a Royal Proclamation as the aim of good government rather than as a provision of a Statute.

A great deal of time and attention had to be given to the thorny question of safeguards, both constitutional and financial. The powers of the Governor-General were clearly defined under three main categories, namely (1) discretionary powers to be used in regard to Legislatures and legislation; (2) special responsibilities relating to emergencies when intervention would be essentially necessary; and (3) powers in regard to reserved subjects such as Defence and External Affairs.

As regards financial safeguards, the Governor-General's previous sanction should be required for the introduction of measures relating to exchange and currency. Further, the establishment of a Reserve Bank as a preliminary to Federation was insisted upon by the Government. Some of the Indian delegates protested against laying down such a condition precedent to Federation, but the Government argued that since they intended to transfer finance to the charge of an Indian Minister responsible to the Legislature, it was necessary to safeguard the Secretary of State's liabilities to British investors, civil servants and pension holders, and also to retain India's financial prestige in the City of London and elsewhere. The Indians were reminded of the need of converting large loans which would mature in the next few years and that the confidence of the City was essential to enable India to secure favourable terms.

Then came the question of protecting British commercial and industrial interests. It was agreed that the Constitution should contain a clause "prohibiting legislative or administrative discrimination in the matters set out . . . and defining those persons and bodies to whom the clause is to apply." The emphasis given to these various provisions in the safeguards caused a degree of uneasiness among some of the Indian delegates. While they were prepared to concede them as the price of responsible government, it was felt that the rigidity[1] of statutory safeguards might deprive the constitutional mechanism of its necessary flexible elements.

Such intricate problems as those of residuary powers (on which Indian opinion was divided, whether they should be Federal or Provincial) and the competence of the Indian

[1] The Indian delegates may be pardoned for not realising what is, of course, the fact that, in so far as the safeguards operate through the novel device of "special responsibilities," that device is not operative unless and until the ordinary machinery for good administration breaks down, *i.e.* they need never *become* operative.

Legislature to amend the Constitution, the Conference left undecided in the hope that the Government might suggest a solution, at least as regards the apportionment of the residuary subjects.

ℭ CONFERENCE ENDS

At the close of the Conference the Secretary of State for India made three important announcements, namely, (1) that the accession to the Federation of about 50 per cent. of the Indian States, in number and population, would be regarded as justifying the inauguration of Federation (that was what Government meant by " effective federation ") ; (2) that the Moslem community would be granted 33⅓ per cent. of the seats in the Central Legislature allotted to British India ; and (3) that Sind and Orissa would be separate new Provinces.

The Indian delegates turned homeward with a feeling, to which some gave expression, that what had been achieved was hardly likely to satisfy the political aspirations of the majority of their countrymen.[1] Some of the Ministers of the Indian States who attended the Conference were not quite sure of adequate guarantees from Federal interference in the event of their accession to the Federation. The formidable array of safeguards continued to be a nightmare to the majority of the delegates on their way to India. The Moslems, however, felt that their 33⅓ per cent. was a distinct victory.

At any rate, the delegates now had with them the draft plans of a Federal Parliamentary system which comprised a Federal Senate and a Federal Assembly for All India.

ℭ A GENERAL REVIEW

We have now come to the end of the review of the three Round Table Conferences. The outstanding gain was the creation of a helpful precedent for free discussion and

[1] Two prominent Indian Liberals left behind, before returning to India, a memorandum stating the minimum demands of the section of Indian political opinion they represented. See Chapter V.

negotiations between the Imperial Government and Indian representatives on questions over which there were wide disagreements. It is claimed that the Conference had initiated a new technique of achieving liberty "through negotiation, by argument." In a letter to the *Spectator*,[1] Tagore wrote:

> "The invitation to a Round Table Conference accorded to the representatives of a people who can with perfect impunity be throttled into silence or trampled into a pulp, is in itself a sign of the time undreamt of even half a century ago."

In any case, the inauguration of the technique by King George in the presence of his Dominion Ministers and of all parties of the Imperial Government should be regarded not only as a pledge that India's future political status would be equal to that of the Dominions, but also as a precedent of first-rate importance to the whole British Commonwealth of Nations.

It must be acknowledged to the credit of the British public and press, that they had shown unfailing courtesy and hospitality to the Indian delegates. Nothing could be more reassuring for the proper solution of Indian problems than the keen interest the Conference evoked among the British people, and there could be no better asset for India's cause than their goodwill. Those who, a decade ago, ridiculed the idea of self-government in India, became enthusiastic sponsors of full provincial Autonomy and even of Central responsibility. The preponderantly conservative complexion of the House of Commons and the strong opposition of a section of the Conservative Party to the policy of the Government in regard to the next phase of the Indian Constitution gave rise, however, to serious misgivings among the delegates. But *The Times*, the premier organ of English opinion, hastened to assure them that "the spirit of the Conservative Party is now more National and less purely Tory than at any period in its history."

[1] *Spectator* (London), November 15, 1930.

Englishmen in India, especially those of the commercial world, who had resisted every single measure of constitutional reforms in the past, heartily co-operated with the Government in their policy, were prepared to recognize that only in a contented India would the interests of British trade be safeguarded, and appeared to be contented with the provisions for protecting their interests. The Indian industrialists found fresh opportunities for striking a bargain and demanded further protection! They welcomed the decisions to place the Railways, the Reserve Bank, and the Tariffs outside the competence of the Legislatures.

The attitude of the Services was, on the whole, equally conciliatory. If the Indian official world moved cautiously, they showed no disinclination towards the policy that was being shaped in the Conferences. The Government knew that the changed conditions in India warranted the application of such methods as would keep the forces of nationalism within bounds, and that the Indian States by their collaboration in the Constitution would provide an adequate element of stability. A feudal-imperialist bloc, under the guise of a federal democratic Constitution, would, to quote Mr. Baldwin's words, " stand against time and weather irrespective of the changes of Government at home."

The British India delegates, on the other hand, attended the Conferences at a time when the bulk of the politically-conscious classes had no faith in the intentions of the Government in regard to granting anything like Dominion Status to India. The co-operating leaders relied on the policy of Lord Irwin, trusted his word and gave him their fullest co-operation. The *raison d'etre* of the Conference was to arrive, *without much delay*, at the maximum amount of agreement on the constitutional issues, and with this end in view, they came to attend the Conferences and Committees.

Through the untiring labour of the Indian Liberals and their leaders, Gandhi was persuaded to attend the second Round Table Conference, but the failure to reconcile their views with those of Gandhi shattered the last vestige of hope of resuscitating the Liberal Federation by winning him over to take up the work of constitution and in acting in a spirit of moderation and reasonableness. The Rt. Hon. V. S. Sastri, in a parting appeal to Gandhi, asked him to recognize that there was some knowledge, some wisdom, some patriotism even outside the ranks of the Congress which he so much worshipped.

But the position taken up by the Indian Liberals had not been at all popular in the country, although they certainly represented some of the most able men in Indian public life. They realized that their voice alone would not be sufficiently powerful in securing the modifications they demanded in the various proposals that came before the Conference. The minority communities were, on the whole, satisfied that their case had won the support of the Government and would, therefore, be adequately safeguarded.

The representatives of the Indian States felt that the conditions of their entry into Federation, as agreed upon, were probably more favourable to them now than they might be at a later stage. They saw some advantage in the offer of remission of the tributes now due to the Government of India and also of territorial concessions, in a few instances, as the reward of supplying the Constitution with stabilizing forces. In the willingness of the Government to re-open negotiations with the State of Hyderabad, in respect of the cession of the Berars—the question which was closed by Lord Reading by his decision that there could be no retrocession—the Princes realized the importance His Majesty's Government attached to their immediate entry into Federation.

Each section of these participants to the Conference knew that the final picture had yet to be drawn, and that before it was finished for presentation to Parliament yet another opportunity would be given to them for the expression of their doubts and demands. They awaited expectantly the emergence of the White Paper from the India Office.

Meanwhile the Government of India felt that the truce period with the Congress was over and decided to counteract its activities with a series of Ordinances. The methods of redressing agrarian grievances which the Congress adopted as "the right of defensive Direct Action," the militant movement in the North-West Frontier Province and the recrudescence of the terrorist movement in Bengal were circumstances that could no longer be tolerated. Besides, the policy of conciliation had, in their judgment, failed in its object, and they justified their determination to take effective measures against Congress activities in a manifesto [1] which ran as follows:

> "They (the Congress) have pronounced the declaration of the Prime Minister to be wholly unsatisfactory and inadequate in terms of the Congress demands, and they have demanded that if their co-operation be accepted, free scope be given to them to prosecute their claim to complete independence. There was clearly no alternative but to reject these demands and to take all measures that were necessary to meet the Campaign of Civil Disobedience."

The Government hoped that by entering upon an open conflict with the Congress they would succeed not only in weakening its hold on a large section of its followers but would bring to play disruptive forces within the organization itself, and that by suppressing its activities, they might be encouraging those Indians who repudiated the claim of Congress to represent them to organize themselves more effectively than in the past. Since the success of the new Constitution, the Government thought, would largely depend upon the formation of Indian political parties outside the Congress influence, the Secretary of State for India in a broadcast talk reassured the Indian Liberals and other groups in the following words: "We shall give the lie once and for all to those in India who say that we never back our friends and that we only yield to threats." In a letter to

[1] January 4, 1932.

his constituents in Chelsea he expressed his belief that in recent times much of the power of the Congress had been due to bluff and that a large section of Indian opinion not associated with Congress (such as the Princes, the Moslems and the Depressed classes) would make its "weight felt in the Government" under the proposed Reforms. "The best way to beat Congress," writes Sir Samuel, "is to give these influences their chance." Confident of the strength that would be supplied by these conservative elements in India, Lord Brabourne[1] expressed his conviction at a debate in the House of Lords that an early constitutional advance on Federal lines would deprive the heterogeneous Congress Party of many of its grievances and much of its cohesion.

But none of these sections of Indian opinion in whose strength and support the Government put so much faith took advantage of the situation that arose from the collapse of the Civil Disobedience Movement to create an effective party machine in order to get into touch with the electorate. The Congress still remains a power, and through its extensive organization commands to a certain degree "the will of the people."

ℂ. THE BURMA ROUND TABLE CONFERENCE

The principle of the separation of Burma from India, as recommended by the Indian Statutory Commission, was accepted by the Burma sub-Committee of the first Round Table Conference. It was, however, necessary to consult the wishes of the Burmese nation in regard to the details involved in the change. Accordingly, on August 20, 1931, the Government announced their intention to convene a Burma Round Table Conference, which met in London on November 27, 1931, under the chairmanship of Lord Peel. The Conference was formally opened by King Edward VIII (then the Prince of Wales).

[1] Now Governor of Bombay.

There were 23 delegates from Burma representing different interests, and their appointed task was to devise the ways and means for a new Constitution based on the separation of Burma from India. At the close of the Conference, the Prime Minister announced the decisions of the Imperial Government, giving an outline of their proposals, the main points of which are stated below:

(1) The Legislature is to be bi-cameral.

(2) The Upper House would consist partly of elected and partly of nominated members and would be about one-third of the size of the Lower House, consisting at the outset of 120 to 130 members.

(3) Members of the Lower House would be directly elected, and the electoral system would be so devised as to ensure the adequate representation of minority communities and of special interests.

(4) The Ministry would consist of about six but not more than eight Ministers appointed by the Governor and collectively responsible to the Legislature.

(5) The Governor must have special powers in regard to:

- (*a*) Defence and External Affairs.
- (*b*) The administration of the Shan States and other "excluded areas."
- (*c*) The administration of reserved subjects.
- (*d*) The direction of monetary policy, including exchange, currency and coinage; the proportion of the rights and interests of officers recruited by the Crown or the Secretary of State.
- (*e*) A continuance of the present discretion on behalf of the Crown to refuse assent to legislative measures and to return Bills for reconsideration.

(6) The Statute would provide for the appointment of a Financial Adviser to the Government and the establishment of a Public Services Commission.

(7) The administration of financial questions, including the power of taxation and raising revenue, fiscal policy and expenditure on subjects outside the sphere of the Governor's special responsibility, would be entrusted to the Ministry.

(8) The Constitution would contain provisions ensuring equal rights and opportunities for any British subject ordinarily resident or carrying on trade or business in Burma.

But the Burmese public had not as yet expressed their views on the issue of the separation of Burma from India. Consequently it was decided to test the verdict of the electorate at the general election of the Burma Legislative Council in the autumn of 1932. The Prime Minister did not miss the opportunity of reminding the Burmese delegates of the nature and extent of the responsibility that would rest on them under the Constitution outlined for a separated Burma, and that they should bear in mind the special conditions of Burma which justified divergence in some details from the Constitution proposed for an Indian province. The Prime Minister observed, in summing up the views of the Government :

> " His Majesty's Government's intention is that, in the event of Burma electing to pursue her political development apart from India, responsibility should be devolved upon her Legislature for the administration not only of the subjects which will fall within the range of Provincial Governments in India, but also of subjects which will be administered in India by the Central authority. But in order that the stability of the realm may be maintained and financial stability secured, the Governor must have the powers already set forth. It will be the endeavour of His Majesty's Government to ensure that these powers shall not be allowed to prejudice the advance of Burma to full self-government."

The Burmese politicians were, however, unsatisfied with the outline of the sort of Constitution they would get in the event of Burma's separation from India; nor could they make up their mind on the question of separation. To them it was a matter of striking a better bargain, of securing a more liberal Constitution than that outlined by the Prime Minister. In the general election the anti-separationists won, but they were not in a mood to agree to enter the proposed Indian Federation without their "right to secede," although the delegates to the Burma Round Table Conference had been warned by the Prime Minister that "members of an Indian Federation could not leave it as and when they chose." The Indian leaders of the Assembly, however, assured the anti-separationists of their right of secession "on terms acceptable to the Federation"!

The Burmese opposition to the severance of political connection with India came to the Government as a surprise. The Burmese delegates, both at the first Indian Round Table Conference and also at the Burma Round Table Conference, appeared to have accepted the principle of separation, and the Burmese Constitution was framed as a "Constitution for a separated Burma." The issue, however, remained undecided at the end of the Burma Round Table Conference, but the matter was left to the Joint Select Committee. The Secretary of State for India submitted to the Committee a full memorandum, setting out in detail proposals for a possible constitutional reform in Burma, if Burma was not to be included in the Indian Federal Scheme. We shall refer to the decision of the Joint Select Committee on this point in a succeeding chapter.

CHAPTER V

THE WHITE PAPER PROPOSALS AND THE RECOMMENDATIONS OF THE JOINT SELECT COMMITTEE AS EMBODIED IN THE GOVERNMENT OF INDIA ACT, 1935

Main Principles—(a) *Federation;* (b) *Provincial Autonomy;* (c) *Franchise;* (d) *Federation and the Units: Safeguards*—(a) *Statutory Restrictions;* (b) *Financial Safeguards;* (c) *Special Responsibilities: Opposition in India: Indian demand for Substantial Modification: The Indian States and the White Paper: Opposition in Great Britain: Supporters of the White Paper: The Joint Select Committee*

THE final proposals of the Government for Indian Constitutional Reform were embodied in the famous White Paper (Cmd. No. 4268 of 1933). It had an explanatory introduction of over 30 pages, and its proposals were tersely put in 202 short paragraphs.

MAIN PRINCIPLES

The underlying principles of the scheme may be defined as Federation, Provincial Autonomy, and Central Responsibility. These were all approved by the Joint Select Committee,[1] and have been embodied in the Act of 1935.

[1] See Chapter VI.

From our discussions in the previous chapters these principles should be familiar to the reader, as also the existence of something like a general agreement to apply them to the solution of the Indian constitutional problems. Controversy centres round the means and methods of the application rather than the principles themselves, and in the following paragraphs I shall state the existing position as embodied in the Act where there are variations between that measure and the proposals of the White Paper, or the recommendations of the Joint Select Committee. A general survey of its report is attempted in the next chapter.

Notwithstanding some cogent reasons for recommending an All-India Federation, the Indian Statutory Commission came to the conclusion that while it was likely to be the *ultimate* form of government, its immediate formation would not be practicable. The recommendation of the White Paper was to proceed to build that structure now with a number of safeguards and reservations. But the risks and vicissitudes of a Federal Constitution, which had to be framed without properly developed Federal units, necessitated something more than the normal precautions usually provided in a Constitution. Before we examine these safeguards we must try to understand the reasons for transforming the unitary form of government, as it exists now, into a Federation.

Let us turn to what Sir John Simon, the Chairman of the Indian Statutory Commission, said in this connection. In a speech in the House of Commons (March 28, 1933) he explained how the Princes' declaration at the first Round Table Conference made it possible to envisage a new development in Indian Constitutional Reforms.

> "We took the view," said Sir John, "when we wrote the Report that it was exceedingly improbable that for, at any rate, a considerable time to come, the Indian Princes and the Indian States would be prepared to come into the greater Indian Federation. . . . I was perfectly confident that the development of a new form of government

at the Centre in India was dependent upon the Indian States coming in, and that consequently, as far as I could see, this was not likely to take place for a considerable time. . . . But there is a new fact . . . which has entered the field of this problem since our Report was presented."

But loyal as he was to the National Government, he was cautious in lending his support to the proposed All-India Federal Scheme. He therefore added :

> " For my part, I want to see the prospects of this new development of a greater India most thoroughly investigated —and the opportunity of these great Indian Princes coming in and playing their part freely tested—before I am prepared to reject the whole scheme."

The situation was further elucidated by Colonel Lane-Fox, one of the members of the Statutory Commission, in a letter to *The Times* (May 6, 1933). He writes :

> " The Princes have accepted the principle of the Federation of India, which our Commission recommended as the ultimate ideal for all India, but which we feared might take long to materialize. They have, however, attached the express condition to their acceptance that responsible government at the Centre must accompany Federation—a form of government which the Commission had not recommended, as being, in their opinion, premature for British India alone, and it was with British India alone that they had to deal. What our Commission's attitude might have been if they had had to suggest a form of central government for the whole of India, including the more conservative elements of the States, I cannot say, but to suggest that in comparing the two plans (*i.e.* the Simon Commission Report and the White Paper proposals) you are comparing like with like is surely dishonest."

As regards provincial autonomy, the White Paper endorsed the recommendations of the Statutory Commission and proceeded to enumerate and delegate such powers as would tend to develop the Provinces as Federal units. That there is a close connection between Federation and provincial autonomy was explained by Sir Samuel Hoare in the House of Commons in the following words. He said :

> " We were driven to the conclusion that there was little or no chance of provincial autonomy starting in a reasonable atmosphere of goodwill if we did not at the same time make proposals that covered the Federal centre." [1]

The logical outcome of the acceptance of the principle of Federation and of provincial autonomy was central responsibility. It was argued that these three principles were closely linked up with each other and that on them alone the future constitutional edifice would have to be erected. But the White Paper stated :

> " The Constitution Act, though treating the Federation as a whole, will contain provisions enabling the Provincial Constitutions for which it provides to be brought into being, if necessary, before the constitution as a whole comes into being."

We shall presently see that the establishment of the Federation is, in the Act as well as in the White Paper, made contingent upon certain factors which involve delay.

(*a*) Federation

The structure of the Central Government is an All-India Federation, the component parts of which are to consist of eleven [2] British Indian Provinces and the Indian States.

The present British Indian Legislature with an irremovable official Executive not responsible to it, is replaced by a Federal All-India Legislature, containing representatives of the Provinces and the States, with an Executive responsible to the Legislature for all departments of administration except Defence and External and

[1] House of Commons Debates, March 27, 1933.

[2] Two new Provinces, Sind and Orissa, are to be created.

Ecclesiastical Affairs, which will be administered by the Governor-General himself.

The present Governor-General's Executive Council consists of seven members appointed under Royal Sign Manual. The portfolios are divided as follows: Army, the Commander-in-Chief, Home, Finance, Industries and Labour, are held by experienced British administrators; the remaining three, Education, Health and Lands, Railways and Commerce, and Law, are entrusted to Indian Counsellors.

It is now proposed that the functions of the Executive Council should be divided somewhat on the lines of the Dyarchic Constitution. The Federal Executive will be composed of the Viceroy and his Counsellors and the Governor-General and his Ministers. The "Reserved" departments, such as Defence, External and Ecclesiastical Affairs, will be under the Crown's representative in his capacity of Viceroy, assisted by not more than three Counsellors to be appointed by him, and the Executive Council of Governor-General of the Federation, consisting of Ministers, will have the control of the remaining branches of administration. The Crown's representative will thus have two separate spheres of administration, one in the capacity of Viceroy and the other of Governor-General. Ministers must be, or become within a stated period, members of one or other Chamber of Federal Legislature and their number will be regulated by this body. The Federal Ministers will be chosen by him, and are to hold office during his pleasure. The Governor-General will be guided by advice tendered to him by Ministers except where the Act provides that he may exercise his individual judgment or act in his discretion.

Although the two sides of the Executive will function separately, it is hoped that

> "a 'prudent Governor-General' would keep his Minister in the closest contact on all matters 'without blurring the line which will necessarily divide' the responsibility of the Governor-General for the reserved departments and that of the Ministers to the Legislatures. His Majesty's Govern-

ment intend to 'secure the embodiment of this principle in appropriate terms in the Governor-General's Instrument of Instructions.'"

The Federal Legislature will be bi-cameral. The Lower Chamber, to be called the Federal Assembly, will consist of 375 and the Upper Chamber, to be known as the Council of State, of 260 members. Out of these, the Princes will nominate 125 in the Lower and 104 in the Upper Chamber, and six seats will be filled by persons chosen by the Governor-General in his discretion. Thus, one part of the Legislature will be elected and the other nominated. The White Paper suggested that the British-Indian members of the Upper Chamber should, in the main, be elected by proportional representation from the Provincial Legislatures, and that in the Lower Chamber the election of British-Indian members should be direct. While the Joint Select Committee approved of the proposal for the adoption of the principle of indirect election to the Upper Federal Chamber, they recommended it also for the Lower Federal Chamber. We have noted in the chapter on Dyarchy that the system of direct election has been adopted under the Government of India Act, 1919; but the difficulty of its continuance with an electorate of the magnitude proposed in the White Paper was realized by the Committee. What reasons they advanced in justification of their recommendation we shall see in the following chapter. In the Act, indirect election is retained for the Lower Federal Chamber, but in an amendment in the House of Lords the principle of direct election to the Upper Federal Chamber has been adopted. The Upper House will not be subject to dissolution, but one-third of the members will retire every third year. The maximum period during which the Lower Chamber may continue without a dissolution is five years. Both Chambers may be summoned or prorogued separately or simultaneously.

The allocation of the 104 seats among the States in the Upper Federal Chamber is based on the relative rank and importance of the State as recognized by the dynastic salute. But in the Lower Federal Chamber the allocation of 125 seats is to be made on the basis of population, that is, the number of seats allotted to each State or group of States should be proportionate to their population.

The distribution of seats among representatives of British India in the Federal Legislatures will be as follows:

	Total Seats.	General Seats	Seats for Scheduled Caste.	Mohammedan Seats.	Sikh Seats.	Women's Seats.	Other Seats.
The Council of State .	150	75	6	49	4	6	10 [1]
The Federal Assembly	250	86	19	82	6	9	48 [2]

The conditions precedent to the establishment of the Federation are stipulated in the Act to be:

1. That at least half the total number of States, comprising not less than half the total population of the States, must consent to enter the Federation. A Ruler of an Indian State who is desirous of acceding to the Federation will transfer to the Crown for the purposes of the Federation his powers and jurisdiction in respect of those matters which he is willing to recognize as Federal matters. The transference in each case will be made by a formal Instrument of Accession. But full liberty will be reserved to the Crown to refuse to accept the accession of any State to the Federation if the terms offered appear to be incompatible with the Scheme of Federation.

2. That an Address has been presented to the Crown by both Houses of Parliament praying that a Proclamation be issued.

[1] Anglo-Indians 1; Europeans 7; and Indian Christians 2.

[2] Anglo-Indians 4; Europeans 8; Indian Christians 8; Labour 10; Commerce 11; and Landholders 7.

(b) Provincial Autonomy

The present Dyarchy, which we have discussed at length in Chapter II, is to be abolished and all departments of the Government will be transferred to the control of Indian Ministers. The statutory allocation of exclusive Provincial legislative subjects marks a departure from the traditional legislative relationship between the Centre and the Provinces. Provincial autonomy will, therefore, have more reality than at present, and the fact that there will be no "reserved" subjects may tend to develop real responsibility of Ministers. The Ministers will be chosen by the Governor, and are to hold office during his pleasure. The Executive Council of a Province will be replaced by a Council of Ministers responsible to the Legislature of the Province. But the Governors will have "special responsibilities" and powers somewhat similar to those of the Governor-General. I shall presently explain the nature of the safeguards provided in the central and provincial spheres.

The Provincial Legislatures will be enlarged. The allocation of seats and methods of election for the Provincial Legislative Assemblies will be made in accordance with the provisions contained in the Communal Award [1] of the Government with such modifications in regard to the Depressed classes as were agreed upon in the Poona Pact on September 24, 1932. The Pact is, the reader may remember, the result of Gandhi's fast, to which a reference has been made in the preceding chapter.

One appropriate change in Provincial Legislatures should be mentioned here. The members will be in all cases elected and no official will be eligible for election. This will remove one of the anomalous situations in the present Legislatures, where the presence of official blocs militates against the establishment of proper relationships with the Ministers.

With a view to securing increased stability on the part

[1] Cmd. 4147, 1932.

of the Executive, the Committee recommended some radical changes in the form and extent of Second Chambers. In the first place, two more Provinces, Bombay and Madras, are to have bi-cameral Legislatures in addition to the three proposed in the White Paper. An amendment to the Bill in Parliament added Assam to the list.

Thus, in six Provinces, namely Madras, Bombay, Bengal, Bihar, the United Provinces, and Assam, where landlordism prevails, the Legislature will be bi-cameral. But provision is made both for the creation of Upper Chambers in other Provinces and the abolition of the Upper Chambers now to be set up in accordance with circumstances that may arise in working the new Constitution.

The technique for the setting up of Provincial Legislatures closely resembles that of the Federal Centre. The Legislative Council, which is to be the designation of the Upper Chamber, will be a permanent body, but one-third of its members will retire every third year. The Legislative Assembly, that is the Lower Chamber, will be elected every five years.

The strength of the Provincial Legislatures will now be as follows:

Provinces.	*Assemblies.*	*Councils.*
Bengal	250	Not more than 65
The United Provinces .	228	,, ,, 60
Madras	215	,, ,, 56
Bombay	175	,, ,, 30
Punjab	175	No Council
Bihar	152	Not more than 30
Central Provinces and Berar	112	No Council
Assam	108	Not more than 22
Sind	60	No Council
Orissa	60	,,
North-Western Provinces .	50	,,

The composition of the Indian Legislatures has been, owing to the existence of the different and conflicting interests and social systems of the country, one of the most intractable problems of the Constitution. That problem is now decided for ten years, with the provision that the Indian communities will be able to renounce separate electorates if they come to an agreement among themselves. The final decision, however, would rest with Parliament. A table showing the distribution of seats in the Provincial Legislative Assemblies is given in Appendix B.

(*c*) Franchise

A high property qualification will be the basis of franchise for the election of the British Indian seats in the Upper Chamber of the Federal Legislature. The Lower Chamber, as stated above, will be filled by indirect election by the Provincial Legislatures. The franchise of the Federal Lower Chamber will therefore remain practically as it is at present for the Provincial Legislatures, excepting certain modifications required in the circumstances of some Provinces. The existing franchise in all Provinces is based on property qualification, but it is proposed to supplement it, as recommended by the Indian Franchise Committee, by an educational qualification. Special provision will be made to secure women members by the reservation of seats. Commerce, labour and other special interests will be represented by special constituencies in the Federal Legislatures.

Provincial franchise has been greatly extended by adopting, in the main, the proposals suggested by the Franchise Committee. The creation of autonomous provinces necessitates an increase of the provincial electorate. It is calculated that the size of the electorate in all the Governor's Provinces will be about 14 per cent. of the total population of British India as compared with the 3 per cent. under the old Constitution, or some 27 per cent. of the adult population. Here also the electoral qualifications are based both on property and education. The ratio of women to men electors will be raised approximately from one in twenty-one to one in seven. Depressed classes will receive special consideration so as to secure an electorate of about 10 per cent. of the community. Commerce, labour, landlord and other special interests, as in the case of the Federal Legislature, will be provided with special electorates. In the opinion of the Joint Select Committee, the extension of franchise provided for in the Act is "calculated to produce an electorate representative of the general mass of the population, and one which will not deprive any important section of the community of the means of giving expression to its opinions and desires."

(*d*) The Federation and the Units

The problem of a distribution of legislative powers between the Centre and the constituent units in a Federal Constitution is one which must of necessity require very careful adjustment.

The respective legislative fields of the Central and Provincial Governments are defined and scheduled in the Act; but certain subjects which are of All-India importance are scheduled as being both Federal and Provincial. There are thus three lists of legislative powers scheduled in the Act, the Federal List, the Provincial List and the Concurrent List. No effort has been spared to make the lists exhaustive, but provision is made in the Act for the Governor-General in his discretion to empower either the Federal or a Provincial Legislature to enact a law with respect to any matter not enumerated in these lists. In other words, residual powers of legislation are by this decree vested in either the Federal or a Provincial Legislature, according as the Governor-General may in any particular case deem the more appropriate body. This is an ingenious refinement on the expedients provided in the Constitutions of Canada and Australia. In the former, powers are vested in the Dominion Legislature; in Australia these powers are vested in the Legislatures of the Federating States. Certain limitations are imposed upon the powers of the Legislatures, which brings us to the most controversial part of the Act, namely the safeguards.

¶ SAFEGUARDS

The provisions designed as Safeguards may be divided into three main groups: (*a*) Statutory restrictions, (*b*) financial safeguards, (*c*) special responsibilities placed upon the Governor-General and the Governors.

(*a*) Statutory Restrictions

They consist in the first place of the administration of certain reserved subjects, such as Defence, External Affairs and Ecclesiastical Affairs, by the Governor-General. That is, on these matters he will act without any interference from his Ministers but with the help of the counsellors appointed by him. These counsellors will be *ex officio* members of both Chambers but will not have the right of voting. These "Reserved" subjects will be financed from Federal revenues, but the demands for grants will be non-votable.

Secondly, the Indian Services, including the two security services, the Indian Civil Service and the Indian Police Service, will enjoy statutory protection. Until Parliament otherwise determines, appointments to the two security services will continue to be made by the Secretary of State, and the conditions of service will be regulated by rules made by him. Although no statutory provision for the purpose has been made, it is proposed to have an enquiry into the question of recruitment for these two services soon after the introduction of provincial autonomy, probably in about five years from that date. In order to guard against the deterioration of the administrative services generally, there will be a statutory obligation on the Federal and Provincial Governments to consult the

Public Services Commissions regarding methods of recruitment, appointments by selection, promotion, etc.

A number of safeguards have also been included to protect the pension rights of all persons in service at present and to secure payment of compensation, emoluments, etc. The assets of the Family Pension Funds are treated as constituting in all cases a definite debt liability of the Government of India and as the property of the subscribers. Grants of salaries, pensions, and emoluments generally, of officers appointed by the Crown and by the Secretary of State, will not be submitted to the vote of the Legislature.

Thirdly, the administration of the railways will be in the hands of a Federal Railway Authority,[1] "so composed and with such powers as will ensure that it is in a position to perform its duties upon business principles and without being subject to political interference," and the Federal Legislature will only exercise a general control over policy.

Should any dispute arise in regard to questions of policy, the decision of the Governor-General in his discretion is to be final. The Federal Legislature is not empowered to alter the provisions of the enactment with respect to services under the Federal Railway Authority without the previous sanction of the Governor-General. Any Bill or amendment which relates to railway rates and fares may be introduced only if it is recommended by the Governor-General. The Act, however, provides that a body called the Railway Tribunal will be set up to safeguard against unfair discrimination between one railway system and another, and to adjudicate upon the complaints in regard to relation of the Railway Authority and a Federated State.

Finally, there are a number of statutory limitations on the power of the Legislatures. The Constitution Act as an Act of the British Parliament cannot, broadly speaking, be amended except by that Parliament. Further limitations are imposed on the Indian Legislatures so that no discriminatory measures will be passed that will affect

[1] See Chapter VII.

any European British subject in British India. A few more instances of restriction of Legislative powers may be cited here. Any Bill or amendment which affects the grant of relief from any Federal tax on income in respect of income taxed or taxable in the United Kingdom, or affects the procedure for criminal proceedings in which European British subjects are concerned, or affects any Act relating to police force, will require previous sanction of the Governor-General or the Governors. Then, there are the usual provisions in regard to assent to Bills passed by the Legislatures, and to the power of the Crown to disallow Acts to which the Governor-General or a Governor may have given his assent. As regards the relations between the Crown and the Indian States, the Federal Legislature will be strictly limited to such matters which are defined as Federal.

(*b*) Financial Safeguards

Perhaps the most important provision to secure the financial safeguards has been the establishment of a Reserve Bank[1] entrusted with the management of currency and exchange. " Reliance on the Bank to play its due part in safeguarding India's financial stability and credit clearly demands," observed the Report of the Committee, " that at all events its essential features should be protected against amendments of the law which would destroy their effect for the purpose in view." The Bank will therefore be free from political influence.

The power of the Federal Legislature is further limited by the statutory check that any Bill or amendment affecting the constitution or functions of the Reserve Bank, or the coinage, currency and exchange, will require the previous consent of the Governor-General before they can be introduced into the Legislature. In order to maintain India's financial position in the loan market, the rights and liabilities arising under statute or contract in existence

[1] See Chapter VII.

when the Act comes into force, including existing immunities of sterling loans from Indian income tax, will be enforceable against the Secretary of State. Such liabilities will remain liabilities on all the revenues of India, Federal and Provincial.

(c) Special Responsibilities

The Governor-General will have power to appoint a Financial Adviser to assist him in the discharge of his "special responsibility" for the safeguarding of the financial stability and credit of the Federation.

A special responsibility exercisable on the individual judgment of the Governor-General and Governors will embrace the specific matters stated below:

(1) The prevention of any grave menace to the peace or tranquillity of India, or any part thereof;

(2) The safeguarding of the legitimate interests of minorities;

(3) The securing to the members of the Public Services and their dependents of any rights provided or preserved for them by the Constitution Act, and the safeguarding of their legitimate interests;

(4) The prevention of commercial discrimination;

(5) The protection of the rights of any Indian State and the rights and dignity of the Rule thereof.

The Governor-General will also have the power, at his discretion, to summon, prorogue, or dissolve the Legislature, to summon joint sessions of the two Houses, and to make any such Ordinances as the circumstances appear to him to require. Lastly, there are the ultimate powers under which he is empowered to assume full control of the Federal Government in case of a breakdown. That is, if and when a situation has arisen in which the Federal Government cannot be carried on in accordance with the provisions of the Act, he may, by Proclamation, which must be laid before both Houses of Parliament, exercise all the powers vested in the Federal authority. Emergency powers, similar to those conferred on the Governor-General, are conferred on the Governors.

The Governor-General's personal responsibility to His Majesty's Government for the efficient operation of the safeguards makes his Instrument of Instructions from the Crown a direct ancillary to the Constitution Act itself, and it and the Instruments of Instructions for the Governors will receive the approval of both Houses of Parliament. The fact that these Instruments, and any amendments thereto, will be subject to British Parliamentary approval should tend to make for a flexibility in the Constitution which may overcome the various difficulties that confront a written Constitution. It will also help to maintain a direct contact between the Indian and British democracies. Any occasion for the exercise of a special responsibility must also, as an ultimate responsibility of the British Parliament, tend also to maintain the same beneficial contact.

In the provincial sphere the main problem has been the transference of Law and Order. We have already noted that the Statutory Commission recommended the transfer, with the suggestion that the Governor should be given discretion to include an official in the Ministry. The idea was that in the event of not finding a suitable Indian Minister, the Governor's nominee might be entrusted with the portfolio of Law and Order. In any case, the Commission came to the conclusion that it would be unwise to retain the administration of police as a "Reserved" Department.

The White Paper, after providing a number of safeguards against the risks of communalism and deterioration of the police service, recommended the transfer of Law and Order as also did the Joint Select Committee, and with the passing of the new Act, that transfer has become an integral part of the scheme for provincial autonomy. In reply to the professional alarmists who foresee the collapse of British rule in India by entrusting Ministers in the Provinces with the responsibility of the administration of police, I cannot do better than refer to the following observations of Sir Samuel Hoare. He recognized the risks involved in the proposal, but pointed out how those risks have been diminished by several provisions in the Constitution.

He said :

> " On the one hand there is the need for making provincial autonomy real self-government and the virtual impossibility of making provincial autonomy real self-government if law and order are not transferred to an Indian Minister. On the other hand, there is the essential need for taking no action that will shake the morale of the police or that will endanger the Indian spirit. Setting on the one side the advantages of a transfer, and on the other side the disadvantages, we came to the same conclusion at which the Simon Commission arrived, namely, that it was both safer and wiser to make this transfer. . . . If you make the transfer of law and order to a responsible Indian Minister, you cannot withhold from his control the administration of the police. . . . We do not intend, nor do Indian public men intend, that the Minister should himself interfere arbitrarily with promotion, postings and discipline. All these matters will be primarily for the executive head of the Service to deal with. The officers at the top, who have been and will continue for a time to be appointed by the Secretary of State, will have their main conditions of service regulated by him and will have a right of appeal to him. The provincial police service proper will have the protection of the Provincial Public Services Commission, and there will, we hope, be strong selection boards for appointments and promotions in the subordinate ranks. The work of the force will be the responsibility of the Minister. He will be deeply concerned in its efficiency, because at every point its work will be subject to criticism. The Governor is given special responsibility in the case of any grave menace to the peace and tranquillity of the Province." [1]

[1] House of Commons Debates, March 28, 1933.

While the Committee endorsed the view that without the transfer of "Law and Order" provincial autonomy would be a sham and a delusion, they proposed to transfer this responsibility to the control of Ministers on two specific conditions: (1) the Constitution Act should provide that any legislation affecting the existing Police Acts and the rules thereunder must have the assent of the Governor, and that he should be empowered to give all directions necessary to ensure that the records of the Intelligence or special branches of the police remain strictly official secrets. It should be noted here that the Central Intelligence Bureau is to be assigned to one of the Governor-General's Reserved Departments and the existing relationship between the Central Bureau and the Provincial Intelligence Departments will continue. (2) There must be a special provision for dealing with the recrudescence of terrorist activities. The Act should specifically empower the Governor to assume charge of any branch of the Government for the purpose of combating such activities, or if necessary to create new machinery for the purpose. The opponents of the proposal for the transfer of the portfolio of "Law and Order" declared that these safeguards for the administration of the police force constituted a considerable improvement on the White Paper recommendations; but to the Indian public these limitations are regarded as a fruitful source for perpetuating distrust and suspicion between the Government and the people.

¶ OPPOSITION IN INDIA

But in these formidable arrays of safeguards, limitations, reservations, special responsibilities, discretionary powers, which are now reproduced in the Constitution Act with some additions, it has been rather difficult for Indian public opinion to discover what was declared to be "the spirit of partnership in a common enterprise." Indeed, the White Paper seemed to please or satisfy or appease no party or group of politicians, or any community in India.

Let us take first of all the present Indian Legislatures, which ought to serve as a guide at least to the opinions of the parties represented. The first legislative body to discuss the White Paper was the Bihar and Orissa Council, and it unanimously adopted (the official members not taking part in the voting) a resolution condemning the proposals. Mr. S. Sinha, formerly Finance Member of the Bihar and Orissa Government, described the White Paper scheme as a "political imposture," and thought that its adoption would "perpetuate British domination, and enthrone pure and unadulterated autocracy, rendering the people far more helpless to resist the despotism of the Government than they are at present."

The other Provincial Legislatures denounced the proposals with equal vehemence. The Central Legislature, on the motion of Sir Abdur Rahim, launched a strong protest against some of the fundamental issues raised by the White Paper. Sir Hari Singh Gour, leader of the Nationalist Party, for example, searched for that phrase "Dominion Status" in the new constitutional proposals, and was disappointed; the Whip of his party found in the scheme only a fraction of responsibility transferred to Indians.

The political organizations were vehement in their opposition. One Indian demagogue described the White Paper as "a damnable piece of British villainy." The attitude of the Indian National Congress, the most influential political organization in India, was definitely hostile to the White Paper. Its leaders expressed their disapproval of the White Paper in unmistakable language, and found in the proposals "the complete negation of the Indian national demand." Their cold indifference to the details of the proposals suggests that Congress would seek to capture the Legislatures, not with the object of working the Constitution, but to make government, through the Assembly and Councils, impossible in India. A generation schooled in this policy of pure obstruction would undermine the basis of the new system as they undermined the basis of the old.

As regards the Indian Liberals, they were in favour of the scheme in its broad outlines, but they and their organizations received the White Paper with "supreme dissatisfaction." The Madras Liberal League declared that the White Paper was inspired throughout by a deep-seated distrust of the capacity and *bona fides* of the Legislatures, and that it was, in effect, designed to perpetuate the present regime. But the Indian Liberals hoped to secure "substantial modifications" of the proposals through further negotiations with the Imperial Government.

The various communal organizations gave their considered judgment against the White Paper proposals. While the All-India Hindu *Mahasabha* smarted under the implications of the Communal Award, which they considered to be "pre-eminently pro-Moslem and highly unjust to the Hindus," the All-India Moslem Conference, at a meeting in Delhi on March 27, 1933, passed a resolution expressing their profound disappointment at the proposals for a Constitution hedged in by numerous safeguards and reserve powers. They demanded radical changes in the scheme before it would be acceptable to the Moslem community. The Moslem League, consisting mainly of Nationalist Moslems, condemned the scheme as a "deception."

Among the divergent reasons for the condemnation of the proposals there was, in the first place, a general agreement in regard to the failure of His Majesty's Government to respect the principle of negotiation. Every section of Indian opinion held the view that the Government had ignored the implications of the statement made by the Prime Minister on December 2, 1931, in which he said that "the Government must carry on these negotiations until a point was reached when the proposed agreement was initialled—a very well-known stage in the negotiation of treaties." But the White Paper proposals did not bear even the semblance of an "initialled" agreement.

Secondly, the responsible Indian leaders of all communities maintained that the proposals virtually left intact the control of Indian affairs by the British Parliament. " Where do we find," they ask, " the fulfilment of the assurance given by the Premier in his statement at the Round Table Conference in which he definitely promised Dominion Status for India ? They refer to the following words of Mr. Ramsay MacDonald :

> " Finally, I hope and I trust and I pray that by our labours together, India will come to possess the only thing which she now lacks to give her the status of a Dominion among the British Commonwealth of Nations—what she now lacks for that—the responsibilities and the cares, the burdens and the difficulties, but the pride and the honour of responsible government."

The opinion of the non-official British communities in India was divided ; but the majority of them felt that the Government could not possibly avoid taking the risks of a further constitutional advance, and trusted that the White Paper scheme would be carefully strengthened by adequate safeguards. They were particularly apprehensive of commercial discrimination which the future Indian Legislatures might enact in such forms as would prejudice the interests of British trade.

Outside the hubub of the active political arena, there were Indians to whom the White Paper proposals did not appear to be either democratic or Federal. While they discovered in them some elements of representative government, they believed that only a small quantum of responsibility had been granted to the Indian Legislatures. In the formidable schedule of safeguards and reservations, they, too, did not find the spirit of working the Constitution as " partners in a common enterprise " ; and they felt that the British Government had taken full advantage of the weaknesses of the Indian situation as revealed by the fear of the minorities and the antagonism between them. They believed that any over-emphasis of safeguards would not only increase hostility towards the new Constitution, but would draw even those who at present owed no definite allegiance to any of the existing political groups into the orbit of Congress or of the parties which derived their main inspiration from that body.

ℂ INDIAN DEMAND FOR SUBSTANTIAL MODIFICATION

But the assurance that the White Paper proposals were only provisional, subject to critical examination by a Joint Select Committee in which the Indian leaders would again be invited for consultation, infused some hope in the minds of Indian Liberals. They at once made it clear that unless the proposals were substantially modified there could be no chance of their acceptance even by those on whom the Government relied for co-operation.

It is worth while to dwell upon the nature of modifications desired by what the Indian Liberals call "progressive opinion in the country." The Right Hon. V. S. Srinivasa Sastri, C.H., one of the distinguished Indian Liberal statesmen, wrote as follows :

> "The defects of the scheme are many; the undermentioned are perhaps among the more important modifications required :
>
> 1. Defence : (i) Indianization to be completed within a fixed period. (ii) Recruitment to be open to all communities and provinces. (iii) Preparation during transition period for responsibility.
> 2. No Governor-General's Acts and no Governor's Acts.
> 3. No special responsibilities and powers to the Governor-General or Governors in the transferred sphere, except for the protection of the interests of minorities or those of a state.
> 4. Exercise of power of previous sanction (if kept) in matters of currency and exchange to be declared by the Instrument of Instructions to be only in the interests of India.
> 5. The services to be in future under the control of the Federal Government.

6. The Constitution Act to be alterable by the Indian Legislature except where Imperial interests are involved.
7. The Railway Board as well as the Reserve Bank to be constituted by Indian legislation.
8. The Secretary of State's Council to be abolished." [1]

But most of these demands had already been insisted upon by some of the Indian Liberals attending the Round Table Conference. At the close of the third session of the Conference, Sir Tej Bahadur Sapru and Mr. Jayakar submitted a memorandum to the Conference setting forth the considered views of Indian Liberals regarding some of the fundamental issues on which they could not come to any agreed solutions in course of the Round Table Conferences. They emphasized " the need for a speedy establishment of the Federation with responsibility at the Centre," and asserted that " mere Provincial Autonomy by itself will not be acceptable to the vast majority of the political classes in India." What troubled them most was the uncertainty in regard to the date for the inauguration of the Federation, and in their opinion the entry of the Indian States into the Federation should not be made a condition precedent to the establishment of responsible government at the Centre.

They considered that there was a need for a declaration of fundamental rights as one of the effective means of allaying the apprehensions of minorities and special interests. Perhaps the important points in the memorandum were those that dealt with the provisions of safeguards. In the first place, the authors suggested that there would be no need for the India Council under the Constitution and that " the powers of the Secretary of State, being strictly limited to matters within the reserved department and the special responsibilities of the Governor-General, should be transferred to the Dominions Office."

Secondly, they foresaw sources of conflict with the Ministers if the special powers and responsibilities vested in

[1] *Indian Review*, Madras.

the Governor-General and Governors were not precisely defined in the Constitution Act, and held the view that even in the exercise of their special powers and responsibilities, it was desirable to consult their Ministers.

On the questions of financial safeguards, they commented as follows :

> " We think there should be real financial responsibility placed on the Finance Ministers of the future. We cannot but feel that the nervousness which has been displayed as regards the capacity of Indians to manage their finances and the general attitude of the Legislature is not justified. . . . We do recognize that it might be necessary during the period of transition to arm the Governor-General with special power, enabling him to intervene, when, and only when, the security of the British, or for that matter of the Indian investor, is impaired or sought to be impaired by any action of the Finance Minister."

Thirdly, it was argued that in matters of commercial safeguards, undue stress was laid on the principle that discrimination in legislation on purely racial grounds should be avoided. They contended that for the future development of Indian industries,

> " it is absolutely necessary to leave in the hands of the Central and Provincial Governments enough power to initiate, subsidize and protect industries which can be briefly described as key or infant industries, even if such initiation, subsidy or protection should occasionally look like discrimination."

Lastly, they claimed that the defence of India

> " should be to an increasing degree the concern of India, and not of Great Britain alone. Consequently they urged that every step should be taken to Indianize the Army within the shortest possible period compatible with the safety of the country and efficiency of the Army."

On the publication of the White Paper, Sir Tej Bahadur Sapru issued a statement representing the views of " moderate-minded " men in political India. He said :

> "It must be recognized that the proposals of the Government cannot be described in any sense of the term as being based on agreements arrived at at the Round Table Conference. A great part of the document seems to be drawn up more with a view to placate that section of the British Conservatives who are frankly opposed to any advance at the Centre and cannot think of India otherwise than in terms of perpetual tutelage." He appealed to his countrymen to work for "material alterations and amendments and not to dissipate our energies in a manner in which at times we have been inclined to."[1]

The Indian Liberal Federation at their annual Conference at Madras (December 1933) recorded their emphatic protest against the proposals of constitutional reform adumbrated in the White Paper and reiterated their demands for modifications. And these were placed before the Joint Select Committee by the Indian Liberal Assessors.

But the Hindus were not alone in demanding modifications in the White Paper. In a memorandum submitted by the representatives of the All-India Moslem Conference and All-India Moslem League, they demanded that

> "the Governor-General and the Governor's powers should be curtailed; the Provincial Governments should have effective control over Imperial and complete control over Provincial and other services; the High Court should be an exclusively Provincial subject; no weightage or other discriminatory privileges should be given to the Indian States; provision should be made for the effective representation of the Moslems in the public services."[2]

They further stated that in their opinion the residuary powers should be vested in the Provinces and that the special powers vested in the Governor-General for safeguarding the financial stability and credit of India and for the prevention of commercial discrimination should not be used in such a way as to prejudice the growth of Indian commerce

[1] *The Times*, March 22, 1933. [2] *Ibid.*, August 4, 1933.

and industry. Then there was the demand for the inclusion of "Fundamental Rights" in the Constitution Act.

ℂ THE INDIAN STATES AND THE WHITE PAPER

The Indian Princes, eager to secure some concrete advantages from the new Constitution, remained unsatisfied with the conditions stipulated for their entry into the Federal scheme. Some of them raised objections in regard to direct taxation and some to constituent powers invested in the Federation. Since the entire Federal scheme hinges upon the "effective accession" of a sufficient number of States, it was desirable to re-assure the Princes. The Princes were, therefore, assured by the Viceroy that the White Paper did not represent the final picture and that they would have ample opportunities to submit their considered views before the Joint Parliamentary Committee. They submitted a memorandum to the Joint Select Committee stating that the liberty of entering into the Federation through a Confederation should be given to those Princes who desired such conditions and that 40 out of 199 members of the Chamber of Princes had already signified their intention to join such a Confederation. The memorandum claimed the full quota of seats reserved for the representatives of the States, irrespective of the number of States joining the Federation, and also immunity from any form of direct taxation. It was further urged that the Federal Senate should enjoy equal powers with the Federal Assembly, including the power of the purse.

It may be interesting here to record the views of the Indian Liberals on the objections raised by the Princes.

> "By excluding paramountcy from the purview of the Federal Government," writes the *Servant of India*,[1] "and by reserving the right to nominate their representatives to the Federal Chambers and reserving also the liberty to join the Federation in only such matters as each Prince

[1] A prominent Liberal paper (Poona), June 29, 1933.

thought fit, the Princes have safeguarded, nay, more than safeguarded, their special rights of Sovereignty and integrity of their dynasties and the character of their administrations. Is it necessary to go further and deliberately weaken the Federation?"

Indeed, a careful study of the White Paper proposals would show that the terms offered to the Princes were overwhelmingly in their favour. In regard to the administrative relations between the Federal Government and the States and also to the financial adjustments, the interests of the Princes had been jealously safeguarded. And yet they were not quite sure of what might be the ultimate result of their entry into the Federation!

In a frank statement, Sir Mirza M. Ismail, Dewan of Mysore (a premier State), wrote:

> "... We have been held in tutelage till now. The Mysore Treaty gives full expression to the measure of the paternal guidance that was thought necessary for an Indian State at the time of the rendition of the State in 1881. In the past half-century we have grown up; the State has long enjoyed the reputation of being the 'model State' in India; and we feel that the time has come for it to be taken out of leading strings."[1]

Thus we see, on the one hand, the Princes' desire to be free from "tutelage" of the Paramount Power and to have the questions of subsidies and cessions of jurisdictions settled in an equitable manner; on the other, their fear that the conflict between their nominees and the progressive elements from British India in the Federal Chambers might offer fresh and recurring stimulants to the influence of the Nationalist movement in their States. Should the position, for instance, of the Congress Party become dominant within the Federal Chambers, it might be difficult for the nominees of the States to resist British Indian political manœuvres. The Princes had to take into consideration the growing

[1] *Morning Post*, July 19, 1934.

political consciousness of their subjects and they could not very well ignore the disapproval of the Indian States' People Association of the conditions under which the States proposed to lend their stabilizing influence to the future Indian Constitution.

ℂ OPPOSITION IN GREAT BRITAIN

We now turn to the opposition in Great Britain. Here the controversy gave rise to a sharp division in the ranks of the Conservative Party. In the first place, the opponents of the White Paper proposals viewed with alarm the change in the procedure of treating the Report of the Statutory Commission; they resented protracted Conferences in which the entire basis of that Commission's recommendations was altered, and when at long last the Government formulated their proposals they raised the cry of abdication of the sovereign responsibility vested in Parliament and argued that the proposals not only transgressed the limitations imposed by the Statutory Commission but definitely departed from the policy laid down by the pronouncement of August 20, 1917. It was clear to them that the policy which was actuated by a disproportionate anxiety on the part of the authorities for placating the organized political groups would only result in weakening the position of the Government in India. They expressed grave doubts and misapprehensions in regard to the future of the proposed Constitution as being cumbrous and unworkable; they believed that the units of Federation were still very much undeveloped and that, in absence of any organic relations between them, the Federation could not proceed on the way to responsible government. On the contrary, the attempt to set up a Federal Constitution under the conditions obtaining in India might result in chaos. It was a "leap in the dark."

Secondly, the hybrid system of administration which was likely to emerge if the so-called Federal Government was hastily introduced in India, might seriously jeopardise the solution of such economic and social problems as were required for the benefit of the masses. It was asserted that since the basic foundation of Indian civilization was totally different from that of the West, Parliamentary democracy would be a risky venture in the Indian Continent. The opponents challenged the view that the White Paper was the logical consequence of all the past constitutional reforms granted to India; and on the presumption that the Act of 1919 was the first step taken for educating India politically on Parliamentary lines, they argued that the time had not come for the advance proposed in the White Paper.

Thirdly, there was the inevitable risk of increasing the cost of maintaining a Federal Government with its necessary ramifications. The imposition of fresh taxation would arouse widespread discontent, and what was more, the Legislature might be forced to increase the customs tariffs, which would affect British trade in India. The experience of the comparatively new Federal Government of Australia showed that it had not been possible to keep down the growing cost of administration. The average State taxation per head of the population was 14s. 1d. in 1901–02; within 25 years it has gradually risen to £3 18s. 3d.

They further pointed out that the British Indian delegates were insistent in their demand for retrenchment in the Army Budget, but it had already been cut down to a figure which experts considered to be dangerously near the "safety limit." The Provincial Budgets were in deficit or very near "a bare subsistence level"; and since provincial revenues were inelastic, the only way of increasing the provincial revenues was by surrender to provincial governments of some of the central revenues. Besides, so their argument ran, the balancing of Budgets was not enough; the expenditure on the essential nation-building services must be increased.

Fourthly, the safeguards provided for in the Constitution would be nugatory in practice and might lead to much confusion. "Our present governmental policy," observed

Dr. A. B. Keith, "seems to seek to meet Indian aspirations by assurances that safeguards are merely formal, and to obviate our anxieties by assurances that the safeguards are real. Both views cannot be correct."[1] Even if the principal States join the Federation, it would be difficult to avoid the fissiparous influences that would arise among the diverse elements composing the Federation. It was dangerous, they maintained, to have "the power at the centre confused and divided" when Provinces were being developed as autonomous units. They believed that so long as the Central Government remained unaffected by the constitutional changes, safeguards could be made effective. Consequently they firmly opposed the view that provincial autonomy and central responsibility must go together.

There was a certain air of unreality about this opposition to the White Paper proposals. The opponents did not produce any alternative scheme ; their only suggestion was that the Provinces should be given autonomy with one reservation, namely, the control of the police and judiciary. They argued that such a proviso was not inconsistent with the principle of provincial autonomy and cited instances of similar reservations proposed by the White Paper (Army, Foreign Affairs, etc.) to the grant of central responsibility. The truth is, that the opponents opposed in order to ensure adequate effective safeguards and prevent the Government from forcing through Parliament their proposals as a *fait accompli*. They knew that only by persistent opposition would they succeed in modifying the proposals to the extent of their not implying political devolution such as had been conceded in the Dominions.

ℭ SUPPORTERS OF THE WHITE PAPER

The supporters of the White Paper lost no opportunity in explaining the *raison d'etre* of the proposals. They claimed that

[1] *The Morning Post*, June 4, 1933.

> "for over a century we (the British people) have been labouring to inspire India with our own political philosophy, and we have largely succeeded. We have welcomed her as an organic part of an Empire which is based on this philosophy. We have helped to create in India habits of thought of which this philosophy is the natural outcome. We cannot exclude her from sharing in what we ourselves regard as the best." [1]

Some took the view that, since the present form of government had outlived its usefulness something must take its place. And they believed that "the triune policy," namely, unity through federation; responsibility with safeguards; and provincial autonomy within the Federation, was the kind of constitution which was practicable. Others took their stand on the pledges of the past and argued that if something was not done to placate the demands of political India, the British Government would forfeit Indian confidence. The best safeguard was to establish an identity of interest between India and Britain.

The leader of the Conservative Party assured his opponents that the proposals had the support of a large body of responsible men on the spot whose considered opinions could not be turned down and that it was now impossible to "go back to the Simon Report." In a speech at the Albert Hall (May 12, 1933) Mr. Stanley Baldwin put his case as follows:

> "When they say 'go back to the Simon Report' they do not mean go back to the words in the Simon Report, but take out of it the whole question of responsibility for law and order, which is of the essence of the recommendations of the Simon Report, and on which they were all unanimous, and on which everyone responsible for the Government of India to-day is unanimous. You cannot as a practical matter go back to an eviscerated Simon Report. I doubt

[1] See Preface by John Buchan, C.H., M.P. (now Lord Tweedsmuir), to "India: The White Paper," 1933, by the late Sir John Thompson, K.C.I.E., K.C.S.I.

> if you can even go back to the Simon Report as it stands, because if you did you would lose the whole support of intellectual and political India. . . . I believe India can be kept in the Empire by going forward, but if we do not adopt the Government's proposals we shall lose India."

But, in order to pacify the opponents belonging to his party, he promised to consult the party before the Government proceeded with the drafting of the Bill.

Further assurance that the final judgment on the Indian constitutional advance rested with Parliament came from Lord Hailsham. He said in the House of Lords:

> "You are not committing yourselves to any scheme at all; you are not pledging yourselves to support any Bill when it comes before this House; . . . and you reserve to yourselves full liberty if, when the solution is brought before you, you think it does not meet the conditions laid down, to reject it."[1]

But the fury of the opposition was not abated; the cry that the White Paper proposals would mean abdication of Parliamentary authority over Indian affairs continued to agitate a large section of the Conservatives. They were repeatedly assured by men qualified to express an opinion on the motive of the Government's India policy that it was not contemplated that the authority of Parliament should be impaired in the slightest degree. The Marquess of Reading at a debate in the House of Lords said that "while being conciliatory, they (the Government) made no concession where it was essential to Imperial interests to be firm."[2]

Sharing the views and anxieties of his Conservative friends, Sir Samuel Hoare, in a letter to his constituents in Chelsea, explained how Imperial interests had been protected under the proposed scheme. He wrote:

[1] House of Lords Debates, December 10, 1931.

[2] *Ibid.*, February 9, 1933.

> "We have no intention of abdicating our responsibilities. We shall certainly not repeat the Irish precedent. While we are prepared to support the cause of Indian self-government, we are certainly not going to sacrifice British and Imperial interests. . . . The Army will remain under the sole control of Parliament . . . the Services, recruited by the Secretary of State, will continue under the guarantee that they now possess of Parliamentary protection. . . . The Governor-General . . . is to exercise all important duties, including the duty of ensuring the peace and tranquillity of the country, its financial stability, and the fair treatment of the Services and British trade. . . . In these all-important fields he will have not only the right but the duty to intervene if the Government is by legislature or administration transgressing any one of them. Similarly in the Provinces, duties corresponding with their responsibilities will be placed on the Provincial Governors."

Similar assurances came from a section of responsible British public who had been trying to remove a certain number of popular misconceptions in regard to the Indian constitutional proposals, which were deliberately fostered by a section of the Conservative Party. Every single item of safeguards was discussed in all its aspects; every aspect was carefully analysed in order to be convinced of its effectiveness; all possible contingencies were assumed to test how the protective provisions in the Constitution would function in practice. It was asserted that the safeguards were real and not of a temporary self-eliminating character. But the result of this over-emphasis on safeguards and limitations only confirmed the suspicions in the minds of Indian political classes that all these safeguarding devices would make the introduction of central responsibility a sham and provincial autonomy illusory.

However, among the supporters of the White Paper proposals, there were men who believed that the scheme was only an unprecedented experiment which might not ultimately work out satisfactorily; but they wanted India to go through this experimental stage under the guidance of the British. In this connection we may refer to an extract from an address delivered before the Royal Empire Society Summer School at Oxford by Sir Malcolm Hailey.[1] He said:

> "I suggest to you that the real justification for the introduction of that form of government (democracy) in India lies in the faith that India must pass through the educative and formative influences of representative institutions before she can evolve the form of government best suited to her own conditions. That, if I may say so, is a very reasonable theory on which to work; it should allow India gradually to evolve her own proper form of government under influences making for the maintenance of order, instead of proceeding by a series of catastrophic experiments.
>
> "But in the end it may very well be that India may find herself best suited with something different from Parliamentary government in our form—something, that is, in the nature of a directorate sufficiently responsive to popular needs and ideas to gain general acquiescence, but not dependent in the constitutional sense on a majority vote."[2]

The White Paper proposals, after full debates in both Houses, were laid before the Joint Select Committee. The Government assured their critics that the Committee would not be restricted in any way so as to prevent it making any fresh proposals. The normal procedure is that a Select Committee has before it the text of the Bill as already introduced into Parliament. The unusual course of asking a Select Committee to examine proposals before their incorporation in a Bill was adopted in order to give the Committee greater freedom in their examination, and in the result this expedient fully justified itself.

[1] Governor of the United Provinces, India, at the time.
[2] *Asiatic Review*, October, 1933.

ℂ THE JOINT SELECT COMMITTEE

The Committee consisted of 16 members from the House of Commons—11 Conservatives, 1 Liberal, 1 National Liberal and 3 Labour; and 16 members of the House of Lords. The Marquess of Linlithgow, who had been Chairman of the Royal Commission on Indian Agriculture (1928), was the Chairman. It was empowered to invite Indians to act as Assessors, and 21 representatives from British India and 7 from the Indian States were called into consultation with the Committee. Of the British Indian Assessors, 8 represented the Hindus, 4 the Moslems, 3 the Legislative Assembly, 1 the Depressed classes, 1 the Sikhs, 1 the Anglo-Indians, 1 Labour, 1 Women, and 1 Europeans.

The Committee held its first sitting on April 12, 1933; and after a series of consultations with the Indian Assessors, it commenced hearing evidence. The exhaustive examination of the witnesses drawn from all representative bodies, —such as the Chamber of Princes, the Civil Service Associations, the European Association of India, Chambers of Commerce—brought into prominent relief many of the aspects of the Indian controversy which made extremely difficult the task of reconciling fundamental differences of opinion on the principles of the White Paper proposals. Perhaps the most noteworthy feature in the proceedings of the Committee was the examination of the Right Hon. Sir Samuel Hoare, Secretary of State for India, who appeared before the Committee on no less than 20 days and answered about 5,594 questions in elaboration of several memoranda he prepared for the guidance of the Committee. His evidence was not only unique in regard to mastery of every detail of almost all the features of this complicated problem, but stood out as a proof of his faith in its solution as outlined in the White Paper. And, judging by the impression he made upon some of his Indian opponents, one may say that Sir Samuel Hoare proved the truth of Lord Elgin's dictum, that "faith, when it is sincere, is always catching."

It is not my purpose to summarize the discussions of the evidence presented before the Committee ; but for the clear understanding of certain aspects of the complexities of the Indian constitutional problems, I propose here to place before the reader the interpretation of some of the essential features of the White Paper proposals given by the Secretary of State for India in his evidence, and leave, as I have already indicated, to the following chapter, the attempt to give a general survey of the Report.

But, before I turn to Sir Samuel Hoare's evidence, a brief reference must be made to the memorandum [1] submitted by the British Indian Assessors (except Sir Hubert Carr), in which they suggested certain essential modifications of the White Paper proposals if the Government desired to "rally the moderates." There was also a separate memorandum by some of the Indian "elder statesmen" in which they demanded certain amendments which, they should have known, could not be adopted without weakening the safeguards. Perhaps the powerful opposition in Great Britain against granting a liberal measure of reforms to India made these elder statesmen apprehensive of the fate of all their efforts during the last eight years ; but they had not as yet lost faith in the sincerity of the National Government.

Let us now turn to some of the main issues which roused a great deal of discussion in the Committee. In the first place, a searching examination of the facts of modern India raised honest doubt and misgivings as to the feasibility of immediate Federation. India is a vast sub-Continent "marching in uneven stages through all the centuries from the fifth to the twentieth," and the fundamental difficulties in the way of an All-India Federation could not be dramatically removed by mere declarations of the Princes that they were willing to join in a federal scheme. The divergent interests of two Indias would have to be reconciled in order to make the Constitution genuinely federal. The Provinces

[1] Record No. 10.

are not as yet autonomous, and the conditions which justified and led to the creation of a Federal Government in other countries (*e.g.* Australia) do not exist in India. The critics asserted that

> " disruptive forces have been very strong in the past history of India. It is the administration of India by a strong central Government that has succeeded in bringing about uniformity of laws and standards of administration and a feeling of common nationality. The separatist tendencies likely to be produced by differences of race, religion, language and custom have been largely overcome, or kept in check, by the influence of a strong centralized government." [1]

Sir Samuel Hoare in his evidence before the Committee said that in essential matters, such as Defence, Transport and general economic factors, there was no wide divergence of interests between British India and Indian States; that the Federal Government would have a limited, definite sphere of activity and would not intervene in the internal affairs of the States " except to the extent that those internal affairs are affected either by paramountcy or by the transfer of the powers to the Federal Government "; and that the prerogatives of paramountcy would ensure proper enforcement of Federal authority upon the State-members.

On the important issue of the right of a State-member to secede from the Federation, Sir Samuel Hoare observed that it was made quite plain in the White Paper that, as long as the terms of the bargain (that is, Treaty of Accession) remain, a State-member, in the interests of the stability of Federation, would not be allowed to do so. As a matter of fact, the Princes made no such demand, and if they did, it would have undermined the basis of applying Federal principles to India.

The witnesses on behalf of the Government of India assured the Committee that there was no great risk of a

[1] " Indian Constitutional Problems," by Sir P. S. Sivaswamy Aiyer, K.C.S.I.

deterioration in the administration of the country consequent upon the creation of a Federal type of government. And since social legislation would belong to Provincial Assemblies, the fear that State-members may stand in the way of enacting such legislation was not justifiable.

Secondly, the proper distribution of subjects between the Federation and the units and the administrative relations between them bristled with formidable difficulties. It raised the problem of residual sovereignty. " It causes trouble in ordinary federations," says the *Observer* (London), " in which only a Central Government and constituent units have to share power. But in India there are four elements, not two—the Provinces, the States, the Central Government, and Downing Street."

The question was fully discussed in the Committee. It was suggested that a number of subjects [1] would be regarded as " the normal field " over which the States should surrender their powers ; but these might vary in accordance with the circumstances of each State. The paramount Power should have, however, the full authority of refusing to accept the terms proposed by a State.

As regards the Provinces, it was pointed out that it was desirable to avoid overlapping between the functions of the Central and Provincial Governments. Autonomy should not, for practical and financial reasons, involve a breach with " the traditional methods and machinery of Indian Administration " ; nor should it divest the Central Government of the power of intervention in an emergency. Part IV of the new Act makes provision for these matters. The Committee were aware of the possibility of conflict between Federal and Provincial legislation with respect to the concurrent subjects, and made the following observation in their Report :

> " We recognize that, in practice, it will be impossible for the Centre to utilize its powers in the concurrent field without satisfying itself in advance that the Governments to whose

[1] Contained in List 1, Appendix VI, of the White Paper.

territories a projected measure will apply are, in fact, satisfied with its provisions and are prepared, in cases where it will throw extra burdens upon Provincial resources, to recommend to their own Legislatures the provision of the necessary supply; but we consider that the practical relationships which are to develop between Centre and Provinces in this limited field must be left to work themselves out by constitutional usage and the influence of public opinion, and that no useful purpose would be served by attempting to prescribe them by means of rigid legal sanctions and prohibitions. Nevertheless, we regard it as essential to satisfactory relations between Centre and Provinces in this field that the Federal Government, before initiating legislation of the kind which we are discussing, should ascertain provincial opinion by calling into conference with themselves representatives of the Governments concerned. At the same time we recommend that, although no statutory limitations should be imposed upon the exercise by the Centre of its legislative powers in the concurrent field, the Governor-General should be given guidance in his Instrument of Instructions as to the manner in which he is to exercise the discretion which is to be vested in him in relation to matters arising in the concurrent field."

Thirdly, we come to the central theme on which the critics of the White Paper were so insistent, namely, the provisions for safeguards. Opposition to the White Paper in Great Britain was chiefly aimed at securing adequate safeguards and stiffening those that were already provided. And it is obvious that Parliament would require definite assurances that the safeguards would be effective.

Sir Samuel Hoare's evidence elucidated how all the protective provisions under the scheme would function, and showed that the criticism that the safeguards were "little better than blinkers for the British public" was wholly unwarranted. He pointed out that the establishment of a Reserve Bank, the creation of a Statutory Federal Railway Authority, and the provisions for placing certain items of supply (*e.g.* defence, the salaries and pensions of Imperial Services, subventions to the Provinces) outside the competence of Indian Legislatures would ensure the maintenance of financial stability and credit of India and safeguard all essential services. Recruitment for the Indian Civil Service and the Indian Police (superior grades) is retained in the hands of the Secretary of State. Then there will be Statutory Public Service Commissions both at the Centre and in the Provinces for controlling and maintaining the standards of efficiency and integrity of the services other than those mentioned above. It was held by some critics that the recruitment for the Indian Civil Service and the Police by the Secretary of State would be inconsistent with the principle of provincial autonomy; but it is the intention that there shall be an enquiry into this matter at an early date after the introduction of provincial autonomy, probably about five years after, if the lead given by the Joint Select Committee is followed up by His Majesty's Government of the day.

For the prevention of discrimination in matters affecting trade, commerce, industry, etc., it is provided that under no circumstances should British traders in India be put in a less favourable position than Indians, and that the Governors and the Governor-General shall have the necessary powers to withhold assent to any discriminatory legislation or even such Bills which "though not discriminatory in form, are, in fact, discriminatory." In course of discussion, Sir Phiroze Sethna, an Indian Liberal, pointed out that the "special provision regarding ships and shipping" had not been discussed in the Round Table Conferences; but the Secretary of State said that it had been found necessary to expand the meaning of the expression "commercial discrimination." As regards ships and shipping, provision will be made for the automatic registration of British ships on the Indian register.

A great deal of discussion took place on the subject of the powers and special responsibilities of the Governor-General in the Federal sphere and of the Governors in the

Provinces. The Committee elicited replies from the Secretary of State on the legal position of the Instruments of Instructions which, he said, were mandatory. Although the Instructions are not part of the Act of Parliament, they must be laid before each House of Parliament. It was further explained that the Instructions passed by Parliament would, as far as possible, be uniform in character, but in order to meet special circumstances, the Secretary of State could add directions to them provided that such added instructions or directions were in conformity with the spirit of the Standing Instructions.

Since there seems to have arisen a great deal of misapprehension as to the nature and use of the "special responsibilities" imposed on the Governor-General and Governors, it may be helpful for understanding the principles on which these powers are based to quote here a few extracts from the evidence of Sir Samuel Hoare. He said:

> "The point I wish to emphasize is that the 'special responsibilities' . . . are not special subjects which are kept out of the purview of Ministers, and reserved for the control of the Governor. I should describe them rather as signposts or labels indicating to the Governor, and incidentally to his Ministers, certain purposes, the fulfilment of which the Governor is directed to secure, if necessary, by refusing to be guided by his Ministers' advice whenever he considers that the advice tendered to him would be inimical to the fulfilment of any of these purposes."

He further stated that "the field of special responsibilities is a field that pervades the general field of administration"; but emphasized throughout his evidence that the special powers are not to be regarded as methods of arbitrary interference on the part of the Governor-General and Governors with the work of the Ministers. These safeguards are provided in case conflicts affecting the matters to which the safeguards relate may arise between a Governor and his Ministers and the Legislature.

The fourth great issue was the subject of finance. The

sub-Committees of the Round Table Conferences failed to offer satisfactory indications of the sources of additional finance necessary for the new regime ; nor were they able to adjust financial relations between the Federation and the units. A financial memorandum was then prepared by Sir Malcolm Hailey, on which Sir Samuel Hoare based his evidence before the Committee. He reviewed the entire budgetary position of the Government of India and of the Provinces and said :

> " I think two significant facts emerge from the figures. The first is that the greater part of this deficit, call it, if you will, from six crores to ten crores, is due not to the setting up of the Federal Government in the centre, but to the setting up of autonomous provinces upon a self-supporting basis. I would lay special emphasis upon this fact, that by far the greater part of the deficit is due to the setting up of the autonomous provinces upon a self-supporting basis. Next, a second fact that emerges is that a very small part of this deficit, take it if you will at the highest figure, say, of ten crores, is due to actual fresh expenditure. If you analyse the figures you will find that, apart from a comparatively small sum, namely, about three-quarters of a crore, for setting up the new machinery in the provinces, and a figure of about the same amount, namely, about three-quarters of a crore, for setting up the Federal institutions in the centre, the rest of the amount is not fresh expenditure at all, and it is due in the main to two changes in the allocation of revenues of India, namely, first of all, the change, supposing Burma is separated from India, of leaving Burma two or three crores that it now contributes to the Indian Central Government. Secondly, it is due to a figure of about the same amount, some two crores, that is necessary whether changes take place in the constitutional field or whether they do not, to put a stop to the permanent deficit in Bengal and the permanent deficit in Assam."

The main conclusions reached on the financial situation were, that it would be necessary to institute an expert enquiry into the financial position before the Constitution came into operation, with a view to readjusting the present state of affairs to the conditions of the time; and that it should be made possible to introduce provincial autonomy with a balanced Budget but without any fresh taxation.

Certain features of Federal finance as drawn by Sir Malcolm Hailey in his memorandum may be stated here. He showed that the Central Government cannot, as things are at the present moment, part with any of the sources available to it, and therefore there is no surplus for the use of Provincial Governments. Barring the excise duty on matches, which would yield some two and a half crores, there is no other immediately reliable source of revenue for the Central Budget. Since the Provinces cannot hope to obtain any relief from the central revenues (except a part of the jute tax for Bengal), the problems to be faced are those of meeting the deficits of certain provinces and of providing for the creation of new provinces. Sir Samuel Hoare declared that the initial deficits of the Provinces would be met by the Federal Government, but his statement of the actual position of the central finance should be borne in mind. He said:

> "I think it is most important to emphasize the fact that, so far as we can see, for quite a number of years to come, there is no orange to divide up in India between the centre and the provinces. The fact that does emerge, anyhow, in my mind, as definitely as any other, is that for some years to come the Central Government, whether it be the present Government or whether it be a Federal Government, will need substantially its present resources if the credit of India is to be maintained and if its financial obligations are to be met."

Fifthly, there was the question of franchise. A great deal of discussion arose over the basis for enfranchising women. The authors of the White Paper did not favour the adoption of a lowered educational test for women,[1] and their reasons

[1] Except in Madras.

for departing from the proposals of the Indian Franchise Committee were that there should be no differential standard between men and women as regards the educational qualification. Sir Samuel Hoare said that "a very formidable argument can be urged against differentation upon grounds of theory, but, over and above that objection, there is the administrative objection."

As regards enfranchising women (wife or widow) on the strength of their husbands' property qualification, it was maintained that under the existing social conditions it would be desirable to provide that claimants themselves should apply to the returning officer for the registration of their names on the electoral roll.

The representatives of Indian and English women's organizations who appeared before the Committee expressed their dissatisfaction at the provision made in the White Paper for the enfranchisement of Indian women. But the suggestions of the Indian Women representatives, in regard to modifications they desired, lacked unity and coherence; one group objected to reservation of seats and put forward a plea for a bare literacy for all voters—Provincial as well as Federal—for a uniform property qualification for both the Provincial and Federal Legislatures, and for adult franchise in urban areas only; the other group insisted upon the Lothian plan and favoured reservation of seats at the initial stage. Both the groups sought to have women's rights protected by inserting a "Fundamental Rights" clause in the Constitution Act.

In their protest against the inadequacy of the White Paper plan, they have had the support of certain English women's organizations. Miss Eleanor Rathbone, M.P., warned the Committee against the proposal of leaving the matter of enfranchisement for Indian women in the hands of the future Indian Legislatures. So much for the franchise for women.

Doubts arose in regard to the geographical size of the proposed constituencies (approximately 17,000 square miles) for the Federal Assembly as being suitable for maintaining proper contact between the elector and the elected. It was explained that the present constituencies were very much larger than those proposed under the White Paper scheme because the number of elected seats is very much smaller; and that, while at present the contact with electors was not adequate, it would probably improve as the sense of responsibility developed.

Some of the members of the Committee wanted to be clear on the point whether further extension of franchise might be effected by the Indian Legislatures "without reference to Parliament." Sir Samuel Hoare observed that for a definite period the proposed franchise should be given a fair trial, but after that the matter ought to be left in the hands of the Indian Governments and Legislatures.

A reference must be made to an alternative franchise proposal, namely, Indirect Elections, which the Franchise Committee rejected on the ground of "administrative difficulties." The majority of the Indian politicians did not favour the proposal, but it was approved of by those who desired to safeguard the interests of the Indian masses against the dominance of the oligarch and the plutocrat.

Lastly, that hideous phase of Indian social life which cast a gloom over almost every progressive measure appeared before the Committee. The Hindu communalists raised the question of the distribution of seats in the Legislatures on a communal basis and protested against the Communal Award [1] and also demanded that the Poona Pact [2] should be abrogated altogether. The Hindus of Bengal argued that an injustice had been done to a Province where even on a population basis, the Moslems would have 109 and the Hindus 90 seats in the Provincial Assembly. Under the Communal Award the respective seats allotted to them are 119 and 80. The Secretary of State for India made it plain in his evidence that the Government stood by

[1] See page 126.
[2] See page 129.

their decision as announced in their Communal Award, and in reply to Sir Nripendra N. Sircar [1] said:

> "I am not going to argue about the communal decision at all. We did not wish to make the decision; it was forced upon us by all the communities in India; we did it with great reluctance. We took into account, of course, the Report of the Statutory Commission; we took into account every conceivable other kind of investigation, and we had in every case the very full reports from the Provincial Governments." [2]

Perhaps the most entertaining evidence upon this question was furnished by a group of Hindu communalists, whose chief demand was that their religion should be "absolutely safeguarded" by a statutory provision to the effect that the future Indian Legislatures should be debarred from passing any measure affecting the personal law or the religious faith, practice, usage, and institutions of any community. The spokesman of this group, which claims to represent 170 million Hindus, asserted that the Child Marriage Act [3] was incompatible with certain fundamentals of Hindu religion. His replies to the questions relating to caste, depressed classes, penance for sea-crossing, suttee and other usages, emphasized the truth that there were serious mal-adjustments in social organization which made the Indian incapable of coping with the demands of a twentieth-century world.

Not being satisfied with their protests against the communal decisions before the Joint Select Committee, the champions of the Hindu Mahasabha proposed to send a deputation to the League of Nations on the ground that the Communal Award violated international decisions on the minority question. Having failed to come to any agreements with various communities, they now declared that

[1] A distinguished lawyer; now Law Member in the Executive Council of the Governor-General.

[2] Vol. II B, p. 856.

[3] Known as the Sarda Act—passed in 1930.

a Constitution vitiated by such measures as were designed to perpetuate differences amongst Indian people was the negation of democracy.

The truth is, the present leaders of Indian communities have utterly failed to root out this disgraceful feature of Indian polity. The only hope now rests with the youth, who must realize the grave consequences of nurturing disruptive forces in the Indian social life, the repercussion of which upon the political future of India would persistently impede progress.

Such is the outline of the problems that confronted the Joint Select Committee. In the following chapter we shall note some of the features of its Report.

CHAPTER VI

THE REPORT OF THE JOINT SELECT COMMITTEE AND THE BILL

The Report : Dissenting Amendments : Certain Features of the Report : The Bill : Amendments in Parliament : Royal Assent : All-India Federation : Dominion Status

ℭ REPORT

AFTER eighteen months' deliberations,[1] the Joint Select Committee published its Report on November 22, 1934. Although the Committee were free to consider the Indian constitutional problems *de novo*, they concentrated their attention on the Government proposals formulated in the White Paper, the principles of which they endorsed. We have noted in Chapter V the matters on which the Majority Report of the Committee corresponded closely with the proposals of the White Paper; but it became necessary for them to devote considerable attention to the various issues which threatened to create a split within the ranks of the Conservative Party.

Rivarol somewhere observed: "Politics is like the sphinx in the fable: it destroys all those who cannot solve its riddles." Perhaps the apprehension that the Indian political riddles might become further complicated persuaded the Committee to recommend additional safeguards and to strengthen the ones proposed in the White Paper so that

[1] The Committee held 159 meetings and examined over 120 witnesses.

the Constitutional changes would not involve any risks in regard to the future position of the British power in India. They made it abundantly clear that the authority of the Imperial Parliament in Indian affairs shall remain unimpaired ; that, as the constitutional head, the Governor-General shall be vested with the whole executive power of the Federation and that his Ministers will be appointed only to " aid and advise him." The Governor-General and the Governors shall have statutory *personal* powers and special responsibilities for safeguarding the essential functions of the Government notwithstanding the changes to be effected in its structure. Even then they failed to satisfy that solid core of opposition within the ranks of the Conservative Party!

But, if the Committee have shown over-caution in transferring political power to Indian Legislatures and reinforced some of the safeguards, it should be admitted that the weight of their argument and their recommendations indicate an adequate recognition of Indian political aspirations. One distinguishing feature of the Report is that its authors do not lay stress on past pledges and commitments[1] but take cognisance of the growth and character of Indian public opinion which, they admit, is " strong enough to affect what has been for generations the main strength of the Government of India — its instinctive acceptance by the mass of the Indian people." While, in their judgment, " it would be a profound error for Parliament to ignore " the forces that are operative in Indian life to-day, they declare that " a recognition of Indian aspirations does not imply that responsible government is an automatic device which can be manufactured to specification."

In an introductory chapter the Committee enunciated " the principles of a constitutional settlement " and came

[1] Commenting upon the passing of the Government of India Bill, *The Observer* (London), August 4, 1935, used the following words : " Out of regard for promises given in an epoch of unsettled emotions, the British people have gone further than naked prudence and reason would have prompted."

to the conclusion that the Preamble to the Government of India Act of 1919 set out *finally and definitely*[1] the ultimate aims of British rule in India. They made no reference to the expression "Dominion Status" in their Report nor did they attempt to explain how the new scope of an All-India Federation was consistent with the constitutional implications of that Preamble and with the pledges given by successive Viceroys since 1919.

The Committee's arguments in support of the main principles[2] on which the White Paper was based may be stated here.

They agreed that the process of devolution of powers and responsibilities in the Provinces must be pressed forward, and recommended the establishment of full responsible government in the eleven Provinces of British India, including the two new Provinces to be created in accordance with the proposals in the White Paper. Since there cannot be full provincial autonomy without responsibility in the Central Government nor responsibility without Federation, the Committee endorsed the White Paper proposal for an All-India Federation as being the corner-stone of the Indian constitutional structure; they concurred in the view that mere grant of provincial autonomy without "responsibility at the Centre" would tend to "give full play to the powerful centrifugal forces without any attempt to counteract them and to ensure the continued unity of India." A responsible Central Government for British India alone is impossible, and the only way to secure a strong Central Government is to bring in a Federal scheme to which the Rulers of the States responsible for at least half the aggregate population of the States would desire to accede. It is obvious that the completion of a long process of negotiations with the States in regard to their entry into the Federal scheme would involve a considerable delay between the establishment of provincial autonomy and the inauguration of Federation. But the form of the

[1] Italics are mine. [2] See Chapter V.

Federal Legislature should be defined in the Act itself. Federation is to be inaugurated by a Royal Proclamation if and when the required number of the Indian States have signified to His Majesty the desire to enter the Federation, and after both Houses of Parliament have presented an Address to the Crown with a prayer for its promulgation. No State is finally committed to enter the Federation until its Instrument of Accession is signed.

Now, the acceptance of these two principles, namely Provincial Autonomy and an All-India Federation, by the Committee brings us to the consideration of the ample provision of safeguards proposed by the White Paper. The Committee approved of these provisions and considerably extended them, mainly on the ground that the four essential factors of Parliamentary government did not exist in India to-day. These are:

> "The principle of majority rule; the willingness of the minority for the time being to accept the decisions of the majority; the existence of great political parties divided by broad issues of policy rather than by sectional interests; and finally, the existence of a mobile body of political opinion, owing no permanent allegiance to any party and therefore able, by its instinctive reaction against extravagant movements on one side or the other, to keep the vessel on an even keel."

In elaborating the series of statutory safeguards which occupy a position of prominence in the Report, the Committee pointed out that these limitations, checks, and counterchecks should be regarded as the substitutes for "the unwritten laws and tacit convention of the British Constitution."

But one should attempt to understand these safeguards in a spirit of objective realism. The general trend of Indian nationalism, the cry of secession from the British Empire, the persistent threats of boycotting British goods, the talk of repudiating public debts and the post-war tendencies among the Dominions, are the circumstances which must needs be taken into account when a large share of the responsibilities of government is handed over to Indian Legislatures. While the activities of the Indian National Congress were held in check by Ordinances, the spirit of extreme nationalism now imbued with "socialistic emotion" dominated a large body of Indian opinion. On the other hand, the opposition within and without Parliament against any real transfer of political power to Indian Legislatures insisted upon considerable modification of the White Paper proposals. Some repercussion of these conflicting tendencies was inevitable in the recommendations of the Committee. The reinforcement of safeguards may be regarded as a compliment both to the Congress Party in India and the Conservative minority in Great Britain!

The Majority Report, however, recognized the utmost importance of securing the effective co-operation of the politically-minded class in the government of the country. It rightly pointed out that the achievements of British rule in India have given her a sense of unity and a national spirit which should now be given a wider scope for expression, and sought to conciliate Indian opposition by declaring that the safeguards provided in the proposed Constitution should not in any way interfere with the growth of healthy conventions, and that they are necessary for the safety of all interests during the process of carrying the administration from one system of Government to another.

ℂ DISSENTING AMENDMENTS

The Report was not, however, without dissenting amendments. One group, headed by Lord Salisbury, laid stress upon the anomalies of creating a Federation with units that have yet to be developed, and asserted the incompatibility of a union of democratic Provinces with autocratic States. The other represented the views of the Labour Party, whose members on the Committee proposed that the new Constitution should be so framed as to enable India to reach the goal of Dominion Status by "a process of internal development " without recourse to future Acts of Parliament. In other words, the former dissented on the grounds that the Committee's recommendations went too far, while the latter submitted a draft alternative Report on the basis that they did not go far enough to satisfy India's demands. These two views constitute the dissenting amendments to which I shall presently refer. Between these two opposite views the Committee laboured to steer a middle course.

> " Is it not the moral," asks Lord Zetland, " that we may draw from these facts this—that the recommendations of the Report embody the golden mean between two extremes, and that they bear for that very reason the hall-mark of what, I think, will be generally admitted to be the peculiar genius of the British people ? "

The Indian Nationalist press, on the other hand, contended that this policy of adopting a middle path would ultimately lead nowhere. Some of the Indian leaders feared that even this middle path might not be followed at the outset, since Federation was made dependent upon so many circumstances stipulated for its inauguration. How soon " responsibility at the Centre " was likely to be granted no one could foretell, and on account of this feeling of uncertainty the Report was not received with any degree of enthusiasm by Indian public.

We shall briefly refer here to the two dissenting amendments to the Majority Report. The four members of the Labour Party in the Committee submitted their amendments in the form of a draft Alternative Report, in which they accepted the general structure of the proposals of the majority but recommended the transfer of all subjects to Legislative control, except Defence. They were not prepared to concede immediate Dominion Status, but considered that the new Constitution should be so framed as to enable India to attain that Status within a reasonable time and without further reference to Parliament. While the Provincial Governments should conform to the Westminster system, the transference of responsibility at the Centre should be effected somewhat on the lines of the Constitution of Ceylon. The provisions for safeguards should be reduced to a minimum, and those that were necessary should be mainly for the protection of the masses from exploitation. They would not, for example, empower the Governor-General to safeguard the financial stability and credit of India, and it is suggested that the Reserve Bank should be under political control. They recommended that there should be provision for the introduction of Adult Franchise as soon as possible but there should be now further extension of the franchise to women and labour. They were strongly opposed to the creation of Second Chambers in the Legislatures and saw no reason for the provision of special electorates.

The second amendment was submitted by the members of the Conservative Party in the Committee who were opposed to the White Paper proposals. They were strongly opposed to conceding responsible government in the Centre but prepared to grant a measure of provincial autonomy. They proposed to establish a Council of Greater India, containing representatives of every Province and State, the advice of which would be sought by the Viceroy on every issue which is of interest to India as a whole. The amendment took the form of protests rather than constructive counterproposals and proceeded to set out " the true character of the Indian problem " in the following sombre words. Lord Salisbury and his small band of colleagues write :

> ". . . The demand for federation without the provision of equality of status in the units ; the claim of Indians to self-government notwithstanding the lack of personal experience and inherited guidance which handicaps them in exercising the higher functions of Government ; the impossibility of any real contact in direct representation between the people and their representatives ; the profound communal differences which split Indian society into fragments impossible to coalesce ; the novelty of provincial

reform and its necessarily tentative character and the reaction of these upon the Central Government," all these constitute problems of great complexities, and they warn the supporters of the majority report that "unless these fundamental difficulties can be met, any federal system in India must be unworkable."

In the final vote on the adoption of the Majority Report nineteen out of the thirty-one surviving members of the Committee voted for it. A group of nine, consisting of five Conservatives and four Labour members, voted against, and three members did not record their votes.

ℂ. CERTAIN FEATURES OF THE REPORT

The recommendations of the majority of the Joint Select Committee modified or supplemented some of the proposals in the White Paper on certain important points, especially in regard to those round which controversy has chiefly raged. Some of these modifications have already been stated. We shall note here certain special features of the recommendations of the Committee.

In the first place, the Committee felt it necessary to provide adequate safeguards for fostering Anglo-Indian trade relations. The question falls into two categories, namely, discrimination against British commercial interests and trade in India, and discrimination against British imports. After laying stress on the fact that this matter was of supreme importance both to Great Britain and India and that they "must approach their trade problems in a spirit of reciprocity which views the trade between the two countries as a whole," the Committee recommended that Statutory provision against discriminatory legislations was necessary. It was, therefore, suggested that the Governor-General and Governors should have a special responsibility for the prevention of both legislative and administrative discrimination in regard to British interests and trade in India. As regards

British imports, the Committee recommended that, while the Indian Legislature should be competent to adopt measures for the development of India's fiscal and economic policy, the Governor-General should have statutory powers to intervene against the imposition of prohibitory tariffs or restrictions on British imports. Both in the Constitution Act and in the Instrument of Instructions the scope of the special responsibilities of the Governor-General in regard to these matters should be enumerated in *precise terms.* For instance, the Instrument of Instructions should make it plain that it would be the duty of the Governor-General and of the Governors in exercising their discretion in the matter of assent to Bills not to feel themselves bound by the terms of the statutory prohibitions in relation to discrimination, but to withhold their assent from any measure which, though not in form discriminatory, would in their judgment have a discriminatory effect.

The Committee argued that the fiscal Autonomy Convention "would never have been evoked to cover an attempt to penalize British imports," and that their recommendations were only framed with the object of allaying fears that the Indian Legislatures might strike at British trade and imports in order to bring political pressure to bear upon the British Government. While British commercial interests were thus reassured, the Indian mercantile community was alarmed at the curtailment of its freedom to develop the nascent industries of India. Sir Pheroze Sethna, a prominent Bombay merchant, declared: "It is sheer mockery to continue British vested interests under the cloak of reciprocity when they are against Indian interests."

Secondly, the future of the Indian Judicature was a subject to which the Committee gave much consideration. It is essential that, as a result of the constitutional changes, the existing machinery for the administration of justice should not in any way be imperilled. An essential element in a Federal Constitution is a Federal Court. The Committee recommended that all disputes arising out of the interpretations of the Constitution Act and of Federal laws, or involving matters of legal right between any of the Federal units, should be included in the jurisdiction of the Federal Court.[1] The question of creating a Supreme Court of Appeal from the Provincial High Courts in civil cases, or of extending the jurisdiction of the Federal Court to deal with such appeals, is left to the Indian Legislature. But the Committee made a number of recommendations with a view to protecting the Judiciary from political influence. Judges of the Federal as well as of the High Courts will be appointed by the Crown and their salaries will not require to be voted by the Legislatures; nor will they be empowered to amend the actual Constitution of the High Courts.

The High Courts will have control over the subordinate Courts and all matters of appointments, posting and promotion will be placed beyond the competence of the Indian Legislatures. Finally, the Governor-General and Governors should be instructed to reserve any Bill which would in their opinion appear to be in any way derogating from the powers of High Courts.

Thirdly, as particular anxiety was widely felt among pensioners as to the future security of the Family Pension Funds, the Committee endorsed the Secretary of State's proposal that arrangements should be made for the transfer into sterling of the accumulations of these funds which are at present held in the rupee balances of the Government of India.

These recommendations were chiefly designed to pacify the Conservative opposition in Great Britain. Let us now turn to certain alterations proposed in the structure of the Constitution itself.

One of the most difficult problems of Indian Constitution building is to make the representative system reasonably representative. The difficulty is enhanced by the increase of the size of the electorate from about 7,315,000 to 35,000,000.

[1] The Bill departed from the recommendation in respect of Federal laws.

The Committee regarded it "as fundamental that the system of election to the Central Legislature should be such as to make the responsibility of a member to those who elect him a real and effective responsibility," and rejected proposals for direct election to the Lower Federal Chamber. They recommended that members from British India to the Federal Lower Chamber should be chosen by a system of indirect election from the Provincial Legislatures, the various communities voting separately for their own representatives. It should be noted here that the proposal for indirect election is a reversion to the scheme of the Indian Statutory Commission and that it has been strenuously opposed by the British India representatives at the Round Table Conferences. The Committee lay emphasis on the special circumstances of India under which a system of direct election would constitute an illogical and consequently unsound basis for constitutional development, and argue that the size of constituencies, lack of communications, widespread illiteracy and diverse characters of Indian social and cultural life are the factors that would reduce the representative system to an absurdity under a scheme of direct election. It is, however, unfortunate that in making the Provincial Legislatures the constituents of the Federal Legislatures it has not been possible to obviate the anomaly of communal electorates. While there is a strong opposition in India against the proposal for indirect election to the Federal Lower Chamber, the various communities (*e.g.* the Depressed classes) feel that they have been unjustly treated in the proposals for their representation in the Upper Houses. An amendment in the House of Lords, as we shall presently see, introduced a novel feature in the Constitution; that is, the Upper Chamber is to be elected directly, while the Lower Chamber is elected on an indirect basis.

As regards a scheme of constitutional reform in Burma, the Committee recommended the separation of the Province from India. They considered the importance of preserving

Burma from injurious economic and financial results during the period of transition, and suggested that agreements in regard to trade and immigration of Indian labour into Burma should be concluded between the present Governments of India and Burma. The importance of readjusting commercial arrangements between India and separated Burma may be realized from the volume of existing trade between these two countries. Since 1930 the imports of Indian cotton textiles into Burma have grown from 23 million yards in 1930–31 to 71 million yards in 1933–34—an increase of over 300 per cent. Over one million Indians reside in Burma.

The Constitution of Burma, the Committee pointed out, must differ in many respects from that proposed for the Indian Provinces. Politically, Burma was a quarter of a century behind India. Strictly speaking, its Constitution would not be autonomous in character although Burma should be excluded from the legal definition of "colonies." The Burmese politicians in the Legislative Council opposed the proposals as being totally inadequate and proposed that Burma should enter the Indian Federation as an autonomous provincial unit.

We must now make a reference to that indispensable element, finance, in the future Constitution of India. It is the very life-blood of government. We have noted how the difficulties in finding the wherewithal for the working of the Reforms of 1921 made the Dyarchical Constitution unpopular and largely ineffective.

The Report of the Joint Select Committee gave an estimate of the cost of the proposed constitutional changes.[1]

[1] The Financial experts differ in their estimate in regard to the extra cost of the new Constitution. Sir Malcolm Hailey put the figure between seven and eight million pounds. Sir George Schuster, in his broadcast speech (January 1935), gave an estimate of about £5,000,000. As regards the budgetary position of the Provinces the figures presented to the House of Commons (March 1935) show that, including Burma, six of the ten Provinces had deficits of over £2,000,000 in 1933–34; eight of the ten had deficits of over £1,000,000 in 1934–35.

The establishment of provincial autonomy would involve additional expenditure of Rs. ¾ crore (£562,500) per annum, and of the Federation a further Rs. ¾ crore. The separation of Burma would probably mean a loss of Rs. 3 crores (£2,250,000) per annum to India, less the yield of any revenue duties imposed upon imports from Burma. On account of financial adjustments with the Indian States there would be a loss of about Rs. 1 crore (£750,000) to Federal revenues.

The Committee laid stress on the importance of introducing provincial autonomy without a deficit, and with sufficient resources for the requirements of each of the eleven Provinces. But the budgetary resources of the Central and Provincial Governments are barely sufficient for attaining this position. The financial horizon is not clear, and owing to the entry of the States the problem has become extremely complicated. Princes desire an assurance of the solvency of Federation before they enter it. The Committee, therefore, hoped that His Majesty's Government would review the financial situation before the new Constitution actually comes into operation. Parliament must be informed how matters stand in regard to the financial resources of the new regime.[1]

In emphatic language the Committee declared that if their main proposals are rejected, " the prospect of an All-India Federation will disappear, perhaps for ever, but certainly for many years to come, and the measure of harmony achieved in British India by the co-operative efforts of the last few years, together with the body of central opinion, will be irretrievably destroyed."

[1] For the special financial enquiry provided for in the Act, the Government of India have now (September 1935) secured Sir Otto Niemeyer, a member and sometime Chairman of the Financial Committee of the League of Nations, to furnish Parliament with an independent review of the financial position of the Provinces and the Centre. Questions such as subventions to meet Provincial deficits, allocation of the proceeds of the jute export duty and the income tax, and financial adjustments consequent upon the separation of Burma, will be dealt with in this enquiry. The final decision on these matters will be taken by Order in Council.

The Committee, therefore, urged the acceptance of its conclusions " as embodying in their broad lines a policy on which responsible public opinion both in this country and in India may unite," and expressed its confidence that Parliament " will make the transfer generously and in no grudging spirit."

But a body of " central opinion," on whose support the Government relied for the working of the new Constitution, found the Report of the Joint Select Committee more reactionary than the White Paper. Even among the political groups which were accustomed to support the Government there was a feeling that the powers given at the Centre were too narrow and restricted, and that the Committee had not formulated their recommendations on the Joint Memorandum of the British Indian Delegates. In a resolution passed by the Conference of the National Liberal Federation of India it was declared that any Constitution based on the lines of the Report would be wholly unacceptable to all shades of Indian political opinion, and would only intensify the present discontent in the country. The Right Hon. V. S. Sastri, P.C., the doyen of the Indian Liberals, in moving the resolution sounded a note of warning in the following words :

> " So far as I could see, the Government would not be able to get the people to work the Constitution with contentment. There would be a continual wrangle between the people and the Government. It might be worked, but there would be no peace in the land, nor peace between India and England. Bitterness would increase. . . . It was impossible for Liberals to give co-operation. Co-operation with friends was noble, but co-operation with those who had treated them with the utmost distrust and were preparing to enact a Constitution in defiance and disregard of their dearest wishes would be suicide."

In the judgment of the Council of the Moslem League, the Report was unsatisfactory as it had not secured them a one-third representation in the Federal Assembly. The

Princes, while recognizing in the Report certain improvements in their favour, did not find in it those conditions which they insisted at the outset were essential if they were to accept the Federal proposals; some aspects of the recommendations in relation to the States and Federation were "still vague and undefined." But they reserved their opinion until the final picture was disclosed to them in the Bill and Instrument of Accession. The truth is, that these criticisms of the Report in India were not indicative of "the measure of harmony" its authors have envisaged as having been achieved in the course of a long period of deliberations over India's constitutional problems.

Indians who were able to take a realistic view of the situation, however, knew that their failure to reconcile their own differences was largely responsible for the character of the Report. In a mood of pessimism they declared that, condemn the Constitution based on the recommendations of the Report as much as they might, there was no alternative for them. "It will work us," wrote Sir Tej Bahadur Sapru, "if we are not prepared to work it." He might have added the remark of the great American Negro leader, Booker T. Washington, that "there is all the difference in the world between working and being worked."

¶ THE BILL

The Bill, based on the recommendations of the majority of the Joint Select Committee, was published on 22 January, 1935. It runs to 451 clauses with 15 schedules, the biggest and the most complicated Bill ever introduced in Parliament.[1]

[1] Mr. Winston Churchill found the Bill voluminous but not luminous. He described it as "a gigantic quilt of jumbled crochet work. There is no theme; there is no pattern; there is no agreement; there is no conviction; there is no simplicity; there is no courage. It is a monstrous monument of shame built by the pygmies."—(Broadcast speech on India, January 29, 1935.)

Two features of the Bill should be noted here: (1) the absence of a Preamble and (2) the proposal to prescribe the new Indian franchise after the passage of the Bill by Orders in Council subject to the approval of both the Houses of Parliament. The Bill repeals the Government of India Act of 1919, but its Preamble over the interpretation of which there has been so much controversy will continue to be regarded as a definition of British policy in India. Let us remind ourselves that the words used in this Preamble were "the gradual establishment of self-governing institutions" in British India. Since they do not imply the eventual establishment of an equation of Status between British India and the Dominions, Indian politicians urged the necessity of a Preamble incorporating Lord Irwin's (now Lord Halifax) pledge that the natural issue of Indian constitutional development is Dominion Status. In introducing the Bill, the Secretary of State for India made a statement to this effect, but Sir John Wardlaw Milne, a member of the Joint Select Committee, made it plain in the course of a debate in the House of Commons that "no pledge given by any Secretary of State or any Viceroy has any real legal bearing on the matter at all. The only thing that Parliament is really bound by is the Act of 1919." Such a pronouncement may be regarded as a good dialectical point in constitutional polemics, but it is not likely to succeed in reconciling political elements in India to the new Constitution. Sir Samuel Hoare's reaffirmation of Dominion Status as the goal of India did not remove the apprehensions of Indian politicians in regard to the Imperial Government's attitude towards Lord Irwin's pledge, and they demanded its inclusion in due form in the Bill.

As regards the franchise, the Government declared their intention to adopt the scheme recommended by the Joint Select Committee, but it did not make any substantial modifications of the franchise proposals in the White Paper except in the case of rural franchise in Bihar and Orissa, and of women's franchise in respect of certain qualifications (*e.g.* the application requirement) stipulated in the White Paper. Since, in working out details of franchise, it might be necessary to make certain changes in accordance with the circumstances of each Province, the matter was not dealt with in the Bill.

The Act departs from the recommendations of the Joint Select Committee in respect of the Judicature. The Act provides that the proposed Federal Court should entertain appeals relating only to the interpretation of the Constitution Act, and not to that of Acts passed by the Federal Legislature. The intricacies of an Act dealing with extremely complicated problems would undoubtedly require the entire resources of a Federal Court; but the refusal "to accord to the Federal Court the decision of the effect of Federal laws" is regarded as a serious defect in the Act.[1]

Perhaps the most important section [2] in the Act is that containing the provisions for the establishment of Federation and the accession of Indian States. One of the distinguishing characteristics of Federal polity is the distribution of powers and functions between the Federal Government and the federating units. It was therefore necessary that the Bill should contain provisions under which the Princes can accede to Federation; but the Princes were not satisfied with the unilateral basis of procedure for their accession and raised objections to Clause 6 of the Bill. They feared that the Federal Government would use their powers to encroach upon their rights and privileges as Rulers of the Federating States and were concerned with the question of paramountcy, which was obviously outside the scope of the Bill. I shall presently refer to the views of the States as expressed at a Conference of Indian Princes and their advisers. It should be noted here that the basis of accession has to be more or less uniform, although it is necessary to offer opportunities to the Princes for acceding upon varying terms, and that basis has to be stipulated in the Act. We need not pause

[1] See Dr. A. B. Keith's letter to the *Scotsman*, January 25, 1935.
[2] Clauses 5 and 6, Chapter I, Part II.

here to consider some of the constitutional difficulties involved in the procedure for the entry of the Princes into Federation, but the nature of the complications may be realized to cite only one example, from the fact that the Constitution Act as such will not be binding upon the Indian States and that the entry of the Princes into the Federation will entirely depend upon their own free will.

At a Conference the Princes adopted a resolution that the Bill and Instrument of Accession were unacceptable to them unless "those vital interests and fundamental requisites of the States on which they had throughout laid great emphasis" were satisfactorily secured. The specific points in the Bill to which the Princes drew the attention of the Government are reported in *The Times*[1] as follows:

> "The form and mode of accession to the Federation; the lack of specific mention and preservation of treaties and agreements concluded with the States; the extent of the executive authority of the Federation in regard to the States; the special responsibilities of the Governor-General *vis-a-vis* the States; provisions consequent upon the possible suspension of the Constitution; the enforcement of Federal laws and the powers vested in the Governor-General to give directions to the rulers of States; the treatment of privileges and immunities in Clauses[2] 145 and 147 of the Bill, and some of the basic provisions of the Bill relating to the finance of the railways."

As the accession of one-half of the Indian States on the basis of population was an essential and integral part of the framework for the All-India Federation,[3] His Majesty's

[1] *The Times*, February 26, 1935.

[2] These clauses deal respectively with cash contributions and ceded territories, and with the value of privileges and immunities as a set off against payments to the Federated States by the Federation.

[3] Dr. A. B. Keith is severe upon Sir Samuel Hoare for insisting that the accession of the Indian Princes is so essential to the working of Indian Reform. He apprehends that the Government will be compelled to make unwise surrenders to them. "But," asks Sir John Marriott, "may not Sir Samuel Hoare possess more of the wisdom of the political serpent than

Government lost no time in assuring the Princes that most of the questions raised by them might be adjusted in course of further consultations with the Government and the legal representatives of the Princes. Some of these points were dealt with by amendments moved by the Government on the Report stage and others by elucidation of such ambiguity as might have crept into the draft Bill.

We shall now follow the course of so complex and controversial a measure in its passage through Parliament.

ℂ AMENDMENTS IN PARLIAMENT

In December 1934 the Government moved a general Resolution in both Houses of Parliament asking authorization for submitting a Bill on the lines indicated in the majority recommendations of the Select Committee. After three days' debate in the House of Commons, and four days' debate in the House of Lords, the resolution was carried by a substantial majority. It was a decisive triumph for the Government, which enabled them to pilot an acutely controversial Bill through Parliament with greater confidence of success.

Although the main principles which underlie the measure stood the test of severe criticism, Parliament made a number of important amendments, adding some twenty-seven new Clauses to the Bill. As the Bill had no Preamble, the Government moved an amendment on the Committee stage to retain the Preamble of the Act of 1919. "To leave the Preamble on the Statute Book after the Act had been repealed," remarked Mr. Hugh Molson, M.P., "appeared to many of us to be like preserving the smile of the Cheshire cat after the Cheshire cat had disappeared."[1] But the inevitability of this arrangement was explained by the Government. They found constitutional difficulty

Dr. Keith appears to suspect ?" See "Imperial Relations, Indian Reform, Constitutional and International Law, 1916–35," by A. B. Keith. Oxford University Press: 1935.

[1] See Proceedings of the East India Association, June 26, 1935.

in drafting a Preamble using the phrase "Dominion Status," and tried to appease Indians by accepting the interpretation given by Lord Irwin (then the Viceroy) in 1929. The character of that declaration and the controversy thereon have been referred to in Chapter III.

The first series of amendments relate to the accession of the Indian States to Federation. By amending Clause 6 it was made clear that a ruler accedes to the Federation by virtue of his Instrument of Accession and not of the Act. It is important to bear in mind that the relation of the States is with the Crown, and that no Acts passed by the British Parliament have validity within the borders of the Princes' territories. The Instrument of Accession will therefore stipulate the extent to which the Federal authorities will exercise legislative and executive power in a State. Since the Princes have again raised the question of paramountcy, it was explained that it is a matter which does not arise in connection with the Bill and the Princes should not expect to secure any concessions in regard to paramountcy as the *quid pro quo* for their entry into the Federation. The Act does not in any way derogate from the paramountcy of the Crown. What it does is that all powers relating to the States are reverted to the Crown, and can no longer be exercised on behalf of His Majesty by the Governor-General in Council. The rights of the Paramount Power should in future be exercised by the representative of the Crown in his capacity as Viceroy.

The situation that might arise on the breakdown of the Constitution was another matter that concerned the Princes, and the relevant clauses were amended with a view to bringing the period of the Viceroy's dictatorial powers under closer Parliamentary control. Approval of Parliament for the beginning and the extension, if necessary, of the period when the Viceroy will be required to assume the legislative powers, in the event of the suspension of the Constitution, will be necessary, and the entire period is to be limited to three years.

The second series of amendments provided further particulars in strengthening safeguarding clauses. The protection of the rights of pensioners was included in the category of the special responsibilities of the Governor-General and the Governors. The opponents to the Bill had raised an alarm in regard to the security of pensions due to retired servants of the Crown and their dependents. It was therefore necessary to provide a "chain of responsibility" for the full and punctual payment of pensions.[1] The Secretary of State will undertake the entire responsibility for the issue of pensions payable outside India, and the Federal Government shall be under statutory obligation to enable the Secretary of State to discharge his liability.

Any alteration in the existing arrangements for the recruitment by the Secretary of State to the Indian Civil Service and the Indian Police will require an Amending Act instead of an Order in Council. A new clause was inserted in order to preserve and extend the protection that public servants enjoy against criminal prosecutions and civil suits. The question of promotion and postings of officers appointed by the Secretary of State will be decided by the Governor-General or Governor exercising an individual judgment; and finally, half the members of a Public Service Commission must be persons who have served for ten years under the Crown in India. So much for safeguards of Services.

Various amendments found their place in the Statute dealing with the restriction of racial and other discriminations. The Bill itself provides a full and complete set of clauses prohibiting discriminatory legislations, especially in the sphere of trade and commerce. But it was thought expedient to provide statutory limitations against discriminatory taxation and measures affecting the professions of alien residents in India.

The third series of amendments deal with the structure of the Legislatures. An amendment in the House of

[1] The total charge under pensions is only 4 per cent. of the Indian revenues.

Commons adds an Upper Chamber to the Assam Legislature; but the House of Lords made a substantial change in the election of the Federal Upper Chamber, to be known as the Council of State. It is to be elected on high franchise qualifications by voters in territorial communal constituencies, similar to those which existed under the old Constitution. The amendment substitutes direct in place of indirect election. Six seats are allotted for the Scheduled castes. The representatives of the Anglo-Indian, European and Indian Christian communities are to be chosen by indirect election from electoral colleges.

As the official *bloc* will disappear from the Legislatures, an amendment provides that the Advocate-General of the Federation and of the Provinces shall have a seat in either Chamber of the Legislature, so that he may be in a position to explain, if necessary, the point of view of the Governor-General and Governors to the Legislature.

In regard to the franchise, particulars of the qualifications for the Provincial Lower Houses are set out in a new schedule. The final and complete scheme of delimitation for constituencies, territorial or special, will be framed after a special committee [1] has submitted its report. By an amendment in the House of Commons, the enfranchisement of retired, pensioned or discharged officers, non-commissioned officers and soldiers of H.M.'s regular military forces is extended to retired officers and men of the Indian Police Force. The proportion of women to men on the

[1] The Indian Delimitation Committee is set up by the Government under the chairmanship of Sir E. L. L. Hammond, formerly Governor of Assam. The terms of reference to the Committee may be summed up as follows: To make recommendations for the delimitation of the constituencies in the Indian Central and Provincial Legislatures under the new Constitution, to make proposals for the nature and location of the constituencies to be established for the return of representatives of certain special interests, *e.g.* women, commerce, industry, mining, planting, labour, landholders, universities and the Scheduled castes, and in the case of seats to represent special interests, to make proposals regarding the qualifications of voters, conduct of elections and the qualifications necessary for candidate where specific provision covering such matters has not been made in the Act and its schedules.

electoral rolls has been raised by amending certain provisions in the Bill in regard to qualifications. Six seats in the Federal Upper Chamber were reserved for women. A new Clause to the effect that "a person shall not be disqualified by sex from being appointed to any civil post under the Crown in India," subject to exceptions which might be prescribed by the Secretary of State, the Governor-General, or the Governor, was inserted in the Bill.

Several amendments were moved in order to simplify, as far as possible, the intricate position of the Judicature under the new Constitution. One important amendment provides that appeal to the Privy Council is to lie as of right in "constitutional cases."

After devoting as many as 61 Parliamentary days to the consideration of the Bill, it obtained a third reading in the House of Lords on July 24 and was passed "amid a congratulatory murmur."

¶ THE ROYAL ASSENT

The Government of India Bill received the Royal Assent on August 2, 1935, and became an Act.[1] From a continuous account of the various stages through which the proposals embodied in the Act emerged, and a survey of facts on which the constitutional edifice is built, such as I have attempted in these pages, the reader is now familiar with the complex character of this "Constitution for a Continent." It should be noted that in the process of the making of Federal India, Indian affairs are brought in closer contact with the British Parliament. The Council of the Secretary of State is abolished, but he may appoint not fewer than three or more than six advisers. For all practical purposes the position of the Secretary of State for India will remain as it is to-day; but the adoption of the Order in Council procedure will be helpful in keeping both the Houses of Parliament informed

[1] 25 and 26 Geo. V, c. 42.

about certain important aspects of the Indian Constitution. These orders, as well as all amendments thereto, will have to be approved by both Houses. Not only are they a valuable means of introducing flexibility into the written Constitution, but the procedure for their approval and amendment, similar as it is to the procedure for the approval and amendment of the Instruments of Instructions, will ensure that through Parliament a contact is maintained between the British and Indian democracies which cannot but be beneficial to both.

Immediate Federation will not result from the Act, for it is made conditional upon the fulfilment of certain essential pre-requisites. Let us remind ourselves of what those conditions are. The existing intricate relationships between British India and the States will have to be readjusted; the Provinces of British India will have acquired internal sovereignty by starting them on the road to autonomy; and the budgetary position of the Central and Provincial Governments will have sufficiently improved. If and when one-half of the Indian States, on the basis of population, should agree to accede to Federation, and the individual ruler will have signed the Instrument of Accession,[1] the *first* important step towards Federation will be taken. Both Houses of Parliament will then be required to present an Address to His Majesty praying that a Federation may be brought into existence. In the next chapter we will see what means and methods are being adopted by the Government in order to facilitate the setting up of a Federation within a reasonable time. It should be noted here that the Act contains transitional provisions for bringing into existence the Federal Court, the Federal Public Service Commission, and the Federal Railway Authority. Provincial autonomy is to be established by Order in Council and will come in force "on such date as His Majesty in Council may appoint."

In commenting upon the Report of the Select Com-

[1] Under the Act the Crown may reject any Instrument of Accession if its terms are inconsistent with the scheme of Federation.

mittee, an important Conservative journal [1] remarked that "India requires an executive system comparable in power with the ruling vigour of the dictatorships, though shielding the growth and encouraging the exercise of ordered freedom." That requirement has been amply fulfilled in the Act by providing the Governor-General and Governors not only with the whole executive power in their respective realm, but also in the legislative sphere. These safeguards, we have seen, take various forms, such as statutory prohibitions, special responsibilities and personal discretion, and so on. Apart from the criticism that some of these safeguards are indefensible because they compromise the principle of responsible government, critics of the Constitution consider that they place on the Governor-General an extremely difficult task. Should he be obliged, for instance, to exercise his special responsibility to prevent the imposition of penal tariffs on British imports against the decision of his Ministers and Federal Legislatures, it may furnish the Opposition with an opportunity for boycott propaganda. Again, the terms under which Law and Order are transferred to Legislatures may prove not only ineffective in day-to-day administration, but may become a constant source of irritation to them. The fundamental safeguard for the working of the Constitution is to avoid crises.

The form of Constitution embodied in the Act is unique and in many respects illogical in theory. It is regarded as "a typical British compromise." [2] While its basic concept —Federation—is not new to India, the actual framing of a Constitution based upon the Federal idea has given India a new basis of political thought and development.

ℭ AN ALL-INDIA FEDERATION

The idea of framing a Constitution for India on a Federal basis occurred to John Bright when the Bill transferring

[1] *The Observer*, Nov. 25, 1934.

[2] Sir George Schuster, formerly Finance member to the Government of India.

the Government of India to the Crown was before Parliament. From time to time proposals were made with a view to converting the provincial administrations into "a sort of Federation of States, invested with equal authority, and subordinate only to the Secretary of State in England." The grounds on which a scheme of a Federation of Provinces was condemned as unworkable were summed up by the Government of India in a despatch [1] to the Secretary of State in 1880. The following quotation from that document may now be of interest to the reader:

> ". . . The army, the railways, the custom duties, the opium, the salt revenue, the post office, the relations with foreign states, whether feudatory or beyond the confines of India, must always be directed by some central authority. The management of these branches of public affairs cannot be parcelled out among the several governments. The financial arrangements of India must also be directed by some central authority; for some provinces are rich, and yield a large surplus, while others are poor, and cannot pay their way. Funds for carrying on the government of the poorer provinces, for the army, for the payment of interest of the public debt, for meeting the home charges, must be found from a common purse for all India, and the necessary control in such matters cannot be exercised from an office in London."

At all events, in the designs of constitutional experiments introduced in various stages one cannot trace the working of "the glowing vision of All-India Federation." There is, for instance, no logical sequence between Dyarchy and an All-India Federation.

But those who were able to perceive the growing sense of nationality among the divergent peoples of a sub-Continent like India envisaged it as an *ultimate* institutional expression of her political life. At the beginning of the present century a distinguished British-Indian official, Sir Henry Cotton, as president of the Indian National Congress, set forth the ideal of "the United States of India,

[1] No. 38 of 1880, June 8, sec. 7.

each with its own local autonomy, cemented together under the aegis of Great Britain." I have already alluded to the attitude of the Indian Nationalist of the early part of this century towards the Federal concept. Some of the Princes, notably the present Maharajas of Bikaner and Baroda, envisaged even as early as 1914 that through an appropriate Federal machinery the interests of the States could be safeguarded consistently with the interests of British India and the Empire. After the War, when the Reform schemes for India were being discussed, many individuals, including some of the Indian Princes, suggested that a Federation of the Provinces and States was the only method by which any real transfer of responsibility could be made. In 1917, at a Conference of Princes and Ministers in the State of Bikaner, a scheme for a Federal form of government was put forward. The idea was very much canvassed in the political circles both in British India and the States during the late Mr. Montagu's visit to India. At a speech delivered on the occasion of a visit of the Viceroy in his State in March 1922, His Highness the Maharaja of Alwar declared:

> "My goal is the United States of India, where every Province and every State, working out its own destiny in accordance with its own environment, its own tradition, history and religion, will combine together for Imperial purposes, each subscribing its little quota of knowledge and experience in a labour of love, freely given for a higher and a noble cause."

But the adoption of a Federal Constitution for India was then scarcely practicable and the ideal remained of academic interest only. Meanwhile the forces of nationalism were gathering strength and, in the face of a growing challenge to the system of government, it became increasingly apparent that its intricate mechanisms would have to be adjusted to new demands. Even among the votaries of Bureaucracy the needs for the reorganization of the system were frankly recognized. "The existing system of government," said a distinguished British official in India, "both in what it has done and what it has not done, has exhausted or completed its potentialities." [1]

And yet the task involved in the transformation of a unitary Government of India into a Federal form of Government is beset with immense difficulties and complications. Even under comparatively favourable circumstances in other parts of the British Commonwealth, Federation has not been working smoothly. Recently a Canadian author [2] observed that a Federal form of Government "is a clumsy device, because it divides authority, decentralizes administration, and from the point of view of getting things done rapidly and effectively, is much less desirable than a unitary system."

The task of decentralization without the risk of undermining the efficiency of administration is difficult. The British North America Act aimed at a form of Government which would actually be a strong centralized Government, but in actual practice the Provinces grew in strength and many matters of national importance came within the competence of the Provinces. The amendment of that Act is now one of the important questions in Canadian politics.

The working of the Australian Constitution shows that all the seven federating units have developed tendencies which are not conducive to good government:

> "The apparatus of Government mechanism," writes a distinguished Australian jurist,[3] "set up by the present constitutional system cannot be relied on, even in cases of capital importance, to do its work cleanly and without a hitch."

But the sponsors of a Federal form of Government for India are fully aware of the difficulties inherent in a political

[1] Speech by Sir James Crerar, Caxton Hall, April 17, 1934.

[2] Professor Norman Mackenzie, University of Toronto. See "Canadian Problems." Oxford University Press: 1933.

[3] See "The Failure of Federalism in Australia," by A. P. Canaway. Oxford University Press: 1930.

system which must of necessity embrace so many divergent units. They realize that no political artistry can smooth over the difficulties involved in readjusting an intricate relationship between the Indian States and British India, and that the conditions out of which the Federal form has to be evolved do not at present exist either in the Provinces or in the States. They know that the constitutional reforms would defeat their very purpose if in the place of a sure foundation for Federation, there should be a form of Central Government which is neither unitary nor truly Federal.

And yet it became evident in the process of investigations lasting over eight years that an All-India Federation alone would offer a wide enough opportunity for putting Indian polity on a stable foundation. It would bring about integration of economic life and make way for lasting unity among the diverse races and interests. One should regard Federation not just as a political contrivance for the division of powers, but as a means of achieving a synthesis in the polity of a country with so many different communities, races and cultures. True, there is no historical precedent for the type of Federation as provided in the Act, but that cannot be an argument against its adoption in Indian conditions. After all, there is no such thing as a pure type of the Federal State.

The question that agitates political India is whether the proposals would eventually tend to political devolution to the extent conceded in the Dominions or not; in other words, will Federation lead India to the goal of Dominion Status?

¶ DOMINION STATUS

Almost all political opinion in India desires a Status in the British Commonwealth as an equal partner like the self-governing Dominions; and the goal of Dominion Status has been recognized in the various declarations and statements since the introduction of the Reforms of 1921.

In the Instrument of Instructions to the Viceroy, issued in that year, the King-Emperor stated as follows :

> " It is our Royal Will and Pleasure that the plans made by Our Parliament for the progressive realization of responsible government as an integral part of Our Empire may come to fruition, to the end that British India may attain its due place among Our Dominions."

In the message addressed to the Indian Legislatures on the occasion of their inauguration, His Majesty declared :

> " For years, it may be for generations, patriotic and loyal Indians have dreamed of Swaraj for their Motherland. To-day you have the beginnings of Swaraj within my Empire, and widest scope and ample opportunity for progress to the liberty which my other Dominions enjoy."

But the phrase " Dominion Status " does not occur in the Preamble, as we have seen, of the Act of 1919. There the promise held out was the responsible government in British India, and consequently the interpretations of these two phrases led to bitter controversy between the spokesmen of the Imperial Government and the Indian political classes. It is argued that the terms of the Preamble do not imply a status greater than what is possessed by the lesser self-governing colonies. In a debate in the Legislative Assembly (1924), Sir Malcolm Hailey, then Home Member to the Government of India, observed :

> " If you analyse the term ' full Dominion Self-Government ' you will see that it is to some extent conveying that not only will the Executive be responsible to the Legislature but the Legislature will, in itself, have the full powers, which are typical of the modern Dominion. I say that there is some difference of substance, because Responsible Government is not necessarily incompatible with a Legislature with limited or restricted powers. It may be that full Dominion Self-Government is the logical outcome of Responsible Government ; nay, it may be the inevitable and historical development of Responsible Government, but it is a further and final step."

The critics of Sir Malcolm Hailey's *obiter dicta* assert that the distinction between Dominion Status and Responsible Government is untenable. Dr. Arthur B. Keith states the case in the following terms :

> " It is forgotten," he says, " that on no occasion had any attempt been made, up to 1917, to discriminate between Dominion Status and Responsible Government. The term Dominion Status was not in current use at that time, and what was promised was a definite system existing in the Empire, whose character was well known as exemplified in the position towards the United Kingdom of the Dominions. . . . It was impossible for the British Government of 1917 to foresee the remarkable development of formal autonomy in external affairs of the Dominions, as a result of the creation of the League of Nations and the grant to the Dominions of distinct membership to that body. But that it never entered the head of the Government responsible for the promise of 1917 to seek to limit India to the measure of authority of the Dominions in 1917 is sufficiently proved by the demand of the Government in 1919 that India should be accorded the full position of a Dominion as a member of the League of Nations." [1]

Whatever may be the subtle distinction between Dominion Status and Dominion Constitution, it should be borne in mind that India now enjoys some of the privileges incidental upon the attainment of Dominion Status. That status is not " ceremonial," as suggested by the Rt. Hon. Winston Churchill in his evidence before the Joint Select Committee. India is represented at all the International and inter-Imperial Conferences as a member of the British Commonwealth ; she was one of the signatories to the Peace Treaties ; her representatives took part in the Imperial War Conferences and attended the five-Power Naval Conference ; she has a seat on the Governing Body of the International Labour Office ; like any other self-governing Dominion, she

[1] See " India Analysed," Vol. I. Gollancz : 1933.

appoints a High Commissioner in London ;[1] and there has grown a Fiscal Autonomy Convention in India somewhat on the analogy of the Dominions. All these achievements conform to the ideal implied in Dominion Status.

But, ever since the controversy raised over Lord Irwin's (now Lord Halifax) declaration that "the natural issue of India's constitutional progress is the attainment of Dominion Status," the Imperial Government in their subsequent conferences and committees have taken care not to use the expression in relation to India's political goal. The suspicion of Indian politicians as regards the intentions of the Imperial Government was roused by this ill-timed controversy, and now the omission of mention of Dominion Status from the Government of India Act of 1935 is regarded by political India as a deliberate equivocation of the pledge given to her in the past. Almost every section of Indian political groups has, as already stated, signified its disapprobation of the Act because of this deliberate avoidance of the expression, "Dominion Status," either in a Preamble of the Act or in its body.

Those who are apprehensive of allowing India to attain that status, point out that the implications of the phrase have undergone a fundamental change by the Statute of Westminster (22 Geo. V, c. 4) in 1931, and that India cannot be given the status which carries with it the right of secession. Therefore the Statute of Westminster has no application to India. We need not enter here into a discussion on the true doctrine of the Imperial relation as expressed in the Preamble to that Statute. But to those who are opposed to India's aspiration to attain Dominion Status, I would say, is it not the inevitable corollary of India's allegiance to a common Sovereign ? What greater mission is there before the British Nation than the elevation of the status

[1] In pursuance of the Act of 1919, a High Commissioner for India resident in London was appointed by the Government of India in 1920, charged with functions similar to those of the High Commissioners for the Dominions.

of India from that of a dependency to a free member of the British Commonwealth? The British Commonwealth numbers some 450 million inhabitants, but 353 millions of these belong to India. Can one envisage the development of this concept of the British Commonwealth of Nations without associating India as an integral part of that system? "What does membership of the British Commonwealth mean to India, to the Commonwealth as a whole, and to the world?" asks Professor Alfred Zimmern.[1] I would ask the reader to ponder over the following reply Professor Zimmern gives to his question. He says:

> "India is the pivot of world politics in the coming generations. To put it more specifically, if India preserves her association with the British Commonwealth, and the Commonwealth, on its side, gives India the place in its system and in its counsels which is due to her, the prospects for world peace and general human progress will be immeasurably increased. If, on the other hand, the effort to establish an equal partnership between India and the other British Dominions should break down, the consequences would recoil, not simply on the parties immediately concerned, but on the whole human family. The stage would be set for an inter-racial conflict of incalculable dimensions."[2]

The controversy over the phrase "Dominion Status" has widened the chasm between India and Great Britain. It may conjure up incidents leading to mutual recrimination and may deepen India's suspicion in regard to the intention of the Imperial Government to fulfil the promise of granting Dominion Status to India. The declaration in definite terms in a Preamble to the Act that the objective aimed at by the new Constitution is to grant Dominion Status to India would have certainly produced a congenial atmosphere for establishing trust and goodwill in the relations between India and Great Britain. It is difficult to persuade Indians that Dominion Status is not susceptible of definition in a

[1] Burton Professor of International Relations, Oxford.

[2] See "India Analysed," Vol. I. Gollancz: 1933.

15

precise constitutional document. "It is misleading to say," writes Dr. Keith, "that the Statute of Westminster did not mention, and did not define Dominion Status. In fact, it alludes in the Preamble to the declaration of that status, and recites that it was enacted to ratify, confirm, and establish *inter alia* the declaration."[1] Those who persistently oppose the very idea of Dominion Status for India believe that such a measure would mean abdication of Imperial authority; they enumerate difficulties that would arise in putting this ideal into practice under conditions obtaining in India; they fear that with the rise of nationalism India will secede from the Commonwealth; and they point to difficulties which have arisen in regard to the constitutional significance of Dominion Status since the passing of the Statute of Westminster. The effective answer to these doubts and apprehensions comes from Lord Halifax, who said:

> "Let us by all means, according to the angle of our minds, have our fears; but for heaven's sake do not let them be such as to strangle our faith; because no great Imperial achievement has been done by this country except by faith."

[1] See his letter to *The Scotsman*, February 12, 1935.

CHAPTER VII

PREPARING THE GROUND

Reserve Bank and other Financial Adjustments : The Ottawa Agreements : India and Lancashire—(a) *Japanese Competition ;* (b) *The Surplus Indian Cotton ;* (c) *Indian Tariff Barriers : Statutory Railway Board : The Indian Sandhurst and Military Expenditure : Negotiations with the Indian States : Government and the Indian National Congress*

IN February 1933, His Excellency Lord Willingdon, in opening the Winter session of the Legislative Assembly, observed that he and the Government of India were "striving with absolute sincerity to advance as rapidly as possible to constitutional reforms." Two main problems were then before the Government—one to prepare a favourable economic background before the inauguration of the new Constitution ; the other to prevent recrudescence of the Civil Disobedience Movement pursued by the Congress. The methods by which the Government proceeded to deal with these problems came to be known as the "dual policy"; that is, the enforcement of Law and Order on the one hand and constitutional advance on the other. We shall briefly survey in this chapter what definite steps were taken to prepare the country for the working of the new Constitution.

RESERVE BANK AND OTHER FINANCIAL ADJUSTMENTS

At the conclusion of the third Round Table Conference the Secretary of State gave an assurance that His Majesty's

Government would do everything within their power to facilitate an early introduction of Federation. The first step in that direction was to make the financial foundations of the Government of India sound.

Owing to the heavy fall in India's exports, her balance of trade had to be maintained by gold shipments, which have now [1] reached a total of about £191 millions since Britain abandoned the Gold Standard in September 1931. These shipments "enabled the international balance to be maintained, relieved distress among the cultivators, and released a certain amount of purchasing power which was expended in low-priced imported goods, mainly of Japanese origin," wrote Sir Thomas Ainscough, senior Trade Commissioner of His Majesty's Government. But the exports of gold from India helped towards the maintenance of sterling values and of India's credit in the London money market.

The outstanding financial measure adopted by the Government of India was the conversion of a large volume of the short-term debt into long-term securities. Within a year or so, about 94 crores of Treasury Bills and Rupee loans were converted into long-term securities. The amount of Treasury Bills now outstanding, including Treasury Bills held in the Issue Department of the Reserve Bank, is about 35 crores.

The reduction of short-term debt, the strengthening of currency reserves and the maintenance of the balance of trade in the midst of the world economic depression, raised Government credit and reduced India's sterling borrowing rate from 5½ per cent. to a little over 3 per cent. The 3½ per cent. sterling stock, quoted as low as 42 in September 1931, has now risen to about 92.

Taking advantage of the substantial improvement in India's credit in the financial markets, the Government of India, since June 1932, have raised three sterling loans in

[1] August 1935.

London aggregating £32 millions, and rupee loans in India aggregating 174¾ crores or £131 millions. The first sterling loan bore interest at 4 per cent., the second at 3½ per cent., and the third at 3 per cent., thus showing the progressive improvement of India's credit on the London market.

It must also be mentioned that there has been a substantial reduction in expenditure. The Defence Estimates have come down from the contract figure of about 55 crores in 1929–30 to Rs. 45 crores in 1935–36. The total net expenditure of the Government of India has also been reduced from Rs. 91 crores in 1929–30 to Rs. 77¼ crores in 1935–36.

Reviewing the financial policy, Sir George Schuster observed that

> "sound principles of finance were the best in the interests of India, not only at present but with an eye to the future and the proposals for a new Constitution. It would have been a poor service to India if they shirked their troubles and left an accumulated weight to burden the new Constitution."

All this is to the good. But how long can India continue to maintain her balance of trade by exports of gold and silver? Her annual oversea commitments total about 42 crores (approximately £31,500,000) but in 1934–35 the balance of trade in merchandise only amounted to 23 crores (approximately £17,250,000). In other words, India is at present unable to meet even her annual oversea obligations through her trade in merchandise. From the point of view of India's economic future it is no comfort to be assured that the outflow of gold since 1931 is not "distress" gold, and that her total holdings of treasure are still so vast that for many years to come she will be able to maintain her trade balance with the help of these assets.

Let us now turn to the efforts for the establishment of a Reserve Bank in India. About seven years ago the Government of India introduced into the Assembly a Bill entitled "The Gold Standard and Reserve Bank of India Bill." The Assembly took up a hostile attitude towards this measure, mainly through scepticism in regard to the Gold Bullion Standard. When the Bill emerged from the Select Committee it had undergone fundamental changes to which the Government could not agree. The Indian Nationalists did not think that it was necessary to create a shareholders' bank and they sought to make the proposed bank responsible to the Legislature. Since no compromise could be effected on the changes demanded by the Indian members of the Committee, the Government withdrew the Bill. It was then decided to institute an exhaustive enquiry into the banking system of the country.

One of the conditions precedent to the inauguration of Federation in India, as stated in the previous chapter, is the establishment of a Reserve Bank. Therefore a Bill to set up a Central Reserve Bank was introduced by the Finance Member on September 1933. In the Preamble to the Bill it is stated that the object of the bank is to "ensure confidence in the management of India's credit and currency" and to "secure monetary stability in India." The Bill was passed in February 1934. The Reserve Bank took over the Government account in April 1935, and before the end of the financial year it should be able to assume its statutory functions in relation to scheduled banks.

The bank is not to encroach on legitimate commercial banking interests. It is to be a shareholders' bank and not a State bank and its management will be free as far as possible from political influence. The total capital is to be 5 crores. One important feature is the inclusion in its organization of a special department for the improvement of agricultural credit facilities.

One of the controversial questions that came up for debate on the Reserve Bank Bill in the Legislative Assembly was the Rupee Ratio. When, on the recommendation of the Hilton Young Currency Commission (1925–26), the

Government of India decided to stabilize the rupee at the then *de facto* rate of 1s. 6d., it was not possible to foresee the present catastrophic fall in gold prices. Although the rupee is still 1s. 6d. in terms of sterling, its value in terms of gold or gold currencies is, in round figures, well under 1s.

But the Finance Member pointed out that the ratio question did not arise on the Bill; as a compromise, however, the following words were inserted in the Preamble:

> "Whereas it is expedient to make temporary provision on the basis of the existing monetary system and to leave the question of the monetary standard best suited to India to be considered when the international monetary position has become sufficiently clear and stable to make it possible to frame permanent measures."

In view of the existing disorganized condition of world currencies, this was a wise decision. When an attempt to stabilize the exchanges takes concrete shape in the principal industrial countries, the authorities of the Reserve Bank will undoubtedly consider the matter of fixing the value of the rupee in terms of gold. For the moment, it is safe for India to hold on to sterling and the present ratio. The question of balanced exchange, however, cannot be left indefinitely to world recovery. "Recent events have reinforced the obvious truth," writes Professor T. E. Gregory, "that there is a limit to the extent to which continual recovery is possible, without new stimuli being applied."[1] The steps towards *de facto* stabilization of exchange, bilateral trade agreements with some of the countries (*e.g.* Germany, Italy) outside the British Empire where trade restrictions prevail, and the re-establishment of silver coinage are regarded as some of the effective means of trade restoration in India. Meanwhile, amid conflicting post-war economic tendencies which resulted in chaos in world-wide trade relationships, it became imperative for the countries within the British Empire to formulate a policy for

[1] See *Independent*, February 9, 1935.

facilitating economic intercourse within its own jurisdiction. We shall now see what plans have been thought out and methods of execution devised for adjusting inter-Imperial trade, bearing in mind the paramount importance of safeguarding India's external market.

¶ THE OTTAWA AGREEMENTS

The Great War shook the entire fabric of Empire trade. Measures, such as the McKenna Duties (5, 6 Geo. V, ch. 89, 1918) and the Safeguarding of Industries Act (11, 12 Geo. V, ch. 47, 1921), were not wholly successful in rehabilitating the industries and trade of Great Britain ; and subsequently it became necessary for her to abandon the Gold Standard in order to maintain her economic position.

But the trade depression continued, industries showed no great sign of revival, and unemployment figures rose to the point of danger. It was then decided to convene the Imperial Conference at Ottawa, a suggestion which the Dominions welcomed as an opportunity for stimulating inter-Imperial trade. The principle of Imperial Preference was recognized in the Colonial Conference of 1902 and in the Imperial War Conference in 1917. India was not represented in the Colonial Conference ; and while, after the Imperial War Conference, mutual preferential tariff rates to a very limited extent were introduced in the trade relations of Great Britain with certain Dominions, India stood aloof from any such negotiation. The question of applying the principle of Imperial Preference to India was first elaborately examined by Lord Curzon's Government in 1903, and they came to the conclusion that "as regards India, the balance of advantage is distinctly adverse." Leaders of public opinion were in agreement with this view, and the matter did not receive much attention until after the War. In 1920 the Fiscal Commission was appointed to examine the Indian Tariff policy, and following the introduction of the Montagu-Chelmsford Reforms, the

Imperial Government recognized the principle of fiscal autonomy for India.

The Majority Report of the Commission supported the principle of Imperial Preference with certain reservations. The exigencies of the devastating economic depression of the post-war period brought to the front the question of adopting Imperial Preference as an integral part of an organized plan for the development of Empire trade, and it was with the object of formulating such a plan that the Conference at Ottawa was held. Empire trade could no longer be left to a policy of *laissez-faire;* the situation demanded a determined effort to explore all the avenues of Imperial economic co-operation and "to clear out the channels of trade."

Two main problems faced the Indian delegation at the Conference, namely, (1) the principal source of Central revenues being the Customs, the adoption of a general scheme of tariff preferences within the Empire might make the position of the Central Budget difficult;[1] and (2) India's trade with non-Empire countries, which is of considerable importance, might be adversely affected.

However, the changes in the fiscal policy of the United Kingdom created "an entirely new situation for India." The Indian delegates put the case clearly when they stated in their Report that

> "it was no longer a question of what India stood to gain from the adoption of a general scheme of trade preferences throughout the Empire. . . . The issue so long debated, whether there should be a general scheme of trade preference within the Empire, was now settled, and the question which those responsible for India's fiscal interests had to face was whether India was justified in maintaining her former attitude of aloofness, whether in fact she could afford to stand out of an agreement which seemed likely to include

[1] The preferences have been granted by reducing the duties on British goods and increasing those on non-British goods; consequently the effect on Customs revenue is negligible.

> most, if not all, Empire countries other than herself. It was no longer a question of what India stood to gain, but of what she stood to lose."

The delegates realized that the principle of reciprocity inherent in the terms of the Agreement held out promise of considerable development of India's export trade, and they entered upon what might be called a pact of economic co-operation with the Empire, subject to its ratification by the Indian Legislative Assembly. The Majority Report of the Committee appointed by the Assembly to examine the question stated that in their judgment "it is definitely in India's interest to accept the Ottawa Agreement."

The Assembly had also the assurance from the Finance Member, Sir George Schuster, that "ratification of the Agreement would have no effect on the prospect of further taxation." He added that India need have no fear of threats of retaliatory measures by other countries, particularly Japan.

The Assembly [1] ratified the Agreement, and subsequently necessary legislation was passed by that body in order to give effect to it. We are not concerned here with the details of the Agreement. What is important to remember is that the decision of the Assembly created a favourable impression on the Imperial Government then engaged in the question of granting constitutional measures to India, and also paved the way to securing the approval of British commercial interests for the policy of the Government.

While the Ottawa Agreements have resulted in stimulating inter-Imperial trade, India's share has not been very encouraging. Canada's trade with the Empire has expanded; Australian exports to the United Kingdom have reached the level of about 55 per cent. as against only 36 per cent. in 1928–29. But the structure of agricultural economy, the character of agricultural exports, the direction of India's

[1] At the time the Indian National Congress had boycotted the Assembly.

foreign trade and the limited growth of industries are some of the factors which place India in a position essentially different from that of the Dominions. Nevertheless, India's export of raw cotton to the United Kingdom has increased; the tea trade has revived, though not substantially, and there has been an increasing use of Indian pig iron in the United Kingdom. Nearly 45 per cent. of all galvanized sheets exported from the United Kingdom from May 1933 to March 1934 were made from Indian steel bars, and the Imperial Government agreed to admit Indian pig iron free of duty in consideration of the preference given to the imports of British galvanized sheets. It is also expected that preferential treatment will be extended to Indian manganese.

The main achievement of the Ottawa Conference, however, is the recognition of the principle of economic federation among the units of the British Empire. The Agreements stand out as a practical demonstration of the truth that the effective bond of trade lies in the better understanding and comprehension of mutual interests. The age of economic Imperialism is over. It is obvious that political coercion can no longer be successfully used in Empire trade relations. That is why the Rt. Hon. Neville Chamberlain, the Chancellor of the Exchequer, said that he was convinced that the proposals for constitutional reforms as formulated in the White Paper offered the best possible prospect of increasing British trade in India.

The views of the Nationalists in India in regard to preferential tariff arrangement with Great Britain may conveniently be stated here. They fear that such an economic pact

> "will greatly increase India's economic dependence upon Great Britain and confirm her political subjection to that country; it will render our fiscal system inflexible, virtually destroying our fiscal freedom; it will isolate India economically . . . ; it will impose an additional burden on Indian

consumers by raising the prices of important articles for the benefit of British industries."[1]

They contend that, while the expansion of India's export trade in the Empire countries is not likely to be stimulated to any great extent by the preferences granted to India under the Ottawa Agreement, her trade with non-Empire countries will suffer a set-back. It is also argued that, in view of the range and number of the articles selected for import into India, her "small scale industries" will be greatly handicapped.

The working of the Ottawa Agreement is to be reviewed in due course. The report reviewing the effect of preferences given in the Agreement on the export and import trade of India will be placed before the Assembly for examination by a committee of the Legislature. One member spoke of this arrangement as "a triumph for the Assembly." Another rejoiced for the reason that "we have, for the first time in the history of constitutional development of this country, made the Executive Government of India responsible to the popular Chamber in this matter."[2]

While the arrangement may be in accordance with Parliamentary procedure, there is a grave risk in allowing these matters of trade and tariff to be *directly* associated with a political body, even though it may not be dominated by Nationalist pugnacities. In shaping the economic policy of India and in adjusting her economic relations to the Empire, the first requisite is dispassionate judgment. It has been wanting in the past, and I hope that Sir Arthur Salter's proposal[3] for the creation of National Economic Councils in India will become a reality and that these bodies will be trusted to supply the Legislatures with expert

[1] "Ottawa Agreement and India," by N. R. Sarker, President, Bengal National Chamber of Commerce, 1932.

[2] Quoted by P. K. Wattal in his article, "The Economic Significance of Ottawa to India." *Asiatic Review*, April 1933.

[3] See "A Scheme for an Economic Advisory Organization in India." Government of India Press: 1931.

knowledge on economic questions. Through the help of these bodies, a means may be found of correlating not only economic policies of federating units in India, but also of the units of the British Empire.

INDIA AND LANCASHIRE

It was not possible to include the cotton piece goods trade in the Ottawa Agreements; but the Indian delegates pointed out that Japan was the largest buyer of the surplus raw cotton of India and that this primary product should increasingly find a market in Lancashire. They asked for a preference for Indian cotton, but it was decided that the matter of using more Indian cotton in Lancashire mills should be investigated by an expert Committee and that India should further explore the possibilities of growing Indian cotton of improved type suitable for Lancashire.

One of the far-reaching effects of the Ottawa Agreements was reflected in the spirit in which India and Lancashire came to an understanding in regard to the cotton trade. After the Conference, a Lancashire-Indian Cotton Enquiry Committee was appointed, and a delegation went to India to discuss the possibility of coming to an agreement between the India and Lancashire cotton industries. The mission was successful in the sense that it brought into focus the fundamental difficulties that face both the countries in the maintenance and development of their cotton trade. It may be a happy augury for the future that the principle of dealing with common problems by direct discussion is now established as between the Indian and British textile industries.

Before we refer to the terms of the Agreement arrived at between them, we may pause to consider some of the main problems of the industry that concern both countries.

(*a*) Japanese Competition

Perhaps the most disturbing factor is the invasion of the Indian market by Japanese textiles. Despite the present slump, Japan was able to treble her exports of cotton piece-goods to the British Empire. In 1932 she exported over 2,000 million yards of cotton piece-goods. In 1928 the import of cotton piece-goods into India from Japan were in the neighbourhood of 306 million yards; in 1932 these imports had risen to 552 million yards, that is, an increase of 80 per cent. in four years! By the spring of 1933 the situation became so serious that the Government had to denounce the Indo-Japanese Trade Agreement. But owing to her assured position in world trade and to her place as a buyer of Indian cotton, the Government of India could not afford to alienate Japan. Therefore they welcomed a deputation from Japan with a view to the preparation of a fresh Agreement which would take account of the existing trade depression.

Under the new Indo-Japanese Trade Agreement, Japan accepts one million bales of Indian raw cotton against India's acceptance of 325 million yards of Japanese piece-goods. It is agreed that each addition of ten thousand bales of raw cotton will allow the export of a further two million yards, subject to an over-riding maximum of 400 million yards. The customs duty on Japanese cotton goods will be 50 per cent., or 5¼ annas a lb., on plain greys and 50 per cent. on others. As a safeguard against currency depreciation, it is agreed that both countries have the right to change their Customs duties in their own interest in the event of variations in exchange values between the *yen* and the *rupee*.

(*b*) The Surplus Indian Cotton

India has a large exportable surplus[1] of short staple cotton. But it is not the type of cotton Lancashire can use to any great extent. In 1928–29 Japan took 287,000

[1] Total export of raw cotton from India:—

1929–30—727,000 tons.
1932–33—375,000 tons.
1933–34—514,000 tons.

tons, valued at 29 crores, but in 1932–33 this had shrunk to 190,000 tons, valued at 11 crores. Throughout the Indian cotton belt Japanese have set up their extensive buying organizations. It is obvious that the shrinkage of exports of raw cotton to Japan would be detrimental to the interests of the Indian cotton grower. The urgent problem for both India and Lancashire is to find an alternative market for this surplus cotton.

Following the assurance given to the Indian delegates by the representatives of Lancashire at Ottawa, that they would do everything in their power to encourage the use of Indian cotton in British mills, a genuine interest in the matter has been roused in Lancashire. An advisory panel, consisting of expert spinners and some of the technicians of the Shirley Institute, has been set up with the object of assisting the mills desirous of using Indian cotton ; a cotton commissioner has been appointed to act as a liaison officer between the raw cotton trade in India and the Lancashire mills ; and the Lancashire Indian Cotton Enquiry Committee has conducted a number of practical experiments with Indian cottons. The Committee obtained six bales of Indian cotton of different varieties and produced about seventy types of cloth for the examination of traders, and detailed information about the cottons used is supplied to any spinner who may be interested in the cloths. The types of cloth so far produced are " weft sateens, reversible satins, striped satin, striped tussores, grey shirtings, plain poplins, plain repps, drills, various twills, cabots, casements, sheets and sheeting finished in the grey state."

Speaking about the use of Indian cotton in Lancashire at a meeting of the Manchester Chamber of Commerce, Sir Richard Jackson said :

> " Of one thing I am convinced, Lancashire can use more Indian cotton. It is the opinion of the Cotton Enquiry Committee that with a proper spirit of interest and co-operation Lancashire's purchases of raw cotton from India will increase."

Since Lancashire mills began to use Indian cotton, the number of cotton bales exported to Lancashire has more than doubled (since 1932), as shown by the figures quoted below :

Year of Export from India to Lancashire.	In thousands of Bales of 400 lbs.
1929–30	270
1930–31	281
1931–32	166
1932–33	167
1933–34	342
1934–35	347

But the responsibility of satisfying Lancashire's demand for raw cotton lies with the Indian Governments. The Indian Central Cotton Committee and Agricultural Departments[1] must now concentrate their attention upon the production of medium and long staple cottons; greater attention must be given to the problem of adulteration and of marketing; and above all, the interests of the cotton growers must be borne in mind. The Report of the Royal Commission on Indian Agriculture pointed out the many advantages attaching to the planting of extensive and homogeneous areas with a single variety of cotton well suited to local conditions. The vast area under the Sukkur Barrage canals should be given to the cultivation of the types of cottons required by the world's markets. The Indian Governments should realize that cottons from other parts of the Empire fields are steadily improving both in quality and yield. The sooner Indian cotton finds a permanent place in the Empire market the better for all concerned.

[1] Recently the Government of Bombay has set aside 300,000 acres for the production of ⅞–1 inch staple, and also proposes to control the planting of some of the shorter lengths of staple throughout the Province. But it would be necessary to institute some form of Government control over ginneries in order to maintain a supply of pure seed.

(*c*) Indian Tariff Barriers

It is urged that the main factor responsible for the decline of the Lancashire cotton trade in India, which since 1928 has dropped by over 1,000 million yards, is the tariff imposed by the Government of India against Lancashire goods. The general rate of tariff before the War was 5 per cent., and it was raised to 11 per cent. in 1921, and to 15 per cent. in 1922. The present rate is between 25 and 30 per cent.

While it may appear that the Indian millowners have developed an insatiable thirst for protective tariffs, it should be remembered that the *primary* aim of increasing the tariff rate has been to raise revenues for the Central Government, and that the protection and encouragement of the Indian textile industry may be regarded as subsidiary motives. The raising of tariff walls is one of the most important "legacies of the War." Despite the protests of the Lancashire cotton industry, the Government of India had to impose a tariff on British cotton goods in order to meet the demands for a larger public revenue. Of course, these "revenue tariffs" had some protective effect which was greatly appreciated by the Indian millowners. Whether for the purpose of "balancing the Central Budget" or for protecting the Indian textile industry, we should remember that tariffs impoverish the peasantry by raising prices and stand in the way of creating an expanded demand in the internal market.

Speaking on the Lancashire textile mission to India, Sir Charles Innes [1] observed:

> "The great buyers of cloth in India are the agricultural population. The agriculturists make up about four-fifths of the total population. You can see in what a plight the cultivators are when I tell you how much less they are receiving now for the agricultural produce which they export from India. Taking again the first six months of 1928–29 and the first six months of the current year (1933), though

[1] Commerce Member to the Government of India (1921–27), and Governor of Burma (1927–32).

the volume of exports of agricultural products has gone down only by 16 per cent., the value of those exports has gone down by nearly 60 per cent. That is to say, the agriculturist's income may be said to be only two-fifths of what it was five years ago. It has been computed that with the agriculturist his fixed charges—rent, water rate, and so on—take up 22½ per cent. of his income; so you can imagine how he is suffering now, and that is the main reason for the reduced imports of cotton cloth." [1]

If we realize that the present-day per capita consumption of cotton fabrics in India is slightly over fifteen yards, that nearly eighteen million people own just a piece of cotton cloth not larger than an ordinary towel, that millions of Indian women do not know what underclothes mean, and that over twenty millions wrap themselves in a piece of cloth that does not reach below the knees—if these facts relating to the potential clothing requirements of the Indian people are borne in mind and considered dispassionately by India and Lancashire, both the countries will then attempt to solve their difficulties not so much by waiting on the doorstep of a Tariff Board as by organizing each and every aspect of their industry. The main difficulty is that certain tariffs imposed by the Government of India are of a revenue character. Their reduction may be possible, provided fresh sources of taxation are courageously explored by the Governments under the new Constitution. At any rate the ultimate advantage of lower prices for the Indian consumer must be the first and foremost consideration of the Federal Assembly.

We will now briefly review the terms of the Agreement concluded between Lancashire and India.

Mr. S. S. Hammersley, M.P., a member of the Lancashire Textile Mission to India, observed that

"the maintenance of the trade link in textiles between India and the United Kingdom is of overwhelming importance to the economic stability of Great Britain. . . . It is the key-

[1] See *Asiatic Review*, January 1934.

stone of the whole of our commercial intercourse with the great dependency."

It was for this reason the Lancashire-India cotton trade was treated as "a political pawn" and evoked so much political passion and prejudice. The opponents to the proposed Constitution along the lines indicated in the White Paper raised a cry of alarm that the Lancashire trade with India was in danger, and that once political power was transferred to Indian Nationalists, they would wage an economic war with Lancashire. And, in order to prejudice the British electorate against the White Paper, they preached from the press and platform—" preserve Lancashire Trade." They refused to believe that the solution might be found in Trade Agreements with India embodying reciprocal economic concessions.

The attitude of responsible Indians towards such propaganda may be gathered from the following extract from the speech of Mr. H. P. Mody, President of the Bombay Millowners' Association. Speaking in Manchester, he said:

> " . . . It would be very difficult to work for co-operation between the two industries if responsible persons in Lancashire were at all to maintain an attitude of hostility towards the legitimate demands of politically minded India; but if Lancashire could be relied on to lend its support to a solution of the political problems of India in harmony with the views held in every responsible Indian quarter, and if Lancashire freely acknowledged the right of India to frame her tariff and other policy with reference to her own needs, the situation would be created in which men of goodwill in both countries could co-operate in formulating a basis of future relations fair and satisfactory to both. The only 'safeguards' of any permanent value to British trade interests must take the form of a better understanding and of agreements freely entered into by both sides to their mutual advantage." [1]

But the problem is not so simple, and one cannot expect too rapid a change in the mental outlook of Lancashire and

[1] *The Times*, July 22, 1933.

Indian industrialists in respect of their share in the Indian textile market. It was, therefore, felt that a frank discussion among the parties concerned in the textile trade was necessary. The decision of the Japanese Government to send a deputation to India to negotiate a new Trading Agreement supplied an opportunity for the Lancashire trade associations to represent their case before the Government of India and the Indian millowners. Thus the object of the Lancashire mission was (1) to secure a reduction in the volume of Japanese exports to the Indian market; (2) to indicate that the import duties on cotton goods are excessively high in India; and (3) to induce the Indian millowners to offer Lancashire a reasonable share in the Indian market.

I have already mentioned the terms of agreement between the Indian and Japanese Governments. After a great deal of discussion the Bombay Millowners' Association and the Lancashire textile delegation came to an agreement which, according to *The Times*, "represents something quite new in the history of our commercial diplomacy, and may with justice be claimed as a triumph of common sense and mutual accommodation. It has shown beyond all possibility of doubt that the method of direct negotiation between industrialists in different portions of the Empire without any Government intervention is capable of achieving important results."

A section of the British public was, however, not happy with this achievement, which it ridiculed as being "petty and temporary concessions." The opponents of the White Paper warned the Manchester Chamber of Commerce not "to sell their vital interests for such an elusive commodity as the goodwill of Gandhi and his patrons, the Indian millowners." They had not forgotten the words of Lord Curzon that "ever since India was ordered to abolish her customs tariff in 1875 it has been in the main in response to Lancashire pressure that the successive readjustments of this policy have been introduced" [1]; but they failed to

[1] *The Times* (London), June 2, 1908.

recognize that "new times" had brought new forces into play which would necessitate certain fundamental changes in their economic relations with India. Not being contented with all the propaganda they carried on, an attempt was made to precipitate a first class political crisis in the National Government by charging the Secretary of State for India with having attempted to tamper with the evidence prepared for the Joint Select Committee by the Manchester Chamber of Commerce. The Committee of Privileges unanimously came to the conclusion that "no breach of privilege has been committed by Sir Samuel Hoare or by the Earl of Derby."

The salient points of the Agreement arrived at with the Bombay Millowners' Association are as follows:

1. Preference on British textiles as against foreign textiles entering India is accepted as a fair and desirable principle on account of the low cost of production in certain countries.

2. When the revenue position of the Government of India would enable them to withdraw the surcharge imposed in October 1931, the millowners would not make fresh proposals with regard to the duties applicable to United Kingdom imports. This would mean reduction of duty from 25 to 20 per cent., and "calls a halt in the process of higher duties against Lancashire." It is agreed that the duty on cotton yarns imported from the United Kingdom may be 5 per cent. *ad valorem*, with a minimum specific duty of 1¼ anna a pound.

3. The millowners agreed to support tariff concessions on British artificial silk goods or on mixed fabrics of cotton and artificial silk.

4. It is agreed that any advantages which might be arranged for British textiles should be extended to Indian textiles; in markets in which India has no independent quota she should be given the opportunity of sharing any quota which might be allotted to the United Kingdom. It is agreed that the Manchester Chamber of Commerce should

use its good offices to bring about contacts between Indian manufacturers and British houses which are already established in those oversea markets in which Indian mills lack established connexions.

5. The Lancashire delegation undertakes to do all that can be done to promote the use of Indian raw cotton.

It should be noted here that the Agreement is limited in duration to December 31, 1935, and that the Ahmedabad and the up-country millowners have not associated themselves with the Agreement. Meanwhile the Government of India have negotiated an Agreement with the British Government to supplement the Ottawa Convention by defining the principles upon which Indian tariff policy in respect of British goods will in future be regulated. Such an Agreement was obviously necessary to secure the adherence of British commercial interests in the support of the constitutional reform proposals. The Agreement, while admitting India's fiscal autonomy, endorses the principle of Imperial Preference and provides means to establish an equitable adjustment of tariffs through the Indian Tariff Board. Under the Agreement the Government of India undertakes, first,

> "not to alter the principles of its protective policy to the disadvantage of the United Kingdom; and secondly, not to impose on British goods protective duties higher than those required to equate the fair selling price of Indian goods with that of imported goods."

In view of the revenue needs of the Indian Budget it was not possible to reduce the duties on British cotton piece-goods, but the Government undertook to remove the surcharge of 5 per cent. "as a general measure" as soon as revenue conditions would permit them to do so. It should be noted here that in drawing up this Agreement, the Government of India did not consult the commercial interests of the country, on the plea that there was nothing in the negotiations which derogated from the existing fiscal policy.

The Indian commercial community raised a strong protest against the Agreement. The President of the Indian Chamber of Commerce declared that it constituted "a national insult" and was drawn "wholly and solely in the interests of the United Kingdom." The Chamber informed the Government that in its opinion the Agreement "involves flagrant violation of the Fiscal Autonomy Convention."

A reference at this point to the Indian Fiscal Autonomy Convention, over which there has been so much controversy, may be of some interest. The tariff policy of the Government of India was long dominated by the maxim of free trade, which fitted so well with the maintenance of the dominant British interests. Since the beginning of the twentieth century the educated classes in India have been demanding a degree of protection for infant industries of the country; and when the time came for considering constitutional reforms, they pressed for a tariff. Their case was summed up in the Montagu-Chelmsford Report as follows:

> "Educated Indian opinion ardently desires a tariff. . . . He believes that as long as we continue to decide for him we shall decide in the interests of England and not according to his wishes; . . . so long as the people who refuse India protection are interested in manufactures with which India might compete, Indian opinion cannot bring itself to believe that the refusal is disinterested or dictated by care for the best interests of India."

The Joint Select Committee set up to consider the Montagu-Chelmsford Report recommended that a Convention should be established so that the constitutional control of the Secretary of State over the Government of India should not be exercised where the Government of India and the Indian Legislature were in agreement upon a question of tariffs. The Committee observed that "whatever be the right fiscal policy for India, for the needs of her consumers as well as for her manufacturers, it is quite clear that she should have the same liberty to consider her interests as Great Britain, Australia, New Zealand, Canada, and South Africa."

The position under the Fiscal Convention was reviewed by the Statutory Commission, which did not recommend any extension of the principles underlying the Convention. Strictly speaking, India does not enjoy fiscal independence; the Convention has been nominal rather than real. The true meaning of the Fiscal Autonomy Convention was explained by Sir George Rainy, a distinguished officer of the Indian Civil Service, in the course of a debate in the Legislative Assembly, as follows:

> "It means this, that, while there is always previous consultation with the Secretary of State, the final decision as to the proposals to be placed before the Legislature rests with the Government of India and with no one else. In this respect, apart from the previous consultation with the Secretary of State, the position of the Government of India is that of a Dominion Government which decides for itself what proposals it will place before the Legislature. To that extent the Government of India are independent, but for how long does this position of independence continue? For exactly the same period as it continues in a Dominion—namely, until the Legislature pronounces upon the proposals placed before it. As soon as the Legislature arrives at a decision, one of two things happens. Either the Government of India and the Legislature are in agreement, and in that case everything proceeds as in a Dominion and no outside interferences can affect the decision. But when the Government of India and the Legislature fail to agree, there is a difference. In a Dominion, if the question is of real importance the difference results in a change of Government, which restores harmony. In India, under the present Constitution, no such result can follow. The actual effect is that the Convention ceases to operate and the Government of India come once more under the control of the Secretary of State, for as soon as the Government of India and the Legislature are not in agreement the Convention is at an end."

Meanwhile, the spirit of the Ottawa Agreement and the manner in which the trade negotiations with Japan was conducted by the Government of India is evidence that India is moving steadily towards the goal of Fiscal Autonomy.

As the growth of transport is a *sine qua non* of industrial development, we should mention here the organization through which Federal India proposes to facilitate extension and control of all forms of transport.

¶ STATUTORY RAILWAY BOARD

The Government of India held a conference in April 1933, to discuss the problems relating to transport and communication in India. The Viceroy in opening the conference observed that it was impossible to develop India fully unless better roads improved all producers' access to markets and the railways. The object of the conference was to formulate a common policy for the co-ordination of all means of transport and communication throughout India.

India has now a great railway system, the beginning of which first appeared in India in 1853. After the Famine Commission of 1880, which urged extension of railways as a powerful factor in the protection of the country from famine, the Railway Companies (domiciled in Great Britain) pursued a liberal policy of construction. At present India has about 43,000 miles of railway; that is, about one mile to each 50 square miles, or 1·3 miles per 10,000 population. The total capital investment, which yields a return of about 3 per cent., exceeds 800 crores of rupees (approximately £600 millions). There are about 7,000 miles of railways built by some of the Indian States within their territories. Thus, three parties are concerned in the railway system of India—the Government of India, owning about 32,000 miles, and operating 18,000 by direct agency; the Companies, operating 18,000 miles, of which they own 4,000; and the Indian States. The integration of these interests into a co-ordinated system of control under a new body with powers laid down by statute may be of great social, political and commercial advantage to India. Provision is made in the Constitution Act for this new body, whose composition and powers will ensure that it is in a position to perform its duties upon business principles and without being subject to political interference.

Indian public opinion demands that the control of the railways should be left to the Central Legislature, but it is considered that continual intervention by a Legislature would not allow the railways to be worked on business lines. It is hoped that it may be possible to develop "a common policy and co-operative course of action" in regard to all problems relating to transport. One hopes that that common policy will embrace the urgent problems of internal communications which are at present undeveloped and disorganized. The Federal Government should endeavour to secure that the provision of intercommunication between the units of federation is treated as *one* problem, and so direct its policy as to promote the co-ordination of road, rail and river transport. Little has been accomplished in exploring the possibilities of such co-ordination of all forms of transport in India, which is so desirable in the interests of the country generally, and particularly of its primary industry, agriculture.

ℭ THE INDIAN SANDHURST AND MILITARY EXPENDITURE

The problem of India's defence has claimed a great deal of attention ever since the question of granting self-government to India came to be discussed. Since India relies on the British Army and Navy for her defence, it is argued that self-government cannot be a reality until and unless an effective substitute for the use of British forces is provided. Leaders of Indian public opinion, on the other hand, have long insisted on providing opportunities for the military training of Indians, so that they may be properly qualified to enter on a military career. The matter, however, received no attention from the Imperial Government until the exigencies of the War changed "the angle of vision" and British Commissions were for the first time granted to Indian officers.

The authors of the Montagu-Chelmsford Report left the question with an observation that, "if our general policy demands that the Indian element in the civil services of the country should be increased, it involves some change also in our military policy." In the new Legislative Assembly, constituted under the Government of India Act of 1919, resolutions were passed urging "that adequate facilities should be provided in India for the preliminary training of Indians to fit them to enter the Royal Military College, Sandhurst ; and that as soon as funds were available steps should be taken to establish in India a Military College, such as Sandhurst, and the desirability of establishing in India training and educational institutions for other branches of the Army should be steadily kept in view." [1]

These resolutions were passed at a time when the House had emphatically protested against the main proposals of the Esher Committee,[2] which was appointed soon after the War to consider the re-organization of the military resources of India in relation with the Imperial General Staff. The Committee made a number of important proposals designed to promote the efficiency and contentment of the Army in India, and to secure that the Government of India would have at its disposal a well-trained and loyal Army fit to take its share in the defence of the Empire. But the policy of Lord Esher's Committee was to remove once and for all the control of the Indian forces from the power of the Assembly. The Government of India, however, felt the need of conciliating public opinion by responding to the modest request for increased facilities for admission to Sandhurst and for a

[1] Resolutions 7 and 8 of the March 28, 1921, Indian Legislative Assembly Debates.

[2] Cmd. Paper 943 of 1920.

Military College in India. Special concessions were granted to suitable Indian candidates for entry into the commissioned ranks of the infantry and cavalry divisions of the Indian Army; and in 1922 the Prince of Wales Royal Indian Military College was established at Dehra Dun for the preparatory training of cadets for King's Commissions.

But these measures were not popular, chiefly because of a feeling of "segregation" evoked by the "most niggardly spirit" in which these concessions were granted. Subsequently, Lord Rawlinson, then Commander-in-Chief, introduced a method of "Indianization of the Army," known as the "Eight Units Scheme." It was a very cautious experiment and provided 5 infantry battalions out of 104, 2 cavalry regiments out of 21, and 1 pioneer unit out of 7, to be gradually placed in charge of Indian officers only.[1] The process would be completed in 1946.

The scheme evoked widespread protest in the Indian press, and the Legislative Assembly passed a resolution urging that a Committee should be appointed to investigate and report what steps should be taken to establish a Military College in India to train Indian officers, and how Indianization of the Army might be accelerated. The Government agreed to appoint a Committee, which is known as the Indian Sandhurst Committee, under the chairmanship of Lieut.-General Sir Andrew Skeen, Chief of the General Staff in India.

The Committee unanimously recommended (1) an immediate doubling of vacancies at Sandhurst, (2) the establishment of a Military College on the lines of Sandhurst in

[1] The total strength of the military force in India is at present as follows:

Regular British troops, about 60,000; consisting of 5 cavalry regiments; 45 infantry battalions, each with an Indian platoon; 60 batteries Royal Artillery; 8 squadrons (96 machines) of the Royal Air Force; Regular Indian troops, about 162,000, consisting of 21 cavalry regiments; 134 infantry battalions (with 34,000 Indian reservists). Indian territory is divided into four Commands, each under a General Officer Commanding-in-Chief.

India, and (3) the abandonment of the "Eight Units Scheme." Besides these main recommendations the Committee made a number of subsidiary proposals, to which we need not refer here. Fifteen months after the publication of the Report, the Government announced their decision that they were unable to accept the recommendation in regard to the "Eight Units Scheme" and that the proposal of an Indian Sandhurst was premature. The Government, however, put into effect the proposal for reservation of places for Indian cadets at Sandhurst, and arranged to make Indians eligible for admission to the Royal Military Academy at Woolwich and the Royal Air Force College at Cranwell.

Once again, in accordance with the recommendation of the Defence Sub-Committee of the First Session of the Round Table Conference, a committee was appointed to re-examine the question of military education of Indian youth. And the Government took immediate steps towards the establishment of an Indian Sandhurst. The Indian Military Academy was opened in October 1932, at Dehra Dun. The intake of candidates will be forty every half-year, and these will be selected as follows:

Twelve by a competitive examination held by the Public Service Commission; three nominated by His Excellency the Commander-in-Chief; fifteen from serving soldiers of the Indian Army; and ten from the Indian States forces. Under the present arrangement it is expected that by 1935 the first group of trained officers from the college will be eligible for the King's commission.

As regards the quality of candidates for commissions, Sir William Ross-Barker, who was chairman of the Indian Public Services Commission, observed that "the successful candidates constitute very promising material for commissions in the Indian Army in respect of character, intelligence and personality." In the very first year, out of 105 candidates who sat for examination, 61 passed both oral and written tests.

It is a matter of great satisfaction to liberal Indian

politicians that the deliberations at the Round Table Conference on the subject of Defence served to hasten the foundation of the Military Academy. If this encouragement of Indian military leadership had been given ten years ago, many difficulties that faced conferences and committees since would not have appeared so complex; and racial antagonism and distrust in regard to the military policy of the British Government in India would not have embittered Indo-British relations. The admission by the Defence Sub-Committee of the Round Table Conference that "the defence of India must to an increasing extent be the concern of the Indian people, and not of the British Government alone," is, let us hope, an indication of a new orientation of British military policy in India. That policy should afford convincing proof of the intention of the Imperial Government to lead India to the goal of the same autonomy in the matters of Defence as is enjoyed by the Dominions.

We now turn to another matter over which there has been a dispute between the Government of India and the British War Office, viz. the capitation payments. After the Sepoy Mutiny (1857), when the troops of the East India Company were brought under the unified control of the Crown, a capitation rate of £10 per year was fixed for every British soldier; but in 1920 the rate stood at £28 10s. Since 1924 India had paid about £1,400,000 per year on this capitation account; that is the amount of India's contribution towards the recruiting and training expenses in England of the British troops and airmen who serve a part of their time in India.

A tribunal was set up in 1932 to examine this matter which had, as Sir Samuel Hoare pointed out, "embittered the relations of the British and Indian Governments." It was composed of Sir Robert Garran (lately Solicitor-General in the Commonwealth of Australia) as chairman, Sir Shadi Lal of the Punjab High Court, and Sir Mahomed Sulaiman of the Allahabad High Court, representing the Government of India; and Lord Dunedin and Lord Tomlin, representing the British Government.

In accordance with the recommendation of the majority of the Tribunal, the Government announced that it was now agreed that a fixed sum of £1,500,000 be granted to India from the British exchequer. It was also agreed that the Air Ministry's payment to India should be increased by £200,000; but that the War Office payment should be reduced by £93,000. As a result of all these adjustments of military expenditure between the Imperial Government and the Government of India, there will be a saving of about two crores (£1,500,000) in the Indian Army Budget.

Since we are enumerating the various activities of the Government of India in this period immediately antecedent to the introduction of the new Constitution, we should mention that a Bill was recently passed in the Indian Legislative Assembly creating a Royal Indian Marine Volunteer Reserve open to Europeans and Indians.

The Cardwell system[1] of reliefs for India came to be examined but no decision could be arrived at till the experimental period was over. The problems of the reorganization of Army units in India and of the mechanization of a number of units for service abroad are now engaging the attention of the military authorities of Great Britain and India.

[1] Under the Cardwell system, British regiments are split into two battalions, of which one is ordinarily abroad and one at home. The home battalion trains recruits and furnishes drafts to the overseas battalion. On the expiry of their service with the Colours, *i.e.* usually after seven years, men return from the overseas battalion and pass into the Reserve at home. In time of emergency transfers to the Reserve are stopped: the drafts that would ordinarily proceed to the linked battalion overseas remain with the home battalion, which is made up to war strength from the Reserve, and becomes available to join the Expeditionary Force, etc. It follows that the two linked battalions must be maintained on much the same scale, though, in fact, minor variations exist.

ℂ NEGOTIATIONS WITH THE INDIAN STATES

Since Federation is made dependent upon the entry of the Rulers of States, representing not less than half the aggregate population of the Indian States, it became necessary for the Government to take certain steps to create a favourable atmosphere and, to quote the Dewan of Mysore, " to remove all financial inequities and inequalities."

But these negotiations have been interpreted by the opponents to the White Paper as the means of " coercing the Princes " to join the Federation. The representatives of the States categorically denied that the Government had exercised any pressure upon the Princes to secure their support to the White Paper proposals. The Right Hon. Winston Churchill gave an ingenious explanation of what was meant by the term " pressure " in his evidence before the Joint Select Committee. He said :

> " Pressure is not necessarily illegitimate pressure. If I use an argument which has any effect upon you, that is legitimate pressure ; and there is no doubt that when the Government of India and His Majesty's Government over here, the Viceroy and all the high officials of the State are known to be anxious that the Princes should come in, the very loyalty of the Princes, their desire to fulfil what may be the general inclinations of the Imperial Government, constitute a form of pressure, not improper pressure, although, as I think, on this occasion unwisely applied. . . ."

The truth is, the Government of India set their mind to some of the problems relating to the States, whose solution was long overdue. One of these problems was the claims of the States to a share of customs duties. The States urge that the Government of India are not entitled to levy any customs duties upon goods not consumed in British territory but in the Indian States. They contend that the principle of exemption of goods destined for the Indian States from customs duties should be recognized, or the yield from the customs duties should be shared with the Indian States on some equitable basis.[1]

A problem of this nature gave rise to a controversy with the State of Nawanagar and other Kathiawar States. In 1927 the Government of India offered to collect the customs on goods which entered at the Kathiawar ports and to make annual fixed payments to each maritime State on the basis of existing custom receipts. The offer was not accepted, and the late Maharaja Jam Sahib (Ranji) protested against the reimposition of the customs line. The matter was then referred to a court of arbitration, of which Lord Dunedin was the sole member. The Government accepted the arbitrator's finding, and it is now (1934) agreed that the State of Nawanagar will retain customs duty on goods passing from the State outside the limits of Kathiawar up to a maximum of Rs. 5 lakhs (£37,500) per annum and that any balance over this amount will go to the Government of India.

Then, the Agreement between His Majesty's Government and His Exalted Highness the Nizam of Hyderabad, Deccan, was concluded in regard to the position of the Berars [2] under the Federal Constitution. The controversy on the retrocession of this territory is of long standing. The Berars and certain districts were mortgaged to the East India Company in lien of the debt incurred by the State of Hyderabad in the early part of the nineteenth century; but in 1860, in consideration of the services rendered by the State during the Mutiny, the British Government remitted a substantial portion of the debt and retroceded certain districts. The Berars, however, continued to be administered by the British Resident. Under the Agreement of 1902, during the Viceroyalty of Lord Curzon, the administration was transferred to the Central Provinces.

[1] The claims of the Indian States were submitted to the Indian Fiscal Commission. See "Minutes of Evidence," Vol. III, p. 1037.

[2] The Province lies to the north of the State of Hyderabad (Deccan). It is larger than Denmark or Switzerland.

The Government of India were prepared to pay an annual rental of Rs. 25 lakhs (£187,500) in respect of the leasing of these territories.

But the Government of the Nizam were never reconciled to these arrangements and asked for the restitution of the Berars. After the War the Nizam hoped that in recognition of his loyalty the Government might reconsider their decision in regard to his claim to these territories. It was, however, made plain to the Nizam that "the Government of India entertain no doubt in regard to the validity of their title to occupy Berar, and they regard themselves as being under an obligation to the inhabitants of the Province to retain it under their own administration." [1]

The Nizam's Government gave full support to the Federal scheme and therefore it became necessary to come to a new agreement in respect of the Berars. Two main factors in this controversy were (1) the recognition of the sovereignty of His Exalted Highness and (2) the *status quo* of about eighty years of British administration of the territory. The settlement arrived at was announced by Lord Willingdon in a speech during his visit to the State of Hyderabad in the following terms. His Excellency the Viceroy said:

> ". . . While His Majesty's Government on their part reaffirm his (the Nizam's) sovereignty over the Berars, His Exalted Highness on his part would, on the bringing into force of the contemplated Constitution Act, or such parts of that Act as become applicable to the Provinces of British India, be prepared to accede to federation in respect of his territories known as the Berars. . . ."

It was also agreed that specific provisions would be made "to give some real as well as ceremonial effect to the sovereignty of the Nizam."

Another definite step towards gaining the confidence of the States was taken by passing the Indian States (Protection) Bill. The object of the Bill and the spirit which

[1] Lord Reading's letter to the Nizam, 1924.

induced the Government to introduce this measure were explained by the Home Member, Sir Harry Haig, in a speech before the Legislative Assembly. He said :

> " In the future, as I see it, British India and the States will each have a contribution to make to the common good. We are endeavouring to evolve a new India. It will not be a mere copy of other countries, which have different traditions and culture. It will be, we hope, distinctly Indian. That hope will not be realized if we discard old traditions and institutions and turn for our model solely to the West. . . . In thinking of the States, I would ask the House not to fail to recognize the distinctive traditional qualities of the system of personal administration where that system is carried on in accordance with its own true principles. This Bill says that the administration of the States is to be protected, and they are entitled to be protected against subversive attacks from beyond their own border. This is not only an obligation which we owe them, but an obligation we owe to the peace of India as a whole—the peace of British India as well as of the Indian States—and as such I commend it with confidence to the acceptance of the House."

II. GOVERNMENT AND THE CONGRESS

We have now to consider how the Government have been dealing with the Civil Disobedience Movement initiated by the Indian National Congress. The Irwin-Gandhi pact created a lull in the Indian political sphere, although a strong section of the Congress disapproved the pact and revolted against the policy of temporary suspension of the movement. Gandhi was, however, able to persuade the Congress that the opportunity of laying before the Round Table Conference in London the demands of the Congress should not be passed by. He argued that the pact opened " a way to peace " and that he would explore every avenue which might lead to settlement of the vital issues the Conference proposed to discuss. We have already noted that the Karachi Session of the Congress nominated him as the sole representative of that body to deliver its mandate before the second Round Table Conference.

Meanwhile the Government planned out their programme to suppress any attempt to revive the Civil Disobedience Movement. The situation in Bengal, the United Provinces, and the North-West Frontier Province led to the promulgation of a number of Ordinances. It became clear to the Government that upon Gandhi's return to India without coming to any settlement in regard to the demands of the Congress, there would be a deliberate attempt to revive Civil Disobedience. Some of the leaders of the extremist section of the Congress were therefore arrested and their followers were made to realize that the Government would no longer tolerate any form of "direct action."

Gandhi returned to India on December 28, 1931, and on the following day telegraphed to the Viceroy for an interview. He expressed surprise at the repressive measures adopted by the Government during the period of the Irwin-Gandhi pact and enquired whether this attitude of the authorities was an indication of the end of the "truce." But Gandhi was informed that the Viceroy was not prepared to discuss with him the measures which the Government had taken in controlling such activities as were necessary to meet the campaign of hostility and disorder. The Viceroy's refusal to see Gandhi inspired the following resolution by the Congress Working Committee which met in Bombay:

> "The Committee is prepared to render co-operation to the Government provided the Viceroy reconsiders his Thursday's telegram to Mahatma Gandhi, adequate relief is granted in respect of Ordinances and its recent acts, free scope is left to Congress in any future negotiations and consultations to prosecute the Congress claim for complete independence and the administration of the country is carried on with popular representatives pending the attainment of such independence."

Gandhi, in a spirited reply to the Viceroy, regretted the Viceroy's decision in regard to the interview he asked for, and after dealing with certain specific charges brought forward by the Government against the Congress, stated that "civil disobedience was the inalienable right of a people, especially when they have no effective voice in their Government."

In a further telegram the Viceroy made the position of the Government clear. He said:

> "Civil Disobedience is wholly unconstitutional; there can be no compromise with it, and the Government cannot enter into any negotiations for its withdrawal. . . . If Congress desires to resume its position as a constitutional party and to put an end to a movement which has brought grave injury and suffering to the country, the way is open to it, as it always has been. It is within the power of Congress to restore peace by withdrawing on its own initiative the Civil Disobedience Movement. . . ."

Since the Congress and Gandhi had declared their intention to carry on the struggle, Gandhi was arrested and interned as a State prisoner under Regulation XXV of 1827; and Ordinances covering almost every form of political hostility were rigorously executed throughout the country. "In the first three months of the operation of the Ordinances the jails in almost every Province were full to overflowing, and special accommodation had to be found for the thousands of prisoners who were incarcerated under the new policy." [1] These Ordinances were promulgated for the period of six months; but, as the Congress had not abandoned its policy of civil disobedience, the Government issued a new consolidated Ordinance including in it some of the principal features of the various Ordinances whose application had proved to be so successful. A considerable number of provisions in the Ordinance have since been included in statutes, so that the Governments, Central and Provincial, under the future Constitution, may have the necessary weapons to combat civil disobedience. "It is no satisfaction to my Government," said the Viceroy in opening the new session of the Legislative Assembly, "to be forced to propose these

[1] "Indian Year Book," Bombay. *Times of India* Press: 1933.

measures for strengthening the law, but we are faced with ideas and methods to which we must offer the most resolute opposition."

The removal of Gandhi to Yeravda Jail, Poona, and "the harsh and repressive measures" adopted against all Congress organizations precipitated a crisis in the Congress. Its failure to carry on the struggle against the Ordinances created a sharp division within its ranks in regard to the advisability of adhering to what a prominent Moslem member of Congress described as the "*reductio ad absurdum* of the principle of non-co-operation and civil disobedience." A section of the Congress held the view that its policy should now be directed towards securing a stronghold within the future Legislatures of the country and that no purpose would be served by ignoring political realism. The extremists, however, thought that the impact of the repression could not undermine the Nationalist forces and that "Ordinance Rule" was bound to fail in the sense that it could never conquer the spirit of passive resistance although it might temporarily suppress its more open manifestations.

In the midst of all these divergent views and differences within the Congress, the Communal Award of the Government was announced. I have already referred to Gandhi's dramatic fast and to the modification of the Award that resulted from his action. Contrary to expectation, Gandhi was not released; but the Government relaxed certain prison regulations to enable him to conduct his campaign for the awakening of the social conscience of the orthodox Hindu communities. He appeared to have left politics outside his mission although the Liberal leaders failed to persuade him to declare the abandonment of civil disobedience.

But trouble began over the pact. The Hindu orthodox party realized that the degree of political concessions granted to the depressed classes might be prejudicial to the interests of Hindu religion, and the Hindu *Mahasabha* resented the pact as well as the Communal Award of the Government as being wholly unsatisfactory. What concerned Gandhi was the manner in which the Caste Hindus attempted to frustrate his campaign against untouchability. In the solitude of his prison cell, he realized that the prevalence of untouchability in the Hindu social structure was a formidable barrier to the attainment of political freedom. He therefore announced that he would now undergo an ordeal of three weeks' "unconditional and irrevocable fast" in connection with the untouchability campaign. He declared that the fast was to be a "process of self-purification" which he would go through "in obedience to a peremptory call from within." In an interview he said:

> "I am not interested in politics at present. My mind is solely concentrated on the untouchability problem. I am not satisfied with the progress that has been made, though I am not altogether dissatisfied. More deeds instead of words are required by my disciples."

In view of the nature and objects of the fast and "the attitude of mind which it discloses," the Government of India decided to release Gandhi and imposed no restrictions upon his movements. This "act of grace" on the part of the Government was quickly responded to by his tendering advice to the Congress, through its acting President, for the suspension for six weeks of the Civil Disobedience Movement. He expressed hope that during this period of suspension, "peace will be arranged between the Government and Congress."

But in a statement issued by the Government it was made clear that

> "a mere temporary suspension of the Civil Disobedience Movement, intended to lead up to negotiations with the Congress leaders, in no way fulfils the conditions which would satisfy the Government of India that in fact the Civil Disobedience Movement has been definitely abandoned. There is no intention of negotiating with the Congress for the withdrawal of the Civil Disobedience Movement. . . ."

Gandhi was disappointed once more at his failure to negotiate with the Government and went through a three weeks' fast. For months after his recovery from the effects of the fast he devoted himself to the cause of the Depressed classes, but it was not possible to leave the Congress in an unsettled state in regard to its policy of civil disobedience. Although the movement had already lost its hold on the majority of the "civil resisters," Gandhi's views about its importance in Indian political life had undergone no change. He was not prepared to regard the suspension of the movement as a confession of failure, and maintained that the Congress workers had not adhered to the principle of Satyagraha.[1] He declared that "the secrecy that has attended the movement is fatal to its success. If, therefore, the movement is to be continued, I would urge those who are guiding the movement in different parts of the country to discard all secrecy."

A Conference of some of the representative leaders of the Congress was convened in Poona to decide whether the Civil Disobedience Movement should be totally abandoned, or suspended for a time, or resumed. Here Gandhi was severely criticized for his guidance in this matter, and opinion in the Conference was in favour of the withdrawal of the movement. But the Conference was adjourned without arriving at a definite decision. The matter was left to the Working Committee of the Congress.

To Gandhi the principle of civil disobedience is as strong and vital as his religious convictions. Although the majority of the Working Committee of the Congress favoured withdrawal of the civil disobedience programme, he warned his followers that any such step would mean the denial of their faith in the movement. It was pointed out to him that, so long as the Government maintained its repressive policy, mass civil disobedience would only aggravate the situation, causing untold misery and suffering to the people who were in any way connected with the Congress. He therefore

[1] Passive resistance.

made a dramatic decision to disband his *ashram* [1] and to organize a march with a band of his followers in order to demonstrate the power of individual civil disobedience. He declared it to be "a fresh sacred mission in life" to which only those would be invited who were prepared to go through the ordeal of suffering. In a letter to the Government he unfolded his programme of individual civil disobedience and offered the immovable property belonging to the *ashram*, worth about £27,000, and movable property (including cash), estimated at about £23,000, to the Government. In appealing to his countrymen he wrote that "without civil disobedience there is no safety and no freedom. Civil disobedience can become impregnable only in the manner pointed out by me"; and to Englishmen his appeal was to the effect that if they wanted peace and goodwill in India, the Government should discard the policy of ruling India by Ordinance.

But the Government did not allow him to carry out his plan this time. They pointed out that there was no real distinction between mass and individual civil disobedience, and that the campaign planned by Gandhi would lead to mass disobedience. He was therefore arrested on the eve of the proposed march under the Bombay Special (Emergency) Powers Act of 1932. While the abandonment of his *ashram* and his arrest excited world sympathy, they did not assist in solving the dilemma in which the Congress found itself. It was then in a "paralytic state of bewilderment." The decision of the acting President to dissolve the Congress organizations and start individual civil disobedience was regarded by the majority of its members as a futile policy. In any case, the Government realized that the vital spark of the movement had been extinguished and it would not be long before the Congress finally abandoned its barren policy of civil disobedience and non-co-operation.

On his return to the prison, Gandhi found that the

[1] Seminary at Sabarmati, near Ahmedabad.

Government had not given him the same facilities for carrying on his campaign against untouchability as he enjoyed during his last imprisonment. But, after a short-lived fast, he was given facilities for direct propaganda for the uplift of the Depressed classes, and after two months he was released, though he was served with an order requiring him to abstain from lawless activities.

At long last, in April 1934, Gandhi advised the Congress to abandon the Civil Disobedience Movement and approved of the council-entry programme. An explanation of this change in his attitude towards civil disobedience was furnished by his own lengthy statement, from which I take the following extracts. Claiming himself to be

> "a *Satyagraha* expert in the making," he said: "After much searching of heart I have arrived at the conclusion that in present circumstances only one, and that myself and no other, should for the time being bear the responsibility of Civil Disobedience if it is to succeed as a means of achieving *Purna Swaraj*.[1] . . . They (all Congressmen) should leave it to me alone. It should be resumed by others in my lifetime only under my direction, unless one arises claiming to know the science better than I do." He then proceeded to advise that civil resisters now freed from the responsibility of civil disobedience "should identify themselves with self-denial and voluntary poverty, and engage in nation-building and society-cleansing activities."

The left wing of the Congress resented the statement. A member of the Congress Committee remarked that Gandhi was imitating Louis XIV by saying, "I am the Congress." Mrs. Sarojini Naidu[2] thought that Gandhi's statement was another public act of self-humiliation and contained ungracious and undeserved indictment of those who underwent intense hardships in trying to follow his lead.

In view of the decision of the Congress to abandon mass civil disobedience, the Government of India once again

[1] Complete independence.
[2] A famous Indian Poetess.

withdrew the notifications outlawing the Congress organizations except in the North-West Frontier Province, where the Red Shirt movement was closely associated with that of the Congress. The collapse of civil disobedience as a means of political expression left a vacuum in Congress politics and, therefore, the Government's announcement in regard to Assembly elections gave the leaders of the Congress a fresh opportunity for a return to the constitutional fold. By abandoning their policy of civil disobedience and by accepting a council-entry programme, the Congress fulfilled the prophecy of Lord Willingdon, who once observed that " . . . in spite of themselves, they (Congress leaders) will find they are caught up in living forces of constructive politics. . . ."

On April 18, 1934, the Congress Committee adopted a council-entry programme and a Parliamentary Board was set up to organize elections to the Legislative Assembly. Although there is wide divergence of opinion in regard to the Communal Award, all the groups formed within the Congress accept the appeal issued by the Working Committee to the electorate on the White Paper proposals. It says:

> "The White Paper in no way expresses the will of the people of India, has been more or less condemned by almost all the Indian political parties, and falls far short of the goal of the Congress, if it does not retard the progress towards it. The only satisfactory alternative to the White Paper is a constitution drawn up by a Constituent Assembly elected on the basis of adult suffrage or as near it as possible with power, if necessary, to the important minorities to have their representatives elected exclusively by the electors belonging to such minorities."

While the Congress has maintained a united front on the question of rejecting the White Paper proposals, its return to practical politics and the election campaign have given rise to sharp division of opinion in regard to the Communal Award. An influential section of the Congress urge that this unjust and unjustifiable Award should be repudiated. The position of the Congress in this regard is explained by a resolution which states that "the Congress claims to represent equally all the communities composing the Indian nation. In view of the division of opinion, the Congress can neither accept nor reject the Communal Award so long as the division of opinion lasts." It is pointed out that in the event of their success in rejecting the White Paper, the Communal Award must lapse automatically.

Perhaps the significant development within the Congress is the rise of the Swaraj Party, organized by the Left wing of the Congress. Its adherents are no longer under the spell of the Mahatma. To them the collapse of civil disobedience is a convincing proof of the failure of "experimenting with Truth" in the field of political realism. They had so far tolerated Gandhi's policy, not with the fervour of a deep conviction in the gospel of Satyagraha but as a means of exploiting his popularity with the masses. They knew that, as Gandhi's influence in the Congress diminished, newer political forces would come into play. Their aim has always been to bring within the orbit of the Congress the Labour and Peasants' Movements; and, during the last few years, the Left wing of the Congress had taken full advantage of the depressing economic situation of the Labour and Peasantry. Its leaders approached them not with abstract political ideas but made them realize that their difficulties would never be solved unless they organized themselves against all forms of exploitation. Behind the scene of Congress diplomacy, they have succeeded in establishing many centres of activity in rural areas and have undoubtedly gained the moral support of the villagers. Indeed, the Left wing of the Congress has proved the truth of the statement of the Statutory Commission that "the politically minded in India are only a tiny minority, but they may be able to sway masses of men in the countryside."

There is another phase of the development of the Congress which should be mentioned here. From the experience of the last decade there has emerged a somewhat clearer comprehension of its political objective. Swaraj is no longer a mystic expression of India's political goal; nor is it subject to various interpretations. I am not saying that there are no conflicts within the Congress. They do exist, but these conflicts are not in relation to the ideologies of the Congress movement. A critical analysis of the various groups within the Congress would show that their differences are chiefly on the methods of attaining the objective.

It would therefore be a mistake to ignore the Congress, which is admitted by Lord Willingdon to be "an extensive organization, which commands, even outside its own ranks, a certain degree of sympathy among many of the educated classes." The assertion that the constitutional proposals are so devised that the Indian Nationalists would fail to make their influence felt, or to become dominant in the Legislatures, suggests that there has been inadequate recognition of the forces latent beneath the present "wreckage" of the Congress. Those who are familiar with the history of the Indian National Congress regret the mistaken attitude of the authorities towards this organization from its very inception. Sir Valentine Chirol rightly observed:

> "Englishmen, official and unofficial, instead of lending them (*i.e.* the leaders of the Congress) a helping and guiding hand, which might have kept the Congress on permanently constitutional lines, viewed that movement with suspicion and resentment and drove it almost inevitably into more and more vehement opposition which has grown to-day into open and bitter antagonism."[1]

Continued hostility towards the Congress would only add fuel to the smouldering flames of agitation suppressed by organized forces at the disposal of the Government; but one hopes that without delay it will be made possible for the Government to withdraw the Ordinances, the rigours of which have undoubtedly caused much bitterness throughout the country. The continuation of these measures would

[1] Lectures on the Harris Foundations 1924.

mean nourishment of a feeling of hostility which is infectious, especially in a country where the masses are peculiarly susceptible to appeals of the "martyrs." The visible antagonism may have been suppressed by the Ordinance rule, but it is well to remember that the chasm between the Government and the people can never be bridged by the assertion of power.

CHAPTER VIII

THE PARTNERSHIP IN A COMMON ENTERPRISE

The Implications of Partnership : Common Enterprise : Tasks before the Partners—(a) *Great Britain, the first Partner ;* (b) *The Indian States, the second Partner ;* (c) *British India, the third Partner*

ℭ THE IMPLICATIONS OF PARTNERSHIP

THE title of this chapter is borrowed from a sentence that occurs in the White Paper in which the Imperial Government elaborated their proposals for the new Constitution for India. It is a happy phrase and implies a recognition of the need of approaching the constitutional problems in a spirit of partnership. The sentiment was also expressed in the Despatch of the Government of India on the Report of the Indian Statutory Commission, where it is stated that "in the future relationship between Great Britain and India the time has come for the relation of partnership to supersede that of subordination." In course of the controversy that raged over the constitutional proposals, Lord Halifax explained the idea more precisely in an address he gave before a meeting at Leeds. He said :

"We had got to get away from the notion of governors and governed and on to the idea of equal partnership. Once we could convince Indians that we were going to get on to that basis, we would find that half our difficulties would disappear."

But Indians ask, "Is the Government of India Act of 1935 really based on the spirit of partnership?" They concur with the view expressed by Major Attlee, a Labour member of the Joint Select Committee, who observed that "throughout the Report and the proposals of the majority of the Committee there was evidence of distrust of the nationalist forces. They were clearly regarded as a potential opposition, not as a co-operating body." Indians condemn most of the safeguards as being measures for the protection of British interests, and affirm that partnership as implied in the Act is just another form of Imperialism. It is held that such concessions as are made in the Act have been granted to India under the tempo of events within and outside India and that the Imperial Government realize that by withholding them they would lose something better.

The reasons for this deep-seated suspicion among them are not far to seek. In answer to the question, Why was there so little enthusiasm among Indians about the Reforms? a distinguished Indian gave the following reply to a British visitor. He said: "Because a certain fatality seems to clog the steps of the Government, so that whenever it does anything useful for the people, it knows not how to do it with a good grace."

The remark is particularly interesting now when a plea for this good grace comes from those who are eager to bridge the gulf between India and Great Britain. Sir Francis Younghusband writes in *The Times:*[1] "What matters now—and matters much—is the temper in which the remainder of our seven years' deliberation is to be conducted. The Joint Committee appeals to our 'characteristic British temper.' To it let us add the spice of grace. . . . On great occasions let our spokesmen in Parliament and the Press and at public meetings show also the winning element of grace. For Indians are sensitive, and while they may admire good sense they will respond to grace."

It has to be admitted that, apart from the occasional

[1] *The Times*, November 28, 1934.

administrative blunders that cause unrest in India, there has grown up a generation of Indians sensitive to any hostile attitude on the part of men in power towards India's political aspirations. Upon the introduction of certain measures of reforms during the Viceroyalty of Lord Ripon, the Anglo-Indian Press declared that "the only people who have any right to India are the British; the so-called Indians have no right whatever."[1] For many years since the introduction of Local Self-Government in 1882, the Bodies created under the Act had no independent life. Most of the officials had not entered upon the task of laying the true foundation of a responsible government in the spirit Lord Ripon conceived the idea. The charge that "official scepticism and unwillingness to work on equal terms with Indians had ruined a valuable educational experiment"[2] cannot be easily refuted. To Lord Curzon the term "self-government" was wholly inapplicable to India. The favourable psychological reactions on Indian opinion consequent upon the passing of the Government of India Act (1919), were, to a great extent, nullified by utterances of responsible British statesmen as soon as Great Britain began to recover from the War fatigue. In the House of Commons, on August 22, 1922, the Prime Minister (Mr. Lloyd George) declared:

> "That Britain under no circumstances will relinquish her responsibility in India is a cardinal principle, not merely for the present Government, but of any Government which will command the confidence of the people in this country. I can see no period when India can dispense with the guidance and the assistance of this small nucleus of the British Civil Service. They are the steel frame of the whole structure."

Lord Irwin's declaration in regard to Dominion Status for India was described in the Tory Press as "the most

[1] Quoted by Sir Valentine Chirol in his book, "Fifty Years in a Changing World."

[2] "Rise and Fulfilment of British Rule in India," by Thompson and Garratt. Macmillan: 1934.

nebulous and mischievous verbiage" and Lord Russell, then Under-Secretary of State for India, stated that there was no question of India attaining the status equal to that of the Dominions. From Lord Birkenhead came the clear statement that he could not imagine India achieving Dominion Status at any time. Indians are thus persuaded to believe that whatever may be the extent and character of political concessions granted to them, the policy of the Imperial Government is based upon the axiom that British supremacy in India must remain unshaken.

Then there is a section of British public both in Great Britain and India which cherishes a supreme contempt for the Indian educated classes. Their liberal education is condemned as being "supremely calculated to turn loyal citizens into political agitators. It was like placing a powder barrel in front of a blazing fire. The inflammable Hindu was astonished as he read the new doctrines of Western democracy."[1] An Anglo-Indian author warns his countrymen of "the soft-soap trick" of the educated Indian who is more subtle than they are but is "a delightful person until you begin to take him too seriously."[2] Similar warning came from Professor Jowett, Master of Balliol, who wrote: "Educated Indians should be treated with the greatest courtesy and even compliment, but of course if they go beyond their tether they have to be stopped." The British communities in India are, as a rule, keen to scent out disloyalty in any independent expression of opinion and are hidebound in prejudices which tend to stabilize the barriers between the two races. One also hears that the best of the two races cannot really understand each other.

It is sometimes asserted that Indian problems are deeply rooted in the psychological differences of the two races, one homogeneous and the other heterogeneous in character. If it be so, then their solution can never be found merely in measures of constitutional reforms granted as concessions

[1] See "Indian Babel," by H. K. Trevaskis, I.C.S. (1935).
[2] "India: The Eleventh Hour," by Hamish Blair, 1935.

under the exigencies of circumstances. On the contrary, political expedients safeguarded with innumerable complex devices may tend to widen rather than bridge the gulf between India and Britain.

The truth, which must be frankly recognized, is that there exists antagonism between India and Britain and that a deeper realization of the true purpose of our mutual relationship is not evident in our dealings with each other. I have therefore no hesitation in affirming that the problem is essentially spiritual and the ultimate bond between us should be spiritual. True, India has been the recipient of a number of political and economic concessions; but these by themselves are of no permanent importance till they spring from a basic understanding between India and Britain and are invested with spiritual values. It is the absence of these values that renders concessions unreliable, gifts devoid of generosity and grace, and tends to encourage the spirit of bargaining. What we give or receive from a bargain counter where affairs are measured only in terms of political values cannot eliminate the causes of errors of judgment in our mutual relationship. I do not underestimate the value of constitutional reforms—they may certainly remove many of the present barriers between us and make a way to avoid bitter conflicts. However, it is a truism, but it must needs be repeated, that constitutional architects may construct with meticulous care an imposing edifice of State, but if it is not consecrated with ethical concepts, it becomes a menace to real peace and understanding among the people. It is with this conviction that the future administrators and politicians in India must approach their problems. Their tasks involve a change in the concepts of State and Society, so that the polity of the State and the structure of the Society may not be devoid of spiritual truth. To-day, both lack this essential quality. Tagore laments that

> " it is not the best ideals of a people that govern a foreign country. The unnaturalness of the situation stands in the

way, and everything tends to encourage the baser passions of man,—the contemptuous pride of power, the greed of acquisition—comes uppermost. . . . It is sure to cause moral degeneracy in men to exercise habitually authority upon an alien people and therefore not to encounter the checks that arise from the relationship of natural sympathy."[1]

These remarks are equally applicable to Indian social life. We, too, have created unwholesome situations among us, and it is the absence of natural sympathy among the various races and social groups that is dragging us down to the abyss of destruction.

The essential step towards the solution of our mutual difficulties must therefore be the recognition of the spiritual values in our relationship. Is this ideal of a great spiritual fulfilment in those relations a mere fantasy of dreamers? Are we to pass it by as being outside the range of a practical policy? Was it not Lord Cromer, an experienced British administrator, who wrote that "the essential points of a sound Imperial policy admit of being embodied in this one statement, that . . . our relations with the various races who are subjects of the King of England should be founded on the granite rock of the Christian code"? In the midst of a world engulfed in a catastrophe of nationalism and racial antagonism, there can be no short cuts to the realization of this ideal. But it is enough if a section of responsible men and women of the two great countries persuade themselves to follow the way of faith. The mission calls for new leadership, and it cannot be trusted to those who ignore the fundamental basis for working towards the harmony of a synthesis. All the partners in the making of Federal India must therefore come forward fortified in the faith that the sympathetic unity of the British Commonwealth of Nations cannot be achieved so long as the tendency to adhere to the worn-out policy of Imperialism remains hidden under the changing mask of liberal spirit; they must approach the problem with a firm determination to harmonize all con-

[1] Andrews, C. F.: Tagore's "Letters to a Friend." Allen & Unwin: 1931.

flicting interests; and on them will rest the responsibility of proving that effective partnership, based on moral ideals and spiritual values, can be a real and supreme arbiter in politics. Such are, in my judgment, the implications of *partnership*.

ℭ COMMON ENTERPRISE

Now, there are three main partners concerned in the making of Federal India,—namely (1) Great Britain, (2) the Indian States, and (3) British India. Since Federation has to be created by the mutual devotion of each partner to the ideal of harmony, it is important to indicate here what is the *common enterprise* which the partners are called upon to pursue. The constitutional terminology of that enterprise is to set up an All-India Federation. But it is more than that—it has two broad aspects which may claim our attention.

In the first place, Federal India should aim at establishing new relations between East and West. It is necessary to remember that Great Britain's achievements in India, great as they have been, should not be evaluated merely in terms of material progress and of stable administration, but by the degree of success she attains in harmonising the antithesis of the Eastern and Western ideals. If and when she succeeds in reconciling their antagonism, her mission of reconcilement in the meeting of the East and the West will be fulfilled. She cannot absolve herself from the responsibility by taking shelter under jingoism, which declares that the "twain shall never meet." Rather she should direct her policy with the conviction that, "Orient und okzident sind nicht mehr zu trennen"[1] (East and West can no longer be separated). In India there should be no trace of racial inequality, and any indication of racial antagonism between the East and West must not be tolerated within the British Commonwealth.

[1] Goethe.

It is equally important that Indian leaders should have a clear comprehension of the significance of partnership with Great Britain and nothing should be done to emphasize the racial aspect. They must realize that " India would have been shorn of fullness if it had missed contact with the West. The lamp of England is still burning; we must kindle our old extinguished lamp at that flame and start again on the road of Time." [1] In moments of political passion they revolt against the impact of the West and seem to think that all would be well if the British Government withdraw from India, if every vestige of its influence is erased from Indian national life, and if they are allowed to live in the peace of " splendid isolation." To Gandhi the civilization of the West is " satanic and perverse." He writes : " It is my firm opinion that Europe to-day represents not the spirit of God or Christianity but the spirit of Satan. And Satan's successes are the greatest when he appears with the name of God on his lips. Europe is to-day nominally Christian. In reality, it is worshipping mammon." In the enthusiasm of vindicating India's culture, Gandhi and those who are known to be his followers preach with frantic insistency that the West is materialistic and the East is all spirit. The West " disowns the spirit," and the East lives for it. They seem to ignore Europe's achievements in the sphere of æsthetics, science and humanitarianism and discern only the Imperialistic designs of the powerful nations of the West in their associations with the East. They forget that Europe has its noble traditions and that she has certainly influenced Asiatic thought by her ideas, the traces of which are to be found behind the forces of renaissance in Asia. They under-estimate the contributions of that " happy breed of men " in Europe whose idealism and sense of justice should inspire courage and faith among the nations of the world. In an unbiassed estimation of the spirit of the West, one cannot fail to discern, amidst all perversions of truth, its persistent urge

[1] Tagore.

towards higher ideals in the service of humanity, and its abiding faith in the freedom of personality.

There are, however, various reasons for the lack of proper evaluation and appreciation of the West by the East. The outward signs of Western influence are tangibly present in India but they do not represent the best and noblest traditions of Western civilization. " By a strange paradox and inversion," laments G. K. Chesterton, " we have claimed superiority in everything except the things in which we are superior. We have extended to Asia all the accidents of Europe ; but we have hardly dared to say a word for the substance of Europe ; least of all for the soul of Europe." [1]

The best minds of Europe and Asia are therefore in complete agreement as to the need for an intimate cultural contact between the West and East. It is in the synthesis of the two main streams of culture that we must look for the ultimate solution of the intricate problem of adjusting our relationships. " The opening of the Suez Canal," wrote Tagore, in a message to the American Friends' Service Committee, " has freed the path of commerce between the two great geographical divisions of the world. My appeal is to open up the channel for the commerce of Culture between the Western continents and my own country, India, which represents the East, for through such freedom of communication will be fulfilled a most important mission of education. Mountains and seas cannot obstruct the fact that deep in our beings we need you and you need us, for we are kin."

But the realization of this relationship is possible only in an atmosphere of fellowship. An American citizen once said to a distinguished Indian visitor that " the West will never appreciate the East unless the East can look the West horizontally in the face." This is, of course, the whole argument of Nationalist India for concentrating its entire resources on the struggle for political freedom. It

[1] See his preface to M. Henri Massis' " Defence of the West." Faber & Gwyer, London : 1927.

is argued that once India succeeds in gaining "Swaraj," the path for the realization of her unity with the West would be made easy. Let us hope that in the working of the new Constitution, it may be discovered that the transfer of political power has now been made real and that it contains within itself adequate provisions for its own development. If the Act has the appearance of, to quote Lord Lloyd's phrase, "combining the maximum of conciliation with the minimum of concession," let us now face the realities of Indian politics with courage and wisdom so that we may speedily acquire the strength necessary to lead India on to the road of freedom. The promotion of understanding between all the partners in Indian Federation should be regarded as the basis of freedom and unity. The consummation of the union of East and West on that basis is, I believe, the first common enterprise for the partners of Federal India, and in that achievement they will have made a lasting contribution to humanity.

The second aspect of the common enterprise is to raise the standard of living of the Indian masses. In the success of this enterprise the partners should find the strength as well as the source of prosperity of the Empire. They should boldly face the fact that the majority of India's population lives in abject poverty and is definitely under-nourished. The millions of untouchables and landless agricultural labourers live in hovels which are no better than the caves of pre-historic humanity. Mr. Sorley, an Indian Civil Servant, tells us in his report on the *Chowls* [1] of Bombay, that some of the conditions of housing in that city "must be more reminiscent of the Black Hole of historical memory than any modern city pretending to sanitary living conditions." In thousands of Indian villages one sees a gruesome spectacle of poverty—that sin of all sins—which is prolific in breeding the evil elements in society. There bad sanitation, bad housing, poor water supply, wasting diseases and deformities of every kind—

[1] Slums.

physical, mental, and moral—are common ; there dominate every kind of vested interest and there also presides the dark spirit of ignorance. So long as this atmosphere remains corrupted with poisonous exhalations from the rural slums of India, there can be no hope of gaining normal health in her political life. Therefore, each and all partners should realize that " while three-fourths of the Empire are weak, the fourth part cannot be strong."

But illiterate and poor as the masses are, there is a clear indication of the spirit of revolt among them. It has already struck a deep root in some Provinces and is bound to spread. They may not possess what is known as political consciousness, but the circumstances of their life and labour tend to undermine their belief in the Government and they are becoming infused with a latent discontent. And, to quote James Russell Lowell, " it is only when the reasonable and practicable are denied that men demand the unreasonable and impracticable ; only when the possible is made difficult that they fancy the impossible to be easy."

Since the beginning of the No-rent Campaign and other symptoms of agrarian unrest, the Government have adopted various measures for the suppression of mass-revolt. With all the resources of the State, it may not be a difficult task ; but, what is important to realize, is that the machinery of Law and Order cannot cope with a spirit of sullen discontent which prevails among the Indian masses. When a weak and docile people sink in utter despair, it creates a situation far more serious than active revolt. As I write, an incident in Delhi comes to my mind. One evening my attention was drawn to a pathetic cry of a woman beggar in the street. Not understanding what she was saying I asked a friend, who said that she was reciting a little verse which meant that she came to the threshold of the home of God for shelter and food but even there bolts were upon His door. It is this spirit of despair that oscillates between the impulse to open revolt and the utter submission to destiny; and it is in this spirit of despair that one finds a true explanation of that monotonous melancholy which broods over the land.

The primary duty of the Provincial Legislatures should be to formulate a coherent policy of rural reconstruction.[1] Acquiescence in things as they are until they become a serious menace or mere adoption of palliative measures will not do. This problem of attacking the poverty of the great bulk of Indian people requires a bold initiative. Indian leaders, on whom lies the responsibility of future Governments, should scrutinize the existing agricultural legislation on land tenures, agricultural credit, control of usury, and marketing of agricultural produce, with a view to bringing it into line with modern requirements.

The Government enact measures for the good of the people, but there is at present no living channel through which they may know the effects of these laws on the people. The official files do not tell the whole story and often tend to conceal the need for enquiry by the pretence of tact and prudence. During the last half-century, for example, various laws, regulations and rules were passed for the benefit of the masses; but recent enquiries as to whether they had fulfilled the purposes for which they were enacted, revealed in some instances a deplorable negligence and indifference towards their enforcement.

It is hoped that the structure of the present Administration may be adapted to the spirit of the new Constitution in such a manner as to make the contact between the official world and the people more real and effective than in the past. The aloofness of the official world from the people develops a peculiar attitude of official nescience, and the people show distrust of anything that emanates from the official hierarchy. The task allotted to Indian leaders is to bridge the gap between the Government and the people.

[1] The Government of India have recently allocated about £700,000 to the Provincial Governments for economic development in rural areas and £112,500 for expansion of the Co-operative movement in India.

For systematic advance towards economic prosperity and social reform, the Provincial Legislatures should direct their attention to the task of framing and carrying out a comprehensive plan for securing a balanced economy for India as a whole. The main features of economic planning vary in accordance with the economic structure and political conditions of the country where the plan is to be worked out. Economic planning in the Russian sense, for instance, has no resemblance to what is being attempted in Great Britain and in the United States of America.

In a sense, a form of economic planning has been in existence in India, where the mediæval type of socio-economic life has predominated since the latter part of the nineteenth century. The State planned irrigation schemes, constructed railroads, encouraged plantations and instituted a famine relief fund. Nevertheless, the State authority was kept within narrow bounds, restricted, for example, to the establishment and maintenance of Law and Order. In accordance with *laissez-faire* ideas, the State interfered as little as possible with industry and commerce; but the settled Government gave private enterprises large scope for development.

The conception of planning, however, signifies something more than these normal functions of a benevolent autocracy. In any real sense it involves an adequately organized control over almost every aspect of economic life. It should aim at bringing all "nation-building" activities into broad harmony with one another in order to minimize wastes and to secure the best results. The partners in Federal India should realize that their problem is not only to reconcile the points of difference among them, but to harmonize individual initiative with the wider interests of India. Here there is no room for over-emphasis of party and sectional interests.

Side by side with the activities of the State, there should be a large number of voluntary associations for promoting the welfare of the people. It is through these voluntary agencies that leaders of all communities are able to assist Government in the realization of its ideal, namely, the welfare of all classes of the community. The existence of innumerable voluntary organizations for education, health, relief and economic betterment is indeed a sure guarantee that the country is ready for a democratic form of government. I believe, as the range of democratic institutions in India expands, there will arise the need of active co-operation of leadership of both Indian and British social service workers. In the domain of voluntary service they will find ample opportunities for an expression of effective public spirit. In that wide field of co-operation, they would be conscious of a general community of aims and interests and thus lay the foundation of a genuine partnership in Indo-British relations. Here, in voluntary organizations for the betterment of the Indian masses, there should be no room for antagonism between India and Britain, and it would be a great disservice to humanity if that co-operation were frustrated by the spirit of intolerance or its ideal distorted by distrust.

II. TASKS BEFORE THE PARTNERS

(*a*) Great Britain, the first Partner

Bearing in mind these two aspects of the common enterprise, we now turn to the partners on whom lies the responsibility of its success. By virtue of her sovereignty over the Indian Continent, Great Britain may be regarded as the first partner. Her primary task is now to win the confidence and goodwill of her Indian partners, and once that basis of confidence is recognized the process of adjustment will be comparatively easy. Some years ago Lord Curzon, in a speech at Southport, said:

> "It is only when you get to see and realize what India is—that she is the strength and the greatness of England—it is only then that you feel that every nerve a man may

strain, every energy he may put forward, cannot be devoted to a nobler purpose than keeping tight the cords that hold India to ourselves."[1]

But what are those cords that would keep India attached to Great Britain? The old system of government inspired by the Imperialistic spirit has failed to strengthen the bond of relationship between Great Britain and India. For the governance of one-fifth of the human race, rescued from the circumstances consequent upon the disintegration of the Moghul Empire, it became necessary to set up a strong and formidable mechanism of administration; but the structure of the Government became "a thing of human invention imposed by foreigners, not an organization growing naturally out of national institution."[2] The form of alien bureaucracy thus established served the purpose well and supplied the efficiency required to consolidate its position and to increase its power of resistance. It became, as Mr. Fielding Hall puts it, "an efficient machine with minds closed rigidly, enforcing the law untempered to the shorn lamb by personalities." But with the least indications of a stir of life among the governed, the machinery of the Government seemed to produce frictions, much to the annoyance and embarrassment of the Imperial authorities and their agents. Their self-complacency and air of racial superiority provoked the intransigent spirit of the educated classes, with the unfortunate result of widening the gulf between the Government and the people.

To-day, in working the new Constitution, the British administrator should evoke a new spirit of reconciliation. His responsibility is now far greater than the past; he can no longer stay aloof from the people with whom he must establish a living link of sympathy; he is required to exercise his moral judgment in the task of transforming the system and methods of administration that have been

[1] Quoted in "Life of Lord Curzon," by Lord Ronaldshay.
[2] "The Lost Dominion," by A. L. Carthill.

established and taken firm root into what is now envisaged by the Government of India Act, 1935. Indians are to be convinced that the Act is really inspired by absolute honesty of purpose and is not just a political manœuvre. Their hostility has to be overcome by impressing on them that the Constitution is designed for the purpose of transforming "a regime of domination to one of understanding, consent, and free co-operation." The task, therefore, demands the courage and conviction of new leadership. Upon the quality of leadership the future of Federal India will depend. "Leadership in the old days," observed Lord Lothian, in an address before an assembly of British youth, "could be summed up as the capacity to say 'go on' and getting other people to do as one thought right. In the modern world, with its democracy, the voting machine, the Press, the wireless, it is a nobler leadership—the capacity to say 'come on' and getting other people to follow."

I believe that in almost every branch of administration Federal India will need, at the initial stage, the services of the picked men Great Britain can offer. Professor Jowett's letters to Lord Lansdowne during his Viceroyalty show what ideals were pursued in the past in training British administrators for India, and what type of administrator was produced. "The English and Indian tempers," he wrote, "can never harmonize. The Englishman has no sympathy with other nations. He cannot govern without asserting his superiority. He has always a latent consciousness of the difference of colour." All that must change now. In the training centres of the young men of both races, there must be a new spirit of service so that they may imbibe the ideals of partnership.

I should state here that the Indian educated classes have a genuine regard for aristocracy of merit. They recognize that young men belonging to the British aristocracy are generally better educated politically than in any other country in the Western world and that they are capable of making great sacrifice for the interests of the Empire. But the majority of them depend more on prestige [1] and power than on their own inner light of imagination when they are called upon to serve a sub-Continent so vast and complex as that of India. New recruits to British leadership in India should have a clear comprehension of the sources from which there has arisen the miasma of suspicion and distrust between Great Britain and India, and should come into closer contact with the cultured aristocracy of India. Through social intercourse between *new* Britain and *new* India, it may be realized that the greatest British asset in India is not British prestige determined by political influence but the registration of goodwill and trust of the people themselves. This is the only way by which it may be possible to "enshrine the continuance of the British connection in the hearts of India."

The British commercial communities in India should reorientate their policy in conformity with the spirit of Partnership. The commercial safeguards in the interests of British trade have been defined in the Act in precise language, but they should remember that the effective safeguard is to establish an identity of interest with their competitors in India. The welfare of India must be the paramount consideration of all interests; and, since prospects for industrial and agricultural production in this vast potential market are so great, there should be ample scope for the adoption of the principle of reciprocity in Indo-British mercantile relationship. Once the parties concerned in the development of trade accept that principle as a basis of arranging matters between them, they will not only avoid the risk of an impasse which may arise in consequence of resorting to the commercial safeguards provided in the Act, but will recognize that the gradual establishment of a reciprocal trade convention is the effective way of promoting their mutual interests. It is to be regretted that the

[1] The late Mr. Montagu observed that prestige, by which he meant the theory of government that produced irresponsibility and arrogance, might be a useful asset in British relations with the Frontier tribes, but should be dismissed as a factor in the relations of the British Government with the educated Indian public.

proposal for a convention based on the principle of reciprocity as a part of the Constitution, made at the first Round Table Conference, was abandoned in favour of providing safeguarding clauses for the safety of British commerce in India. At any rate in practice it would be an unwise policy to place much reliance on them, and the British commercial communities should aim at winning Indian opposition by conciliation and by offering their co-operation in attacking India's essential economic problems.

Our fellow-citizens in the Dominions can also render a great service to the creation of the new order in India by their recognition of her status in the British Commonwealth. The participation of Indians in the economic life of the Dominions and Colonies involves the British Commonwealth in questions which are of great importance. It should be admitted that the disabilities imposed on Indians are based on distinction of colour and are regarded by them as being badges of racial inferiority. At the Imperial Conference of 1921, the Prime Minister of Great Britain held forth the ideal of Imperial citizenship in the following words:

> "No greater calamity could overtake the world than any further accentuation of the world's divisions upon the lines of race. The British Empire has done signal service to humanity in bridging those divisions in the past; the loyalty of the King-Emperor's Asiatic peoples is the proof. To depart from that policy, to fail in that duty, would not only greatly increase the dangers of international war; it would divide the British Empire against itself. Our foreign policy can never arrange itself in any sense upon the differences of race and civilization between East and West. It would be fatal to the Empire."

Unfortunately the position of His Majesty's Indian subjects domiciled in the Dominions still remains unsatisfactory, and on this question all organized public opinion in India is unanimous in its protests. At the Imperial

Conference in 1923, Sir Tej Bahadur Sapru presented India's case and observed: "Let me tell you frankly, as a subject of King George, that I fight for a place in his household and will not be content with a place in his stables." The Imperial Conference recognized that there was an incongruity between the position of India as an equal partner of the British Commonwealth and the existence of disabilities upon British Indians in the Dominions and Colonies. There are, however, economic and social problems arising from different standards of living and different levels of culture, which are not easy to solve; but I am not disposed to believe that it is not possible to find a just and reasonable *modus vivendi* for harmonizing the conflicting interests involved in the grant of citizenship to Indians in the Empire overseas. The real touchstone of British statesmanship lies in making the British Commonwealth a free association of peoples without distinction of race or creed. The Dominions and Colonies should realize that it would be a difficult task to resist measures of retaliation from the Asiatic units of the Commonwealth if they become convinced that their position in South Africa, Canada, Australia and East Africa will never conform, in practice, to the ideal of Imperial Citizenship.

(*b*) The Indian States, the second Partner

Since the accession of the Indian States to Federation is the corner-stone of that structure, the Princes occupy the place of a second partner in the making of Federal India. Those who are familiar with the structure and traditions of the Indian States should sympathize with the Princes for not being able to reconcile their position easily with the proposal for a Federal Government of India. It means, in the words of Lord Bryce, "the existence of a double government, a double allegiance, a double patriotism," and calls for fresh adjustments in the relations of the two Indias.

The Princes, however, realize that they can no longer

keep themselves aloof from the main currents of Indian politics and that their willing co-operation is necessary to enhance India's status in the British Commonwealth. The trend of events in the last quarter of a century has shown that neither British India nor the Indian States can prosper without mutual aid. By sharing the responsibilities of the future government of India with Indian representatives of British India, the Princes will doubtless make the bond of co-operation more intimate and vital and will greatly assist in the revival of India's cultural aristocracy.

At the beginning of the century, Lord Curzon described the Indian Princes "as partners in the British administration of India." He writes:

"As time passes they will be less and less sleeping partners, and more and more joint managers of that mighty estate. But, equally with the British Governors, will they have to make up their minds as to their attitude and to take their stand. A number of Philippe Egalités in India might place the princely structure in India in grave peril." [1]

To-day the Princes are invited to be partners in a common enterprise. Their partnership is desired by the Imperial Government for the creation of a permanently conservative Central Legislature and for the support of Imperial interests. As we have seen, the Act itself amply safeguards the position of the Princes in every important respect within the Federal sphere, and in matters not ceded to the Federation their relations will be with the Crown. All this is to the good; but it would be unwise to put so much emphasis on the slogan that the main purpose of affiliating the States with the Federation is to allow "Indian autocracy to check Indian democracy." It is an entirely wrong assumption that the Princes' support may be used to defeat Indian Nationalism and that they will not be influenced by a steady infiltration of democratic ideas across the frontiers between British India and their own States. What we should

[1] "British Government in India," by Lord Curzon of Kedleston, 1925.

earnestly hope is that their participation will not only strengthen but *vitalize* the Federal plan, which aims at co-ordination of the two Indias for the supreme interests of India as a whole. As early as possible the leading Princes should establish representative Assemblies in their domains in recognition of their subjects' rights to assume some responsibility of self-government. Through leadership in their own domains the Princes will exercise a sober influence over their partners in British India.

(*c*) British India, the third Partner

The third partner is the educated and propertied classes of British India. The new Constitution throws a serious responsibility on the leaders of Indian public life. Their insistent demand for self-government is justifiable mainly on the ground that it is a moral necessity for India's development. She needs it for evolving unity among her diverse people presenting, to use the words of Lord Zetland, "an ethnologic pageant epitomizing the gradual growth of civilization through centuries of time"; she realizes that without self-government she can neither follow her own destiny nor make her contribution in the world of humanity; and she demands this, not for political and commercial aggressiveness, but for the revitalization of the life of her masses. It would be a wrong estimate of self-government if it was considered as a means of securing privileges from a paramount power; for mere acquisition of a political nationality will not solve her social needs. Indian leaders must realize that the immobility of social structures is one of the serious obstacles to political emancipation.

> "We must remember," warns Tagore, "whatever weakness we cherish in our society will become the source of danger in politics. The same inertia which leads us to our idolatry of dead forms in social institutions will create in our politics prison-houses with immovable walls." [1]

[1] "Nationalism," by Rabindranath Tagore.

If the new Constitution is to grow out of its limitations, there should be a vigorous campaign throughout the country for social reforms. That is, in my judgment, the *first* task to which Indian leaders must devote their attention.

There are fatal defects in our social structure which certainly stand in the way of developing "community of ideas" and offer resistance to partnership with the West. We have set up innumerable barriers against intercourse with the units of humanity which found their way to India; we have erred in approaching the solution of the various problems of adjustment that have risen in consequence of our contact with Britain. Our outlook is narrow, our minds timid and our spiritual life buried under the debris of dead traditions. No sophistry can hide the fact that there is a lack of vitality, a spiritual flagging among us. "To-day," as Professor Radhakrishnan puts it, "we seem to be afraid of ourselves, and are therefore clinging to the shell of our religion for self-preservation." No honest Indians can deny that their failure to bring about a speedy adjustment in the social structures, in conformity with modern conditions, has undoubtedly given rise to some of the intractable problems in shaping the new Constitution. While extraordinarily alive to the deficiencies of the British rule in India, they do not seem to recognize their own failure to develop those qualities so necessary for the remoulding of their social life. And it is a great temptation for them to attribute all their shortcomings to an alien rule.

About a quarter of a century ago, a Japanese statesman, Count Okuma, made the following observation on India. He said:

> "India was at the head of all civilized countries in ancient times, but what was the cause by which she was reduced to her present state? She brought it about herself. She fell behind, because her social organization did not conform to the international standard. From the reprehensible caste institution, from religious superstitions, from the discordance of languages, conjoined with various

> other causes, the Indian nation has been unable to withstand the international competition. The rise or fall of a nation is brought about by the people themselves, and no other force is responsible for a nation's downfall. Rome was not brought to its destruction by the northern barbarians, but by the Romans themselves. Therefore I always give advice to my most beloved Indian friends to cease from their aversion to England, and to recognize their own weak points and to cultivate the knowledge and morality that corresponded to the present world requirements." [1]

These words are profoundly true. The complications of our social problems disturb the very basis of our national life. As we come into closer grips with the political realities, we begin to realize that the gravest danger ahead lies in communal antagonism, which has appeared in malignant forms. The most ominous feature of the Constitution is the perpetuation of the system of communal electorates. So long as this wholly undemocratic element in Indian franchise persists, so long there can be no hope of the unification of the country. It was this element which was primarily responsible for the lack of unity among British Indian representatives at the Round Table Conferences and exposed them to humiliations. We have therefore no right to complain if the framers of the Constitution have taken advantage of our communal dissensions; nor can we justifiably accuse them of not trusting us, because mistrust and suspicion dominate our own relations with the various communities.

Let there be now a determined and persistent effort to root out this ugly feature from our social life. The very nature of this communal antagonism fosters political dissensions. That is why during the first outburst of the non-co-operation movement led by Gandhi, Tagore enjoined his countrymen to set their houses in order. To him the agitation was "only another form of begging." "Do not mind the waves of the sea," he said, "but mind the leaks in your vessel."

[1] See "Journal of the Indo-Japanese Association," July, 1910.

Federation in its proper sense rests on a social ideal; it aims at establishing an organic unity among the diverse elements which compose it. But it cannot evolve itself into a stable polity in the welter of confusions and conflicts that may constantly arise from social mal-adjustments.

We should, therefore, recognize the fact that the socio-economic life of Indian society is not endowed with those liberal traditions which exist in the countries where a democratic form of government functions; and admitting that our conception of a form of government has been dominated largely by that of the parliamentary system working in Great Britain and in the self-governing Dominions, we should lose no time in translating the basic principles of democracy into the relations between the various classes, castes and creeds. In commenting upon the unreality of Indian political aspirations, it is asserted that the ferment in our political life is not really an indication of an urge for a democratic form of government and that it is only a symptom of revolt against a preponderance of British control of Indian affairs. Those who are in sympathy with Indian aspirations remind us that the political system of a country has its roots in the society where it is applied and that the introduction of the ballot-box alone cannot lead to democracy in a country where, to use an appropriate phrase of Professor Laski, "the religion of inequality" dominates the social outlook. That outlook must change if India wants a democratic political state. The fissiparous tendency of the Hindu social system, the rigidity of social customs sanctioned by mediæval traditions, the poverty and ignorance of the bulk of the population, and the diversity of the claims of various minorities—all these circumstances make one doubtful of the practicability of setting up a democratic form of government in India.

And yet democracy offers India the best possible scope for harmonising the varied alignment of interests, and with its ethical conception she may yet succeed in accomplishing the tasks of unifying the diverse elements of her national life. But, in this connection we should bear in mind the truth of an observation made by Lord Balfour. In his introduction to the new edition of Bagehot's "English Constitution," he writes:

> "If we would find the true basis of the long-drawn process which has gradually converted medieval monarchy into a modern democracy, the process by which so much has been changed and so little destroyed, *we must study temperament and character rather than intellect and theory.*[1] This is a truth which those who recommend the wholesale adoption of British institutions in strange lands might remember with advantage. Such an experiment can hardly be without dangers. Constitutions are easily copied, temperaments are not; and if it should happen that the borrowed constitution and native temperament fail to correspond, the misfit may have serious results. It matters little what other gifts a people may possess if they are wanting in those which, from this point of view, are of most importance."

I commend these words to the propertied and privileged classes of India. With the establishment of British rule in India, after a period of anarchical chaos, their position was made more secure than that of the cultivators, artisans and labourers. Taking the full advantages of land laws, education, commercial facilities and settled government, they were able to strengthen their hold on the masses and to use the power and prestige thus acquired for their own interest. A great lover of Indian villagers, Sir Daniel Hamilton, describes India as being "the paradise of the parasites who feed and fatten on the labour of the people." Mr. Montagu observed that the aristocracy created by Land Tenure systems in India "stands upon a conception of social order which is not easily reconcilable with the hustings and the ballot-box." The landlords, merchants, money-lenders and other privileged classes in India have now the onerous duty of refuting the charge that in demanding a democratic

[1] Italics are mine.

form of government their sole motive is to render their own position secure in the circumstances of changing India and that the interests of the masses cannot be entrusted to their care. It is for them to remove a reproach to the new Constitution which has entrenched vested interests to a degree of making the appearance of the constitutional structure devoid of the substance of democracy notwithstanding its forms and formalities. Indian leaders must realize that the quintessence of democracy is justice and that justice implies harmony. For the attainment of that ideal, let us remind ourselves of Asoka's favourite dictum: "Let small and great exert themselves."

Their *second* task is to avoid sterile methods of non-co-operation for creating an effective opposition within and without the Legislatures. It would be a folly to waste our energy in quarrels over the limits of political concessions granted to India; or to use the Constitution "as an instrument for uninterrupted pressure and leverage." We have not, as the Right Hon. V. S. Sastri puts it, the capacity to reject the new Constitution. I believe that any attempt to do so will be the surest means of frustrating the purpose of the Indian National Congress; for the political life of a party cannot solely be made up of protests. It should be organized on sound principles, directing its energy towards the evolution of a constructive and co-operative policy.

Gandhi's choice of non-co-operation was not dictated by political wisdom. The technique of redressing grievances, which he perfected during the period of his apprenticeship in South Africa as a political leader of the Indian settlers there, was considered by him equally suitable in the wider field of Indian politics. He failed to realize that the passive resistance which might be effective in redressing a *local* grievance could not be applicable to the circumstances which inspired him to try it in India. It was, indeed, the most serious of all his miscalculations when he claimed the responsibility of "mending or ending" a highly organized State by non-co-operation or by a series of "experiments with truth."

But it was not long before some of his followers perceived the errors of his judgment. They saw that Gandhi had greatly under-estimated the complex character of the problems with which he was faced in India, and that he was vainly struggling to find an effective common grievance in order to make his technique of " warfare " applicable. In 1923, about three years after the inauguration of the non-co-operation movement, the policy of entering the Legislature was adopted by the Congress. The motive behind the policy was, however, to obstruct the working of the Reforms and to use the Legislatures for the Congress propaganda. The obvious result of the policy was deadlocks in the working of the Reforms. The futility of the non-co-operation movement became evident to those who observed in the spread of the movement the working of a blind force. It created a quasi-religious mood among the youth, under the impulse of which hundreds embraced martyrdom and courted imprisonment. And when it was resuscitated by the Civil Disobedience Movement, the struggle became aggressive. It was then followed by reckless persecution, which only begot a tense atmosphere and widened the gulf between the Government and the people. "Non-co-operation," Gandhi avowed, " though a religious and strictly moral movement, deliberately aims at the overthrow of the Government." The positive result of the movement was just the opposite—it only made the Government jealous of its power and prestige and conscious of the need of strengthening its hold by some concessions to the Indian propertied classes. As regards its repercussion on socio-religious reforms, it may have stirred the surface film of our society, but has not moved the depth where the evil lies. With the advent of Gandhi in Indian public life the social reformers had hoped for a real advance in the renovation of the worn-out social structures ; but that was not to be. " That such a precious treasure of power should be put into the mean and frail vessel of our politics, allowing it to sail across endless waves of angry recrimination, is terribly unfortunate for our country, when our mission is to revile the dead with the fire of the soul "—thus laments Tagore in a letter to a friend during the excitement of the non-co-operation movement. It would have been a wise course to adopt if Gandhi had given a moral direction to the new Legislatures. With his spiritual magnetism, he might have succeeded in forming a *real* National party within the Indian Parliamentary life and eventually developed a tradition of self-less devotion to the cause of the country. His guidance in working the Reforms would have evoked the natural humanity and piety of a large section of the British people with whose co-operation the process of transforming the " Satanic Government of India " would have been more effective than the methods chosen by him. The champions of liberty have fought their battles and won the victory within the constitutional bodies that are set up to govern a country. Burke, Lincoln, Shaftesbury, Gladstone, Bradlaugh, Mill, Morley—all these men enriched Parliamentary history by co-operating with the Government. They knew that the process of political evolution was dynamic and could never stand apart from other forms of evolutionary progress.

But that co-operation can be fruitful if political parties are drawn within the orbit of the constitutional sphere and make their influence felt both in the executive and legislative fields. Indian leaders must therefore direct their attention to the organization of political parties based on some particular principle involved in political programmes, avoiding as far as possible the lines of cleavage between the parties on the grounds of racial and religious differences. Responsible government presupposes party government, but we must adopt every possible means of arresting the dominance of communal and sectional interests. The introduction of responsibility in the Provinces should furnish sufficient stimulus for the formation of genuine political parties both in the Legislatures and in the electorates.

The *third* task before Indian leaders is to proceed

cautiously on the road to Federation. Provincial autonomy throws a heavy burden of responsibility upon them and offers a vast field for service to men and women of the right calibre in every sphere of activity. They will now have control over nine-tenths of the State activities that concern the lives of the people. The enfranchisement of nearly 35 million people, the size and character of the Legislatures both in the Provinces and the Centre, without the presence of official blocs and the formation of Ministries fully responsible to the Provincial Legislatures, in the place of the Executive Councils, are measures that lead India on to the open road for her journey towards the ultimate goal of Dominion Status. It is my firm conviction that no power would be able to resist India's attainment of Dominion Status once the great Indian Provinces began to function as autonomous bodies. That status is, as *The Times* tells us, " a consequence of growth." To the Right Hon. Sir Thomas Inskip, M.P., it is " a thing of life, of spirit. . . ." Therefore it cannot be granted as a gift to any people. " The chief test, indeed, of Indian statesmanship in the coming years," writes Professor R. Coupland, " may well be its capacity to recognize that its path to Dominion Status is more a question of practice than of precedent." [1] While close analogies with the Dominions may not be apt because of " the distinctive conditions which separate India from the Dominions," it must be admitted that there are safeguards in the Government of India Act, 1935, which are unknown in Dominion history.

To Indian critics of the Constitution the entire scheme is indeed a Penelope's web. In its intricacies they find that responsibility conferred on Indian Legislatures is neutralized by ingenious devices.[2] But it is well for Indian leaders to realize that the solution of their difficulties lies in the kind of constructive statesmanship, which may prove that the workman can be trusted to use his tools properly. A Constitution may bristle with limitations, but for its actual

[1] " The Empire in these Days " : R. Coupland, C.I.E., M.A., 1935.

[2] See the footnote on p. 136.

working, the political leaders should look to the establishment of such constitutional usages as will obviate the necessity of enforcing the various safeguards and reserved powers under normal conditions. It is regrettable that so much emphasis has been laid upon the provisions for safeguards in the Constitution. They arose from distrust and scepticism of each other's motives; but, if all the parties concerned in the welfare of India genuinely cherish the ideal of partnership and are able to invest their powers and responsibilities with the dignity of grace, if the political realities are faced with the spirit of co-operation and not with the cult of economic Imperialism, and above all, if the differences between Government and people do not churn up passion, racial hatred and senseless assertion of physical strength—then all these formidable safeguards will not appear to be incompatible with the measure of self-government granted to India. We should be prepared to admit that most of the safeguards are, to quote the words of Sir Tej Bahadur Sapru, "as much due to our want of faith in ourselves as to British want of faith in our capacity to govern ourselves." The growth of political parties, the spread of education, the extensive use of the vernacular press in order to enable the electorate to follow the proceedings of the Legislatures, and the creation of public opinion in regard to the basic problems would effectively safeguard the Indian Legislatures against unjustifiable intrusion. After all, the whole purpose of the Constitution may be frustrated if the dictatorial powers of the Governor-General and the Governors are frequently applied in defiance of Ministers and Legislatures.

As regards the stability of a responsible form of government, Indian leaders must now devote their attention to the development of local self-government. Their task is to remove deficiencies that have so far retarded the progress of local bodies wherein lies the foundation of corporate life among the various classes of the population. To ignore this foundation is to under-estimate the psychology of the masses and to overlook the importance of habituating them to the tasks of self-government.

From the point of view of rural welfare, we know that it is essentially important that there should be efficient local bodies through which the advantages of irrigation, forest co-operative organization, education and other benevolent activities of the State Departments may reach the rural population. The formation of irrigation and forest *panchayats* in certain Provinces indicates the way of training the cultivator in collective action. The Royal Commission on Indian Agriculture held the view that by encouraging the *panchayat* system, it would be possible to develop communal management of affairs that concern the village, and heartily welcomed the foundation of a Local Self-Government Institute in Bombay.

No time should therefore be lost in searching the root-causes of chaos and confusion that now prevail in the machinery of local self-government throughout India. The authors of the Montagu-Chelmsford Report observed: "Responsible institutions will not be stably rooted until they become broad-based, and far-sighted Indian politicians will find no field into which their energies can be more profitably thrown than in developing the boroughs and communes of their country." But the subject of local self-government received no serious consideration in the discussions and debates of the Round Table Conferences. The Joint Select Committee left this matter with a short paragraph, in which they just alluded to the importance of developing local self-governing institutions and observed: "It is thus that the great mass of the Indian peasantry, constituting a vast majority of the people, whose welfare has been constantly in our minds during the whole course of our discussions, can be trained in those qualities of responsible citizenship which may hereafter entitle them to the full provincial franchise. These (*i.e.* the problems relating to the development of local self-governing institutions) are matters upon which Indians must form their own conclusions." They should remember that the basis of democracy in Great Britain lies in her system of local government, which is undoubtedly one of the remarkable achievements in the last century of British history. It is within the sphere of local self-government that the British politicians and electors receive their training for the realization of democratic ideals. The extent to which the local authorities touch the life of every citizen may be judged from the fact that in England and Wales alone they expend each year some £500,000,000 on services such as education, public health, transport and housing.

As regards Federation, its future will depend largely upon the degree of success attained by Indian Legislatures in promoting cohesion of the parts constituting Federal India. Indian leaders must bear in mind two important postulates to which their tasks should conform with a view to arresting the disastrous tendency of provincialism which, if allowed to develop, may gravely weaken the Federal bonds.

The first is that in the spheres of legislative and administrative action there must be a degree of uniformity based upon some coherent scheme of policy. The national well-being of India depends upon due co-ordination of all forms of nation-building activities, and nothing should be done to limit the sphere of action of the Federal Government in any way which might make it impossible to take initiative in matters that concern the welfare of India as a whole. Provincial autonomy does not mean that each of the eleven British Indian Provinces should develop, so to speak, in insulated compartments. The task of bringing about whole-hearted co-operation between them and of co-ordinating their activities in the interests of India must rest with the Federal Government. There need be no apprehension that the Federal Executive will in any way encroach upon the sphere of provincial autonomy if they are given powers to strive for harmony and unity in matters relating to the welfare of India.

The second is that every possible means should be

adopted to establish an organic link between British India and the Indian States. Not only is it impossible to ignore the Princely Houses in any plans for the regeneration of India; their co-operation is of fundamental importance in the growth and stability of Indian national life. I esteem their co-operation not merely as an invaluable asset to political India in its struggle to attain Dominion Status, but I believe that only with their support can an Indian renaissance be really fruitful. One curious feature of the non-co-operation movement was that it left the Indian States out of its consideration, and that irresponsible slogans, such as secession from the Empire and complete independence, were raised with the result that our Princely Houses became alarmed at the attitude of British India towards them. Instead of bringing them closer, the national movement only widened the chasm between the two Indias.

It is a happy augury for the future of India that the Princes realize that the spirit of isolation can no longer be maintained and that they are prepared to establish a constitutional relationship with British India. They are naturally concerned with clear recognition of the sovereignty of the States and the formulation of an exact estimate of their liabilities and responsibilities in entering the Federation. Indian leaders should respect their anxiety, and if the terms under which they are prepared to join British India in a constitutional scheme appear to be a compromise of the principle of a responsible government, it would be an act of statesmanship to recognize this compromise. For the advent of the Princes into the Federation would ultimately be a source of strength to the development of Indian national life as a whole, and at this stage of political growth their co-operation would tend to keep the development of various forces in equilibrium.

Lastly, political India must identify its activities more closely than ever with the cultural forces that are slowly but perceptibly becoming operative in Indian life. Civilization cannot live on politics alone. The advanced States in the world to-day are becoming more and more aware of the ineffectiveness of mere political systems when they are cut off from the springs of ethico-religious inspiration. Without a sense of growing solidarity between politics and culture, it is almost impossible to humanize the machinery of State. In India we must keep in view the ideal of cultural unity among her diverse people, so that we may succeed in creating healthy reactions in her political life, despite all impediments of our present circumstances. Our difficulties are immense, and there are indeed serious obstacles in the way of reaching our goal. But let us not be disheartened; let these obstacles be, in the words of our poet, "like blocks of marble with which those who are artists amongst men fashion the best living images of truth."[1] We have to prove that in the midst of her poverty, defeat, humiliation and social disintegration, India still retains her capacity for a creative synthesis of her varying cultures and civilizations. She must assemble all her forces in order to extricate her social life from the tyranny of the dead hand. Even if her present seems gloomy and uncertain, let my countrymen realize the truth of what Nietzsche wrote about his people: "The Germans have as yet no to-day; they are of the day before yesterday and of the day after to-morrow." The cultural heritage of the past and the vision of the future will give us hope and courage. The future is indeed within us and is to be shaped by ourselves. To those who tell us that the inauguration of the new Constitution for India is "a leap in the dark" or "a voyage into unknown country," we shall offer a challenge asserting that India is conscious of her destiny and destination. And our prayer is:

"Our voyage is begun, Captain, we bow to Thee!
The storm howls and the waves are wicked and wild, but we sail on.
The menace of danger waits in the way to yield to Thee its offerings of pain,

[1] Tagore.

And a voice in the heart of the tempest cries,
    'Come to conquer fear!'
Let us not linger to look back for the laggards
    Or benumb the quickening hours with dread and doubt.
For Thy time is our time and Thy burden is our own,
    And life and death are but Thy breath
    Playing upon the Eternal sea of Life.

"Let us not wear our hearts away in picking small help
    And taking slow count of friends,
Let us know more than all else that Thou art with us
    And we are Thine for ever."[1]

[1] Tagore.

APPENDIX A

CERTAIN ASPECTS OF THE POPULATION PROBLEM IN INDIA

A.—THE GROWTH AND ITS TWO MAIN SECTIONS

Year of Census.	Total Population (in millions).	Real Increase (in millions).	Rate Per Cent. of Real Increase (in millions).	Percentage of Total Population.	
				Urban.	Rural.
1881	253·8	3·0	1·5 (a)	—	—
1891	287·3	24·3	9·6	9·5	90·5
1901	294·3	4·1	1·4 (b)	9·9	90·1
1911	315·0	18·9	6·4	9·4	90·6
1921	318·8	3·7	1·2 (c)	10·2	89·8
1931	352·8	34·0 (d)	10·6	11·0 (e)	89·0

NOTE.—(a) *The rate of increase was affected by the great Indian famine of* 1876-1878. (b) *Famine is responsible for the low figure.* (c) *The low figure in this case is due to the influenza epidemic of* 1918. (d) *This increase is more than three times the total population of Canada, whose area is double that of India.* (e) *The increase is largely due to the natural increase of the pre-existing population and partly to migration from rural areas to industrial centres.*

B.—RELIGIOUS CENSUS

Religious Creeds.	British India (in millions).	Indian States (in millions).	Number per 1000 who are Literate (a).
Hindus	177·7	61·5	84
Muslims	67·0	10·7	64
Buddhists	12·7	0·1	90
Christians	3·9	2·4	279
Sikhs	3·2	1·1	91
Jains	·452	·80	353
Parsis	·096	·014	791
Tribal	5·8	2·5	7
Not enumerated . .	·4	2·2	—

NOTE.—(a) *The standard of literacy prescribed in the census is extremely low.*

C.—Educational Census

Year of Census.	Total Students in all Educational Institutions (in millions).			Number of Literate Per Mille over 5 Years of Age.	
	Males.	Females.	Total.	Males.	Females.
1901	?	?	?	?	?
1911	5·8	·95	6·75	122	12
1921	6·9	1·4	8·3	139	21
1931	10·2	2·5	12·7	156	29

NOTE.—*Over three millions can read and write in English. All proceedings in the Legislatures are to be conducted in the English language. But it is provided in the Act that members who are unacquainted with English may use another language.*

D.—Occupational Census (British India and States)

Year of Census.	Agriculture.	Industry and Trade.	Other Occupations.
1901	91,289,000	26,575,000	8,481,000
1911	106,777,000	30,821,000	10,408,000
1921	106,147,000	27,829,000	10,947,000
1931	110,760,000	30,044,000	23,269,000

NOTE.—*The very large increase under the head of "Other Occupations" is more apparent than real, being due in the main to more accurate returns of those employed in domestic service of all kinds.*

APPENDIX B

DISTRIBUTION OF SEATS IN PROVINCIAL LEGISLATIVE ASSEMBLIES

Provinces.	*Total Seats.*	*General Seats.*		*Seats for Representatives of Backward Areas and Tribes.*	*Sikh Seats.*	*Mohammedan Seats.*	*Anglo-Indian Seats.*	*European Seats.*	*Seats for Representatives of Commerce, Industry, Mining and Planting.*	*Indian Christian Seats.*	*Landholders' Seats.*	*University Seats.*	*Seats for Representatives of Labour.*	*Seats for Women.*				
		Total General Seats.	*General Seats Reserved for Scheduled Castes.*											*General.*	*Sikh.*	*Mohammedan.*	*Anglo-Indian.*	*Indian Christian.*
BENGAL	250	78	30	—	—	117	3	11	19	2	5	2	8	2	—	2	1	—
UNITED PROVINCES	228	140	20	—	—	64	1	2	3	2	6	1	3	4	—	2	—	—
MADRAS	215	146	30	1	—	28	2	3	6	8	6	1	6	6	—	1	—	1
BOMBAY	175	114	15	1	—	29	2	3	7	3	2	1	7	5	—	1	—	—
PUNJAB	175	42	8	—	31	84	1	1	1	2	5	1	3	1	1	2	—	—
BIHAR	152	86	15	7	—	39	1	2	4	1	4	1	3	3	—	1	—	—
CENT. PROV. AND BERAR	112	84	20	1	—	14	1	1	2	—	3	1	2	3	—	—	—	—
ASSAM	108	47	7	9	—	34	—	1	11	1	—	—	4	1	—	—	—	—
SIND	60	18	—	—	—	33	—	2	2	—	2	—	1	1	—	1	—	—
ORISSA	60	44	6	5	—	4	—	—	1	1	2	—	1	2	—	—	—	—
NORTH-WESTERN FRONTIER PROVINCE	50	9	—	—	3	36	—	—	—	—	2	—	—	—	—	—	—	—

NOTE—*In Bombay seven of the general seats are to be reserved for Marathas. In the Punjab one of the Landholders' seats is to be a seat to be filled by a Fumandar. In Assam and Orissa the seats reserved for women are to be non-communal seats.*

APPENDIX C

CHRONICLE OF EVENTS RELATING TO THE INDIAN CONSTITUTIONAL DEVELOPMENT (1911–1935)

1910–1916 – *Lord Hardinge, Viceroy*

1911 – Their Majesties King George V. and Queen Mary left Portsmouth for India on November 11. The Coronation Durbar was held at Delhi on December 12 and Their Majesties laid the foundation of the new Capital of India on the 15th.

1912 – Their Majesties left India on January 10. In the following month Lord Curzon initiated a debate in the House of Lords on the Durbar announcements and the change of Capital. In April, Mr. Montagu, the Under-Secretary of State for India, presented the India Bill, which proposed to make such amendment in the laws relating to the Government of India as are consequential on the administrative changes effected by the Durbar announcements. The Bill was passed in June. Public meetings were held in Calcutta and other important centres to consider Lord Crewe's interpretation on the Government of India Despatch dealing with administrative changes. The appointment of the Royal Commission on the Public Services in India was announced in the House of Commons (Chairman—Lord Islington). Regulations for the Councils under the Morley-Minto Reform scheme were published. The position of Indians in South Africa became a matter of serious concern to Political India.

In December the State entry of the Viceroy to Delhi was marred by a bomb outrage.

1913 – The first meeting of the newly-constituted Imperial Legislative Council was held in January at Delhi. Indian public opinion became greatly stirred by the news of the treatment of Indians in South Africa, and of their struggle under the leadership of Mr. Gandhi. The All-India Muslim League held a conference in Lucknow and suggested means of bringing about a friendly feeling between the Hindus and Muslims. In June, Lord Crewe proposed to take steps to consolidate the enactments relating to the Government of India, the main object of which was to rid the Statute Book of confusion and obsolete phraseology in reference to India.

The Government of India discovered the existence of widespread conspiracies which aimed at the overthrow of British power in India. A Bill to amend the law relating to conspiracy was passed into law by the Imperial Legislative Council.

1914 – A deputation to England from the Indian National Congress left Bombay in April and was received informally by Lord Crewe. In the House of Lords, Lord Crewe introduced the Council of India Bill in order to provide for the representation of Indians on the Secretary of State's Council. Lord Curzon moved the rejection of the Bill and received messages from the European Association of Calcutta protesting against the measure. The Bill was rejected by the House of Lords by 96 votes to 38.

The War broke out in August.

On the 3rd of August the Viceroy assured the Imperial Government that they could count on every man and every gun of the Indian Army; and two days later issued a Proclamation of War. The Indian Princes made loyal offers of troops and other assistance and the leaders of the Indian Congress addressed an appeal to the people of India reminding them of their duty to stand by the Imperial Government in the hour of crisis. On the 28th of August the first battalion of Indian troops left India for the war-zone. The National Congress at its annual gathering made certain proposals for constitutional reforms.

1915 – Defence of India Act was passed. Under the Indian Councils Act of 1909 the Viceroy could create by Proclamation an Executive Council in a Province of a Lieutenant-Governor, on condition that the draft Proclamation be laid before each House of Parliament. The House of Lords rejected the proposal for instituting an Executive Council for the United Provinces by 47 votes to 26. Indian public opinion was alarmed at this refusal and demanded provincial self-government. The Legislative Council passed a Resolution asking that India should be officially represented at the next Imperial Conference. The Government accepted the Resolution. An Act of the Imperial Parliament—the Government of India Act, 1915—repealed in whole or in part nearly all the previous Statutes that affected the government of India.

1916–1921 – *Lord Chelmsford, Viceroy.*

Lord Hardinge before leaving India in March announced Government's intention to abolish the system of Indentured labour from India.

In October 1916, the Viceroy received a notable memorandum submitted to him by nineteen of the twenty-seven members of the Imperial Legislative Council. The memorandum stated that what India wanted was "not merely good government or efficient administration, but government that is acceptable to the people because it is responsible to them." An Act of the Imperial Parliament amended the Government of India Act,

1917 – India's War contribution of £100,000,000 was announced. Mr. Austen Chamberlain (now Sir) appointed two Indians to his Council in London. He also announced that India should be fully represented at all future Imperial Conferences. The Imperial War Conference was held in London. Several leading Congressmen and members of the Muslim League joined the Home Rule movement initiated by Mrs. Annie Besant. The Committee of the Congress and the League pressed for an early adoption of the policy of making India a self-governing unit in the Empire. The Imperial Government accepted the principle of granting Army Commissions to Indians. In July Mr. E. S. Montagu became the Secretary of State for India. On August 20 he made a pronouncement in regard to a measure of constitutional reforms to be granted to India. In November he visited India for making a preliminary survey in regard to post-war reforms. Indentured emigration of Indian labour was abolished.

1918 – The Premier—Mr. Lloyd George—made an appeal to India, and another conference was held in Delhi to mobilize all necessary resources for the War. Mr. Montagu reached England in May and his Report was published in July. The Report of the Sedition Committee (Rowlatt) was also published. A special session of the Indian National Congress was convened to consider the Montagu-Chelmsford Report. The Congress deputation to England was prohibited. In October two Committees were appointed to work out details in regard to Franchise and to Division of Functions. Lord Sinha (then Sir S. P. Sinha) was invited to represent India in the Peace Conference. The War Cabinet paid a warm tribute to India for her services in the War.

1919 – Sir Reginald Craddock published his scheme for constitutional reforms in Burma, in which he urged the complete separation of the Province from India. A Conference of the Ruling Princes was held at Delhi to consider the relations of the States to the Government of India under the proposed Constitution. In March the Criminal Amendment Act based on the Rowlatt Report was certified by the Viceroy. Under Mr. Gandhi's leadership Passive Resistance Movement was inaugurated. In April General Dyer enacted the Amritsar tragedy. A punitive expedition was sent to Waziristan to suppress the revolt of the Mahsuds. A strong body of Indian Muslims protested against the proposal of the Peace Conference to dismember the Turkish Empire and to form Palestine into a Jewish State. Thus India was in a state of great unrest. In December the Government announced their decision on the question of the membership of the Chamber of Princes. The Government of India Bill, 1919, was introduced in Parliament; the Committee stage was taken on December 3, and its third reading on December 5. No division was taken on the third reading. The Bill received the Royal Assent on December 23. His Majesty addressed a Proclamation to the Princes and peoples of India.

1920 – A Committee of Enquiry was appointed to investigate into the Amritsar tragedy under the presidency of Lord Hunter. The publication of its report was followed by a debate in the House of Commons. Mr. Asquith—the Premier—considered that General Dyer had been guilty of an error of judgment and supported the course which the Government of India had taken. But in the House of Lords, Lord Finlay moved a Resolution deploring the treatment that had been accorded to General

Dyer, which was agreed to by a majority of 43. A special session of the Congress adopted Mr. Gandhi's Non-Co-operation policy. In November-December there began preparations for elections under the new constitutional scheme. Lord Sinha was appointed Governor of Bihar and Orissa. He was the first Indian to hold the post. Mr. Alexander Frederick Whyte (now Sir) was appointed as President of the Legislative Assembly.

1921-1926 – *Lord Reading, Viceroy*

1921 – Provincial Legislative Councils were opened in January. In the following month the Legislative Assembly and the Chamber of Princes were inaugurated by H.R.H. the Duke of Connaught. The Council of State adopted a Resolution recommending that the Government of India be granted full fiscal autonomy subject to the provisions of the Government of India Act of 1919. By means of a notification the Government of India applied the provisions of the Act to Burma. Non-Co-operation movement was in full swing. H.R.H. the Prince of Wales visited India in November.

1922 – The Indian National Congress began preparation for mass Civil Disobedience; but Mr. Gandhi was arrested and sentenced to six years' simple imprisonment. In March the Government of India made a representation to the Imperial Government for a revision of the Treaty of Sèvres. The publication of this document led to Mr. Montagu's resignation. In August the Premier—Mr. Lloyd George—made his famous "steel-frame" speech. The problems arising from the disabilities of Indians in the Dominions continued to agitate Indian opinion. The Government of India sent the Hon. V. S. Sastri to the Dominions to consult with the leaders of the Dominions the ways and means of solving the question. A college for military training was established in Dehra Dun.

1923 – The Indian Legislature asked for the introduction of the system of compulsory national military training. Lord Rawlinson, Commander-in-Chief, announced his "Eight Units Scheme" for the Indianization of the Army. A Royal Commission to enquire into the conditions of service of the superior civil services in India was appointed (Chairman—Lord Lee).

The Commerce Member outlined the views of Government as to future fiscal policy and proposed to set up a Tariff Board. The Indian Legislature considered the question of the Governor-General's emergency powers of certification which had been evoked and also of the control of the Secretary of State over the Government of India. Indian leaders urged the revision of the Government of India Act. The position of Indians overseas continued to agitate public opinion in India. Towards the closing of the year, preparation was made for the fresh election for the Assembly.

1924 – The Swarajists obtained 50 out of a total of 145 seats in the Assembly, and the demand for a fresh enquiry into constitutional position became insistent. The Labour Government came in power in Great Britain, but the Premier—Mr. Ramsay MacDonald—sent a message to India stating in clear terms that no party in Great Britain would be cowed by threats of force or by policy such as the Indian National Congress advocated. Gandhi was released on the grounds of ill-health. The Swarajists formed an effective coalition with a number of Liberals and Independents and maintained a united front against the Government. At last the Reforms Enquiry Committee (Muddiman) was appointed. The revolt of the Akali Sikhs in the Punjab added to the general feeling of unrest throughout India. The Government announced its intention of separating the railway from the general finances. The Steel Protection Bill was passed. The Government proposal to adopt the recommendations of the Royal Commission on the superior civil services was rejected by the Assembly. The Finance Bill was also refused, but the Governor-General, acting in accordance with the special powers conferred upon him by section 67 B of the Government of India Act, laid it before the Council of State and the Bill was passed without amendment. The Bill provided for the levy of the salt tax at the rate of one rupee four annas per maund. The status and welfare of Indians in Kenya caused much anxiety, and a committee was appointed to confer with the Colonial Office in London on the matter raised by the Kenya White Paper (Cmd. 1922). The Legislative Rules were amended with a view to allowing re-submission of rejected votes. The Swarajists, who obtained a phenomenal success in the 1923 elections in Bengal, created a deadlock and the Governor prorogued the Council. In Bengal and the Central Provinces the Dyarchical system broke down. The Government of Bengal issued an Ordinance to deal with the situation created by the increased activities of revolutionary bodies.

1925 – There was no sign of *rapprochement* between the Government and the Congress. The Government refused to accede to the demand for the immediate stabilization of the rupee; but the Finance Member announced the appointment of a Royal Commission to consider the question of Currency and Exchange (Chairman—The Rt. Hon. E. H. Young, M.P.). From this year there came into force for five years a scheme for the amortization of the Public Debt of the Government of India. A minimum sum of 3 million sterling was provided each year for the purpose of redemption. A bounty on steel manufactured in India was granted. The Assembly carried a motion for the reduction of the salt tax but it was restored by the Council of State. The Reforms Enquiry Committee issued its Report and the Viceroy sailed for England to confer with the Secretary of State. The Minority Report asserted that Dyarchy was unworkable and should be replaced by full provincial autonomy. The Council of State debated a motion for the immediate appointment of a Royal Commission to enquire into the Indian constitutional questions. A Swarajist leader (the late Sardar V. J. Patel) succeeded Sir Frederick Whyte as President of the Assembly.

1926–1931 – *Lord Irwin (now Lord Halifax), Viceroy*

1926 – The Legislative Assembly passed the Removal of Sex-disqualification Bill and the Indian Trade Union Act. The Public Service Commission was inaugurated. The Imperial Conference met in London. India was also represented on the Empire Parliamentary Delegation in Australia. The Report of the Royal Commission on Indian Currency was issued and the Government accepted its recommendations as a whole. The Government announced the appointment of the Royal Commission on Agriculture in India (Chairman—the Marquess of Linlithgow). At the elections in November-December the Swaraj Party lost one-third of their strength in the Assembly.

The election campaign was marked by bitter communal antagonism, and the differences among the various political parties led to fatal cleavages within the Congress.

1927 – The Assembly began its sessions in Delhi in the new Council House. The Currency Bill, fixing the ratio of the rupee to 1s. 6d., was passed by a narrow majority. The Indian Reserve Bank Bill was withdrawn. An agreement was reached at the Round Table Conference held at Capetown between an Indian Delegation and members of the Union Government. At the suggestion of Mr. Gandhi, the Government of India selected as its first agent in South Africa the Rt. Hon. Srinivas Sastri. Report of the Indian Sandhurst Committee (Skeen) was published. An Act of the Imperial Parliament provided for a Royal Indian Navy mainly for the purpose of the training of Indian cadets. An Act of the Imperial Parliament repealed the law under which the Anglican Church in India has so long been subject to "the general superintendence and revision" of the Archbishop of Canterbury. Under the new Act, the Anglican Church in India will be entitled to manage its own affairs. The Viceroy announced the decision of the Secretary of State to appoint the Indian States Enquiry Committee (Chairman—Sir Harcourt Butler). In November, appointment of the Statutory Commission on Indian Reforms was announced. Political India vehemently protested against the exclusion of Indians from the Commission. The sessions of the National Congress and Liberal Federation passed resolutions of boycotting the enquiry; but sharp division of opinion among the ranks of Indian communities and their leaders resulted in serious conflicts between the Hindus and Moslems.

1928 – Sir John Simon and his colleagues in the Statutory Commission on Indian Reforms left London on January 19 for a preliminary tour in India. Their arrival was followed by public demonstrations to boycott them. On February 6 Sir John Simon in a letter to the Viceroy suggested a plan of co-operation with representatives of Indian Legislatures. An All-India Central Committee and Provincial Committee were appointed to sit with the Commission. The All-Parties Conference met in Bombay and appointed a Committee (Chairman—the late Pandit Motilal Nehru) to outline a scheme for a Constitution for India. The Report of the Committee is known as the Nehru Report. The Congress passed a Resolution that if by the end of 1929 the British Government had not accepted the Dominion Status Constitution drafted by the Nehru Committee, the Congress would organize a Non-Co-operation movement and would recommend the non-payment of taxes. The All-India Moslem Conference met at Delhi on December 31, recommended a Federal Constitution for India and urged the necessity of maintaining separate Moslem electorates for legislative and local bodies. The Commander-in-Chief announced to the Assembly the decision of the Government on the proposals of the Indian Sandhurst Committee. The Finance Member in his Budget provided for the remission of provincial contributions to Central revenues. The Secretary of State sanctioned a separate Secretariat for the Assembly. The Report of the Royal Commission on Agriculture was published in the summer.

1929 – The Assembly refused to allow debate on the Public Safety Bill when the Meerut trials were proceeding; the Government withdrew the Bill and the Viceroy issued an Ordinance to deal with the Criminal Procedure. The life of the Assembly and Provincial Councils (except in Bengal) was extended. Report of the Indian States Enquiry Committee was published. The Viceroy left India to confer with the Labour Government, and on his return to India made an announcement to the effect that Dominion Status was the goal of British policy in India. Sir John Simon suggested to the Premier—Mr. Ramsay MacDonald—that after the publication of the Report of the Statutory Commission the Government should hold a Round Table Conference inviting representatives of the Indian States and of British India. The Cabinet decided to convene a Conference in London. The Report of the Auxiliary Committee was issued, in which it was shown that there was a great deal of waste and ineffectiveness in the educational system. The Congress met at Lahore and declared that the attainment of complete independence was its goal. Indian Liberals held their meeting in Madras and urged all parties in India to combine for the purpose of securing for India a Dominion Status.

1930 – The Congress fixed January 26 as " Independence Day " for political demonstrations throughout the country. The

Viceroy announced to the Legislative Assembly that His Majesty's Government would hold a Round Table Conference in the autumn. In March Mr. Gandhi inaugurated the Civil Disobedience campaign by breaches of the law relating to the production and sale of salt. He was arrested and interned at Yeravda jail. The Viceroy issued Ordinances proscribing the Congress and its working Committee. Widespread disturbances throughout the country led to arrests of Congress leaders and their followers. From April to December no less than 54,000 persons were convicted of offences resulting from Civil Disobedience Movement. Mr. V. J. Patel resigned his Presidentship of the Assembly and later was sentenced to six months' imprisonment for breaches of law. In June the Report of the Statutory Commission was published, but its reception in India was unfavourable. The import duty on cotton piece-goods was raised from 11 to 15 per cent. and an additional protective duty was levied on certain classes of piece-goods of non-British origin. The Governor-General dissolved the Assembly. The Congress Party boycotted the elections. On the 8th of July, India House (office of the High Commissioner for India) was opened by His Majesty the King-Emperor, accompanied by Queen Mary.

Indian Liberals attempted to come to an agreement with the Congress leaders who were still in prison. Their demand was that the Round Table Conference should undertake to draw up a scheme for Dominion Status Constitution for India. Sir Tej Bahadur and Mr. Jayakar issued a statement in regard to their negotiations with Congress. The statement was presented to Parliament (Cmd. 3728). On November 12 the First Round Table Conference was opened by His Majesty. The announcement was made of Lord Willingdon's appointment as the next Viceroy.

1931-1936 – *Lord Willingdon, Viceroy*

1931 – The First Round Table Conference concluded its session on January 19. Mr. Gandhi and other Congress leaders were released. After the " Delhi Pact " was concluded between the Viceroy (Lord Irwin) and Mr. Gandhi, the Assembly recorded its satisfaction that a settlement had been reached. The Finance

Bill was not passed by the Assembly and was certified by the Viceroy. The census taken on the night of February 26 showed a decennial growth of population of 10·6 per cent. The Congress authorized Mr. Gandhi to proceed to London as its sole representative at the Second Round Table Conference. In August the Labour Government resigned, the National Government was formed in Great Britain, and the Gold Standard abandoned. The Viceroy issued an Ordinance providing for similar action in India, but without establishing any relation between the value of sterling and the rupee. The Assembly passed a vote of censure on the Government's financial policy. The Second Round Table Conference met on September 7 and closed on December 1. The Burma Round Table Conference was opened by H.R.H. the Prince of Wales and presided over by Lord Peel. The Government's India policy was debated in both the Houses of Parliament. The Commons, after rejecting an amendment by Mr. Winston Churchill by 369 votes to 43, approved the Government's policy without a division. The Lords passed a motion approving the policy by 100 votes to 58.

1932 – The Congress decided to revive Civil Disobedience campaign. The Viceroy promulgated four Ordinances empowering Governments to meet political disorders. Some of the essential provisions of these Ordinances were, on expiry of six months, incorporated in the ordinary law. Mr. Gandhi was arrested and the Congress was declared an unlawful Association. Nearly 67,000 persons were convicted of Civil Disobedience offences. The three Committees appointed by the Round Table Conference proceeded to India: (1) The Franchise Committee—Chairman, Lord Lothian; (2) the Federal Finance Committee—Chairman, Lord Eustace Percy; (3) the Indian States Enquiry (Financial) Committee—Chairman, Mr. J. C. C. Davidson, M.P. A Consultative Committee of nineteen members was also appointed under the chairmanship of the Viceroy. The dyarchical system of administration was introduced in the North-Western Frontier Province, and the Imperial Government approved of the creation of Sind and Orissa as two separate Provinces under the new Constitution. In August the Prime Minister announced the Communal Award. Mr. Gandhi protested against it and announced that he would fast unto death. Negotiations among the Indian communities were concluded at Poona, known as "Poona Pact," which was accepted by the Government. In the House of Commons the Secretary of State announced the intention of the Government to embody the principles of the new Constitution for India in a single Bill providing alike for Provincial Autonomy and for an All-India Federation. It was also decided to set up a Joint Select Committee of Parliament to examine the proposals formulated by the Government, and the Committee would be asked to consult Indian representatives. The announcement disappointed Indian Liberals, and consequently the Viceroy announced the decision of the Government to hold a Third Round Table Conference. The Conference met on November 17 and ended in December 24. There were no representatives of the Indian National Congress or of the Labour Party of Great Britain in this Conference. In Burma the anti-separationist agitation was started and succeeded in producing a deadlock in the Legislative Council. At the Imperial Economic Conference at Ottawa India signed a Trade Agreement, which was ratified by the Assembly, for a period of three years, by 77 votes to 25.

1933 – The Government proposals were published in the White Paper (Cmd. 4268). Both the Houses of Parliament debated on the proposals. In April, the Joint Select Committee was appointed. The term of life of the Assembly and of certain Provincial Legislatures was prolonged. The Congress was not allowed to hold a session, but the majority of its leaders rejected Mr. Gandhi's plan for "individual" Civil Disobedience. A Trade Agreement was signed between Lancashire and the Bombay Mill-owners. India negotiated directly with Japan in regard to the cotton trade. A protective tariff from 50 to 75 per cent. *ad valorem* was levied on cotton goods of non-British origin. The Imperial Government came to an understanding with the Government of the Nizam in respect of the administration of Berar. The Imperial Government announced their decision to make an annual grant of £1,500,000 as a contribution to the cost of the Army in India. The Indian Legislative Assembly passed the Reserve Bank Bill.

1934 – In April Mr. Gandhi advised the Congress to suspend the Civil Disobedience campaign. A Parliamentary Board was appointed to direct elections of Congress nominees to Legislatures. On the abandonment of Civil Disobedience, the Government of

India withdrew the ban on the Congress and its constituent parts. After a lapse of three years, the annual general session of the Congress was held at Bombay and it re-affirmed India's goal of complete independence. Mr. Gandhi retired from leadership of the Congress and directed his attention solely to the question of untouchability in Hindu social life. In the autumn the Viceroy left India for a visit to England. The Assembly passed the Indian States (Protection) Bill. The Indian Army Act (Amendment) received the approval of the Assembly; it provides that Indian students of the Military Academy at Dehra Dun may receive Dominion Commissions in the King's name but "over the signature of the Governor-General." The Reserve Bank Bill was passed by the Assembly. The Assembly was prorogued. In the election the Congress Party gained 44 out of the 105 elective seats in the Assembly. Similar success was recorded in Provincial elections. In Burma a bitter controversy arose over the question of separation from India. On November 1 the Report of the Joint Select Committee was laid before Parliament and three weeks later it was published simultaneously in England and in India. On December 3, at a meeting of the Council of the National Union of the Conservative and Unionist Associations, Mr. Stanley Baldwin explained the main principles underlying the recommendations of the Majority Report of the Committee and asked for their approval by the Conservative Party. The Opposition was defeated by 1102 votes to 390. A week later a debate on the Report continued for three days in the House of Commons. The Opposition (the Labour Party) moved an amendment that provision should be made in the new Indian Constitution for the recognition of the right of India to Dominion Status. The amendment was defeated by 491 votes to 49. A Conservative motion for the rejection of the Report was defeated by 410 votes to 127. In the House of Lords, Lord Halifax's motion for the acceptance of the Report as a basis for a constitutional settlement was carried by 239 votes to 62.

1935 – The Government of India Bill was published on January 25. The second reading of the Bill was approved by the House of Commons by 404 votes to 133 and third reading by 386 votes to 122. On June 7 the Bill came to the Lords and the first reading was approved without a division. On June 11 the Marquess of

Zetland assumed office as Secretary of State for India. The House of Lords approved of the second reading by 236 votes to 55 but passed the third reading without a division on June 24. The Bill received the Royal Assent on August 2. On the 7th, Lord Linlithgow's appointment as Lord Willingdon's successor was announced. The Indian Central Delimitation Committee (Chairman—Sir Laurie Hammond) was appointed. Sir Otto Niemeyer was invited to examine the financial position of the Central and Provincial Governments. The Report on Indo-Burma financial relations was issued. Steps were being taken to develop the Cabinet system in connexion with the Central Government. The term of the Council of State was extended. The Government set up a Tariff Board to review the duties on British textiles. The Assembly refused to consider the Criminal Law Amendment Bill but it was passed by the Council of State as certified by the Governor-General. The Viceroy addressed a joint session of both Houses of the Legislature and urged that "nothing was to be gained by working the Constitution in a spirit of mere destruction or by the abandonment of constitutional methods."

1936 – A beginning has been made with the passing of the numerous Orders in Council required under the Act of 1935 to set the new constitutional machinery in motion. The Orders constituting Sind and Orissa as new Provinces from the 1st April, 1936, and the Order delimiting the Excluded Areas have already been passed, and it is abundantly clear from the spirit in which these three Orders were considered in draft form by Parliament that there will be no drawing back on the part of the British nation from their intentions as manifested in that Act. The omens in the Indian sky are also not unfavourable. Congress has not been able to maintain an unbroken front against accepting office under the new Constitution. The farewell tour of Lord Willingdon in the Indian States has been an unqualified success. The financial outlook is rapidly clearing, as is evidenced by the fact that the Finance Member has been able to declare this year a surplus of no less than Rs. 242 lakhs. Last, but by no means least, the universality of the mourning at the passing of King George V is evidence, if evidence were needed, of the profound devotion of all classes of my countrymen to the Crown, the essential link under the new Constitution between England and India.

SELECTED BIBLIOGRAPHY

(NOTE.—*In preparing the bibliography I have taken care to select relevant literature on Indian constitutional developments covering the period dealt with in the book. The list, though not complete, may be helpful to those who wish to make a serious study of the Indian questions. For a more comprehensive selection of modern books relating to India, the reader may apply to the published lists distributed by the National Book Council,* 3 *Henrietta Street, Covent Garden, London, W.C.*2.)

A—BOOKS

Aga Khan, H.H. The . INDIA IN TRANSITION: A STUDY IN POLITICAL EVOLUTION, 1918.

Anderson, Sir George . BRITISH ADMINISTRATION IN INDIA, 1920.

Andrews, C. F. . . INDIA AND THE SIMON REPORT, 1930.

Archbold, W. A. J. . OUTLINES OF INDIAN CONSTITUTIONAL HISTORY, 1930.

Archer, William . . INDIA AND THE FUTURE, 1917.

Banerji, Sir Albion . THE INDIAN TANGLE, 1933.

Banerji, D. N. . . THE INDIAN CONSTITUTION AND ITS ACTUAL WORKING, 1926.

Barton, Sir W. P. . . THE PRINCES OF INDIA, 1934.

Besant, Mrs. Annie . HOW INDIA WROUGHT FOR FREEDOM: THE STORY OF THE NATIONAL CONGRESS, 1915.

BIRTH OF NEW INDIA, 1917.

INDIA: BOND OR FREE, 1926.

INDIA: A NATION, 1930.

Bevan, E. R. . . INDIAN NATIONALISM: AN INDEPENDENT ESTIMATE, 1913.

THOUGHTS ON INDIAN DISCONTENTS, 1929.

Bolton, G. . . . THE TRAGEDY OF GHANDI, 1934.

Bose, Subash Chandra . THE INDIAN STRUGGLE (1920–34), 1935.

Butler, Sir Harcourt . INDIA INSISTENT, 1931.

Chamber of Princes . THE BRITISH CROWN AND THE INDIAN STATES, 1929.
Coatman, J. . . YEARS OF DESTINY, 1932.
Coomerswamy, A. K. . ESSAYS IN NATIONAL IDEALISM, 1910.
Coupland, R. . . THE BRITISH EMPIRE, 1933.
THE EMPIRE IN THESE DAYS, 1935.
Craddock, Sir R. H. . THE DILEMMA IN INDIA, 1929.
Chirol, Sir Valentine . INDIAN UNREST, 1910
INDIA OLD AND NEW, 1921.
INDIA, 1926.
FIFTY YEARS IN A CHANGING WORLD, 1927.
Cromer, Earl of . . REFLECTIONS ON INDIA, 1914.
Cumming, Sir J. G. (Editor) POLITICAL INDIA (1832–1932)—A CO-OPERATIVE SURVEY OF A CENTURY, 1932.
MODERN INDIA, 1931.
Curtis, Lionel . . A LETTER TO THE PEOPLE OF INDIA, 1917.
DYARCHY, 1920.
Curzon, Lord . . THE PLACE OF INDIA IN THE EMPIRE.
BRITISH GOVERNMENT OF INDIA, 1925.
Eddy, J. P., and Lawton, F. H. INDIA'S NEW CONSTITUTION, 1935.
Ellam, J. E. . . SWARAJ, THE PROBLEM OF INDIA, 1930.
Fraser, L. . . . INDIA UNDER CURZON AND AFTER, 1911.
Fisher, F. B. . . INDIA'S SILENT REVOLUTION, 1919.
Fuller, Major-General J. F. C. INDIA IN REVOLT, 1931.
Gangulee, N. . . NOTES ON INDIAN CONSTITUTIONAL REFORMS, 1928.
INDIA: WHAT NOW?—1933.
Garratt, G. T. . . AN INDIAN COMMENTARY, 1930.
Gilchrist, R. N. . . INDIAN NATIONALITY, 1920.
Gwynn, J. T. . . INDIAN POLITICS, 1924.
Haksar, Col. Sir K. N., and K. M. Panikkar FEDERAL INDIA, 1930.
Hall, H. Fielding . . PASSING OF EMPIRE OR THE REDEMPTION OF INDIA, 1914.
Hammond, Sir E. L. . THE INDIAN CANDIDATE AND THE RETURNING OFFICERS, 1923.
Horne, E. A. . . THE POLITICAL SYSTEM OF BRITISH INDIA, 1922.
Houghton, B. . . BUREAUCRATIC GOVERNMENT: A STUDY IN INDIAN POLITY, 1913.

Hull, W. I. . . . INDIA'S POLITICAL CRISIS, 1930.

Ilbert, Sir Courtenay . THE GOVERNMENT OF INDIA, 1922.

Ilbert, Sir Courtenay and Lord Meston . . THE NEW CONSTITUTION OF INDIA, 1923.

Irwin, Lord (now Viscount Halifax) INDIAN PROBLEMS, 1932.
SOME ASPECTS OF THE INDIAN PROBLEM, 1932.

Keith, A. B. . . . SPEECHES AND DOCUMENTS ON INDIAN POLICY (1750–1921), 2 VOLS., 1922.
LETTERS ON IMPERIAL RELATIONS (1916–35), 1935.

Krishnaswami, A. . . THE NEW INDIAN CONSTITUTION, 1933.

Lajpat Rai . . . THE POLITICAL FUTURE OF INDIA, 1919.
INDIA'S WILL TO FREEDOM, 1921.

Lee-Warner, Sir William THE NATIVE STATES OF INDIA.

Lovett, Sir H. V. . . HISTORY OF THE INDIAN NATIONALIST MOVEMENT, 1921.

Low, Sir Sidney . . THE INDIAN STATES AND RULING PRINCES, 1929.

MacDonald, J. R. . THE AWAKENING OF INDIA, 1910.
THE GOVERNMENT OF INDIA.

Marriott, Sir J. A. R. . THE ENGLISH IN INDIA: A PROBLEM IN POLITICS, 1932.

Marvin, F. S. . . INDIA AND THE WEST, 1933.

Meston, Lord . . NATIONHOOD FOR INDIA, 1931.

Montagu, E. S. . . AN INDIAN DIARY, 1930.

Morley, Viscount . . SPEECHES ON INDIAN AFFAIRS, 1909.
RECOLLECTIONS, 2 VOLS., 1917.

Mukerji, P. . . . THE INDIAN CONSTITUTION, CONTAINING RELEVANT DOCUMENTS RELATING TO THE INDIAN CONSTITUTIONAL REFORMS OF 1919, 1920.

Nevinson, H. W. . . THE NEW SPIRIT IN INDIA, 1908.

O'Donnell, C. J. . . CAUSES OF PRESENT DISCONTENTS IN INDIA, 1908.
THE FAILURE OF LORD CURZON, 1905.

Panikkar, K. M. . . WORKING OF DYARCHY IN INDIA, (1919–28), 1928.
INTRODUCTION TO THE STUDY OF THE RELATIONS OF INDIAN STATES WITH THE GOVERNMENT OF INDIA, 1932.

Pole, D. Graham . . INDIA IN TRANSITION, 1932.
I REFER TO INDIA, 1933.

Pradhan, R. G. . . INDIA'S STRUGGLE FOR SWARAJ (MADRAS), 1930.

Ranga Iyer, C. S. . INDIA: PEACE OR WAR, 1930.

Ratcliffe, S. K. . . SIR WILLIAM WEDDERBURN AND THE INDIAN REFORM MOVEMENT, 1923.
WHAT THE SIMON REPORT MEANS, 1930.

Reed, Sir Stanley, and Cadell, P. R. INDIA: THE NEW PHASE, 1928.

Rees, Sir J. D. . . THE REAL INDIA, 1908.
MODERN INDIA, 1910.

Ruthnaswamy, M. . . THE MAKING OF THE STATE, 1932.

Sapru, Sir T. B. . . THE INDIAN CONSTITUTION, 1919.

Sastri, Rt. Hon. V. S. Srinivas SELF-GOVERNMENT FOR INDIA UNDER THE BRITISH FLAG, 1916.
LECTURES ON INDIAN STATES, 1924.
RIGHTS AND DUTIES OF THE INDIAN CITIZEN, 1927.

Sen, D. K. . . . THE INDIAN STATES: THEIR STATUS, RIGHTS, AND OBLIGATIONS, 1930.

Seton, Sir Malcolm . THE INDIA OFFICE, 1926.

Simon, Rt. Hon. Sir John TWO BROADCAST TALKS ON INDIA, 1930.

Sivaswamy Aiyer, Sir P. S. INDIAN CONSTITUTIONAL PROBLEMS, 1928.

Spender, J. A. . . INDIAN SCENE, 1912.
THE CHANGING EAST, 1926.

Tagore, Dr. Rabindranath NATIONALISM, 1917.

Thompson, E. J. . . A LETTER FROM INDIA, 1932.
THE RECONSTRUCTION OF INDIA, 1931; (AND WITH GARRETT, G. T.) THE RISE AND FULFILMENT OF BRITISH RULE IN INDIA, 1934.

Thompson, Sir John P. . . INDIA: THE WHITE PAPER, 1933.

Whyte, Sir Frederick . INDIA: A FEDERATION, 1926.

Winslow, J. C., and Elwin, V. THE DAWN OF INDIAN FREEDOM, 1931.

Zetland, The Marquess of (formerly Earl of Ronaldshay) INDIA. A BIRD'S-EYE VIEW, 1924.
THE HEART OF ARYAVARTA, 1925.
THE LIFE OF LORD CURZON, 3 VOLS., 1928.
STEPS TOWARDS INDIAN HOME RULE, 1935.

B—OFFICIAL PUBLICATIONS

Report on Indian Constitutional Reforms by Mr. Montagu and Lord Chelmsford. Cd. 9109. 1918.

Correspondence relating to the Montagu-Chelmsford Report, between the Secretary of State and the Government of India.

Report of the Southborough Committee (Franchise). Cmd. 141. 1919.

Report of East India Sedition Committee. Cd. 9190. 1918.

Report of the Feetham Committee (Division of Functions). Cmd. 103. 1919.

Report of the Meston Committee (Financial Relations). Cmd. 724. 1920.

Government of India Act, 1919. *Reports of the Joint Select Committee,* 1920.

Report of the Muddiman Committee (Reforms Enquiry). Cmd. 2360. 1925.

Report of the Indian Fiscal Commission. Cmd. 1764. 1922.

Report of the Royal Commission on Indian Currency and Finance. Cmd. 2687. 1926.

Report of Indian Sandhurst (Skeen) Committee. 1927.

Report of the Committee appointed by the All-Parties Conference (known as the Nehru Report). 1928.

Report of the Indian States Committee. Cmd. 3302. 1929.

Report of Growth of Education in British India by the Auxiliary Committee appointed by the Indian Statutory Commission. Cmd. 3407. 1929.

Reports, Surveys, Recommendations, Evidence, and Memoranda of the Indian Statutory (Simon) Commission. 17 vols.

Vol. I—*Survey.* 1930. Cmd. 3568.

Vol. II—*Recommendations.* 1930. Cmd. 3569.

Vol. III—*Reports of the Committee.* 1930. Cmd. 3572.

Report of the Indian Central (Nair) Committee, 1928–29. Cmd. 3451.

Supplementary Note by Dr. A. Suhrawardy. Cmd. 3525. 1930.

East India Constitutional Reforms: Government of India's Despatch, September 20, 1930. Cmd. 3700. 1930.

East India: Events Preliminary to the Round Table Conference: Conversations with Congress Leaders. Sir Tej Bahadur Sapru and M. R. Jayakai. Cmd. 3728. 1930.

East India Constitutional Reforms: Despatches from Provincial Governments. Cmd. 3712. 1930.

India from a Back Bench . . . 1934.

Indian Round Table Conference : Reports and Proceedings :

First Session.

Part I. 1931. Cmd. 3772. Part II. 1931. Cmd. 3778.

Second Session. Cmd. 3997. 1932.

Proceedings of Federal Structure Committee and Minorities Committee. 1932.

Third Session. Cmd. 4238. 1933.

Indian Student of Political Science, a . . . Key to Freedom and Security in India, 1933.

Report of the Indian Franchise (Lothian) Committee. 1932. 5 vols.

Report of the Federal Finance (Lord Eustace Percy) Committee. Cmd. 4069. 1932.

Report of the Indian States Enquiry (Davidson) Committee. Cmd. 4103. 1932.

Proposals for Indian Constitutional Reform. The " White Paper." Cmd. 4268. 1933.

Report of the Joint Committee on Indian Constitutional Reform (Session 1932–33) : Minutes and Index. 1933–34. 5 vols.

Report and Proceedings of the Joint Committee on Indian Constitutional Reform (Session 1933–34). 1934. 2 vols.

INDEX